S0-FLO-909

The Cool Greenhouse Today

by the same author

THE TOAD IN THE GREENHOUSE
THE TORTOISE IN THE ROCKERY

Rechsteineria Leucotricha

The
Cool Greenhouse
Today

Deenagh Goold-Adams

London
FABER AND FABER

*First published in 1969
by Faber and Faber Limited
24 Russell Square London WC1
Printed in Great Britain by
Latimer Trend & Co Ltd Plymouth
All rights reserved*

SBN 571 09160 1

Contents

	Preface	page 11
1.	The Greenhouse Today	13
2.	The Structure	18
3.	Automation in the Greenhouse	28
4.	Heating	33
5.	Ventilation and Humidity	47
6.	Pots, Soil and Feeding	54
7.	Automatic Watering and Capillary Benches	66
8.	Lighting	73
9.	Buying Greenhouse Plants	76
10.	Plants from Cuttings	80
11.	Mist Propagation	87
12.	Plants from Seed	93
13.	Bulbous Plants	100
14.	Cacti and Succulents	105
15.	Pests and Diseases	111
16.	Specialisation	119
17.	Encyclopaedia of Cool Greenhouse Plants	125
	Index	249

Illustrations

Rechsteineria leucotricha	*frontispiece*
1. Hartley aluminium alloy greenhouse	*facing page* 16
2. Hartley Clear Span Lean-to	16
3. C. H. Whitehouse three-quarter span greenhouse	17
4. C. H. Whitehouse all-cedar greenhouse	17
5. G.E.C. combined steriliser and heater	32
6. Para boiler	32
7. Para boiler (detail)	32
8. Aladdin greenhouse heater	*after page* 32
9. Camplex 3-kW. floor standing fan heater	32
10. LO-heat convector heater	32
11. Humex capillary trays and tank	32
12. Ekco Hawkins Thermotubes	*facing page* 33
13. Bayliss Autovent Mark III	33
14. Author's mist unit	48
15. Author's capillary bench	49
16. *Thunbergia alata*	128
17. *Torenia fournieri*	128
18. Salpiglossis	129
19. *Trachelium caeruleum*	129
20. Calceolaria	144

9

ILLUSTRATIONS

21. *Primula kewensis*	*facing page* 144
22. *Zinnias*	145
23. *Gerbera*	145
24. *Lachenalias*	160
25. *Cyclamen persicum*	160
26. *Tigridia pavonia*	161
27. *Pleione formosana*	161
28. *Begonia*	176
29. *Vallota purpurea*	176
30. *Pimelea*	177
31. Fuchsia 'Mrs. Marshall'	177
32. *Plumbago*	192
33. *Tibouchina semidecandra*	192
34. *Clianthus puniceus*	193
35. *Tolmiea menziesii*	193
36. *Datura*	208
37. *Passiflora*	208
38. Collection of Cacti	209
39. *Cotyledon undulata*	209
40. *Aporocactus flagelliformis* and *Cleistocactus strausii*	224
41. *Aloe variegata*	224
42. Collection of succulents	225
43. Cretan Mullein *Celsia cretica*	240
44. *Streptocarpus* 'Constant Nymph'	240
45. *Hedychium gardnerianum*	241
46. *Cestrum purpureum*	241
47. *Rehmannia angulata*	241

Preface

MY AIM in this book is both to stimulate fresh thought in the amateur's greenhouse and to provide a reference book of value to anyone with a greenhouse that is kept free from frost.

So many private greenhouses are virtually abandoned, largely because there is no integration between the day-to-day activities of the owner and the day-to-day needs of the plants. No two people live identical lives and very few of us live primarily for the greenhouse. It must be adapted to suit the type of attention it will actually be given. I have tried to suggest a variety of ways of doing this.

There is no single correct way of growing anything, and many of the best plants are grown by people who never read a book. Nevertheless, it takes a long time to discover the many possibilities and it is hard to remember the details even of what has been learnt by experience. With varying degrees of success and enthusiasm, I have myself grown more than 90 per cent of the 250 genera described in this book. I now know what I like and what likes me, but I wish I had reached this point much sooner. If the fruits of my experience help others to enjoy a fascinating hobby, I shall feel well rewarded.

This book is a successor to *The Cool Greenhouse and Conservatory* published in 1959. I have used my previous book as a basis but have re-written it, as well as adding extra chapters and new photographs, and bringing it up to date. In this work I am indebted to Mr. L. A. Pottinger for certain advice on electricity.

DEENAGH GOOLD-ADAMS

I
The Greenhouse Today

I BELIEVE that history will show that the middle of the twentieth century was a period of exceptional development in cultivation under glass. By 1950 great improvements had been made in the construction and heating of greenhouses, and the John Innes scientifically devised potting composts had done much to simplify the management of pot plants, particularly for the amateur. Since then the age of automation, in which we are now living, has begun to make an impact on greenhouses of all sizes.

Today, it is at last possible for the amateur to have a greenhouse that runs itself so far as essential daily maintenance is concerned. This means that new possibilities are opened up for busy people who have never embarked on a greenhouse before. The young and technically minded may well be interested for the first time in what is sometimes thought of as a hobby of old age. At the same time there have been developments which make the care of a greenhouse easier for the elderly or disabled.

Greenhouse gardening in the traditional style first became fashionable and perhaps reached its zenith about a hundred years ago. For the more affluent Victorians those were the days of cheap labour and cheap coal, while glass itself had only recently become reasonable in cost. There was also the excitement of many new plants being introduced in the 'golden age' of explorers and plant hunters.

Once the basic needs of plants were understood and sufficient light, heat and ventilation were provided, a good gardener could apply his skill to growing plants to perfection. It was, however, necessary to attend to the greenhouse at all hours of the day and night, in order to keep the climate under control with the equipment then available. The successful greenhouse became the domain of the professional gardener, and so it remained for several decades. This led to traditional practices which continued to demand constant attendance and considerable skill. It also encouraged the mystique that tends to surround professional skills.

In recent years inexorable economic forces have persuaded the larger commercial and research establishments to turn to automatic controls in order to save labour and to produce uniform results. Although the problems are different both in nature and in scale, there is much to be learnt from this greenhouse revolution.

In Britain at the present time there are some two million privately owned greenhouses in an affluent, but 'do it yourself', society. This book is intended for all those who are interested in growing ornamental plants under glass, whether by traditional or by modern methods. For anyone buying a new greenhouse today some fairly searching thought is necessary if it is not to prove inadequate for the demands of tomorrow.

Automation is a word that conjures up visions of computers and vast expense. This is totally misleading so far as greenhouses are concerned. Complete automation is still expensive, but almost anyone with a greenhouse can afford the simpler forms of automatic watering and ventilation if they want to.

I am not under any illusion that all of us want to do anything of the kind. Nevertheless, I am quite sure that it is high time that more thought was given to the greenhouse of the future, if it is to develop along lines that are going to be useful to the amateur. Few of us today are, in fact, either able or willing to give enough regular attention to a greenhouse throughout the year to get the best results. Thousands of greenhouses produce a very poor return, either in plants or pleasure. It is often only the retired or housebound amateur who can hope to emulate the successes of the past in a wholly traditional manner. Although we already have baby-sitters and even dog-sitters, I hope that automation has come in time to avoid plant sitters!

At the same time I do realise that there are amateur gardeners who positively welcome a daily routine of watering and ventilation, which in itself provides the pleasure or mental and physical therapy they seek in gardening. Such people can comfort themselves with the knowledge that there is, as yet, no device so sensitive to greenhouse atmosphere as the human nose, though there are automatic aids far more efficient than the average person with a watering can.

Unfortunately, there are those who scorn any form of what they call gadgetry in gardening, in much the same way that the horseman scorned the early motor-car. If you are the kind of person who would not have wished to own a motor-car until the horse had disappeared from the streets, automation in the greenhouse is probably not for you. Whether or not to rely on mechanical and electrical devices, rather than the individual, is a matter of temperament, as well as cost and common sense. Both people and gadgets have their failings, and automation in the greenhouse is still an adventure.

Most forms of greenhouse automation have been devised to meet large-scale commercial needs, which still dominate all thought on the subject. Today, after more than ten years of development, there are a growing variety of aids available to the amateur. These are sometimes scaled-down models of the commercial version, or made-up kits of ideas that nurserymen would probably fix up for themselves. There is still plenty of scope for private ingenuity.

Some people will say that they do not want to save labour or to produce thousands of plants. Others may feel that the greenhouse should be a refuge from the pressures of technological advance. I do not argue with them. There is no one way to grow any plant well, and there are extremely few years in the human span that are too early or too late for enjoying a greenhouse.

In an earlier book I described the possibilities of the entirely unheated greenhouse; these are far greater than most people realise, particularly in a lean-to against a house wall. At the same time the scope is enormously increased the moment the temperature can be controlled, and I am writing this book for the amateur with a greenhouse or conservatory which can be heated enough to ensure a minimum temperature of 4° C. (40° F.) on the coldest winter night, in other words what is known as a 'cool' greenhouse. The precise temperature at which a cool greenhouse is kept is a subject of debate and of individual preference. If resources are adequate, both in heating equipment and willingness to pay for fuel, there is a tendency for the winter temperature to creep up from year to year so that new plants from warmer climates can be tried. The spread of central heating in homes has also had an effect on greenhouse climate in two ways. First of all, it is easier to run a warmer conservatory attached to a warmer house, and secondly the warmer house is apt to lead to the growing of tropical plants indoors, which soon spread into the greenhouse.

Unfortunately, the fact that an extra 5° F. of heat can double the electricity bill is a powerful deterrent to many of us who would otherwise make the cool greenhouse warm. I find that few people actually keep the minimum night temperature in winter above 10° C. (50° F.) today, even when they grow plants that would do better in a warm greenhouse.

In order to discover what plants could be grown in my own cool greenhouse, I found that I had to consult many books, and grow many plants to see if they would be happy in the cool conditions I describe in this book. Obviously the 200 genera I have chosen do not all like exactly the same conditions; so I will mention their preferences and leave the choice to you. In the dictionary of plants at the end of the book I have tried to include all those plants that are both available and worth growing in the cool greenhouse or conservatory with minimum temperatures from 4° C. (40° F.) to 10° C. (50° F.).

I make no apologies for using Latin names. When it comes to greenhouse plants, Latin names are unavoidable and must be mastered. Some, like primula and begonia, are so well known that there is no problem. Others, like *Coronilla glauca*, are less familiar; but there is no more homely way to describe this and many other plants. You can take courage from the fact that the differing views about Latin pronunciation mean that few people will ever know for certain that you are wrong, if you name any plant as it is

Hartley Clear Span enamelled aluminium alloy greenhouses require no maintenance and can be erected by the manufacturers, Hartley Clear Span Ltd., of Greenfield, near Oldham

Interior of Hartley Clear Span 10 ft. wide greenhouse

C. H. Whitehouse Ltd., of Frant, Sussex, made this ¾ span greenhouse to suit a client. It gives ventilation from two directions

This solidly constructed Western Red Cedar greenhouse on a brick base is a standard model of C. H. Whitehouse, who also make all-cedar houses

written in a firm and confident voice. I fear that the purists will question this advice. But I know I am right when I say that you will never have an interesting collection of greenhouse plants if you insist that they shall all have names like 'Black-eyed Susan', or 'Mind your own business'!

# 2

The Structure

Many factors combine to make a greenhouse or conservatory a pleasure or a disappointment, and it is hard to provide a definite formula for success. I can, however, remind you of the various points that help to create conditions in which plants will flourish under glass. I will also mention some advantages and disadvantages of the various materials of which greenhouses are made.

The days of the greenhouse hidden away at the bottom of the garden must surely be numbered. In the future almost all greenhouses will need to be close to electricity and water. Usually this also means close to the dwelling-house. I believe, too, that the former sharp distinctions between the propagating house, the greenhouse, the vinery and the conservatory are already largely irrelevant in most private gardens today. Although specially designed structures may be better and cheaper to run for certain specific activities, the general-purpose greenhouse is all that most of us are likely to have. Further development must surely lie in adding to the variety of possible climates within one structure, rather than in multiplying the types of different greenhouse.

In an age of affluence it is possible that the conservatory may return to popularity in some other form better adapted to life today. Although prefabricated building methods have already produced glass-walled extensions to the home, I have yet to see one that is as well adapted to growing plants as the more traditional greenhouse shapes. It is sometimes forgotten that, if the moisture from condensation is not to drip on the plants, the roof must have an angle of at least 26° to the horizontal for water to run down to the eaves.

Unfortunately plants are more particular than people about ventilation and humidity control. When I look up at modern office buildings on a hot summer day, I always think: 'There are the unfortunate guinea pigs, being frizzled up in the essential research into how to control environment in sealed glass structures.' When they have got it right for people, we will be well on the way to getting it right for plants!

It is curious that, at the very moment when more people than ever before are living in buildings made of glass, the future for plants may lie in artificially lighted and heated growth rooms with well-insulated walls. Although this idea has little charm for the amateur, it is beginning to be considered commercially as fuel costs continue to rise and more is learnt about the light, humidity and ventilation requirements of plant life. Even now I would advise those who are determined to grow tropical plants needing high winter temperatures to consider an indoor winter home for them rather than a greenhouse. In the United States, where the winters are colder and the electrical industry more helpful than in this country, there are already many amateurs with artificially lighted plant-growing rooms.

For the general run of cool greenhouse plants the first consideration is light. During the winter months in Britain the limiting factor on growth is more likely to be lack of light than lack of heat. No greenhouse should have buildings or trees between it and the low arc of the winter sun. At the same time shelter from the north and east saves fuel bills. A free-standing greenhouse exposed to wind can cost a great deal to heat.

A span-roofed greenhouse is lighter than a lean-to, but if it is going to be placed close to the wall of a building there is not a great deal of difference. Ideally, a lean-to should face south and be open to the east and west. It is possible to have a three-quarter span which is wider, lighter and better ventilated than a lean-to, but it has to be specially made to fit the wall it rests on. It is also worth remembering that there is no compelling reason why a conservatory should not be on an upper floor. With modern lightweight composts there is no necessity for a great weight of soil to be used. Of course, access from outside is highly desirable. Any specially constructed greenhouse will naturally cost more than the standard product, but we do have manufacturers who carry out this kind of work to a high standard.

I believe that a general-purpose span-roofed greenhouse standing on its own is best sited running east and west, giving one sunny side and one cooler side. This arrangement also gives the maximum of light in winter and is certainly best for propagation early in the year. Although controversy has raged for years, there still seems to be no final agreement on this subject, and many people prefer a north–south alignment. In practice a conservatory is often put in the only convenient place, and we can but hope that it will get enough sun in winter. If the siting is very poor, you may have to concentrate on shade-loving plants.

If you are anxious to have a very large greenhouse at the lowest cost in order to grow plants in the ground, it is worth considering a type of house often used commercially which is made up of standard Dutch lights bolted together. A Dutch light consists of a piece of glass 56 inches by 28¾ inches in a wooden frame. When supported on low walls, these are often used for raising early vegetables. They are a commercial form of garden frame. The Dutch light house consists of a framework on to which these lights can be bolted to form a temporary and removable structure. One can buy these structures complete and they are of more squat form than the ordinary greenhouse. There are also greenhouses of the Dutch light type that are not made up of individual lights, but have a similar shape and superficially the same appearance.

Plants need air as well as light, and ventilation is one of the trickiest points for the beginner. For success with plants the temperature has to be kept reasonably steady and ventilation plays an important part in this. The larger the volume of air within a greenhouse, the easier it is to avoid sudden rises and falls in temperature. Unfortunately the beginner all too often starts with the very smallest size of greenhouse and this is by far the most difficult to manage successfully. In a lean-to a great deal of sun heat is absorbed and stored up during the day by the back wall. Although this helps to reduce the cost of heating, a small lean-to can become like an oven on a hot day unless there is ample ventilation.

With every kind of glasshouse it is vital that the ventilation should be adequate. Although ventilators are often sold as extras, they are absolutely essential, and the cheaper houses always need more than they are provided with. Ideally, the ventilator in the roof of a span-type house should run the whole length of both sides of the ridge, while half this amount equally divided between the two sides should be regarded as a minimum. In a lean-to a ventilator running the whole length of the roof is not a bit too much. But you may not be able to get it. To ensure effective circulation of the air, there should also be a ventilator in at least one side wall of the greenhouse. This is frequently provided on a level with the staging; but it is much more satisfactory lower down where the incoming air will not cause a draught on the plants. It is worth paying a little extra to have box or panel ventilators put in under the staging. If a greenhouse rests on a brick wall the box ventilators are easily built into the brickwork, while the manufacturers will fit them to wooden-based houses. The manufacturer too should provide some low-down ventilation in the all-metal greenhouses with glass to the ground. You may be told that this is not necessary; but it is obvious that air will circulate better if cool air comes in low down. It is sometimes suggested that one should remove a pane of glass in the summer. This is an absurdly inconvenient suggestion. All ventilation must be adjustable or it is pointless.

If the ventilation of your greenhouse is going to be automatically controlled, this must be considered at the outset. Extractor-fan ventilation and fan heating do enable air to be kept moving in conditions which are otherwise unfavourable, and other forms of automatic ventilation need ventilation control gear that can be adapted to automation, or light-weight ventilators that are easily lifted. For the points to watch, please turn to Chapter 5, Ventilation and Humidity.

Another important factor in choosing a new greenhouse is maintenance. Although the white-painted softwood greenhouse can be both the cheapest to buy and the most pleasing in appearance, it can be expensive to maintain. It needs to be painted with a high-quality paint every three years. If someone has to be paid to do this the cost mounts up over the years. All the same, if you have a large old-fashioned greenhouse built in the age when only the finest materials and workmanship were used, do not lightly tear it down. The needs of plants came before the needs of mass production in those days and greenhouses were built to last.

A possible alternative to white paint for greenhouses is aluminium paint; this gives a silver metallic finish which is long lasting in adverse circumstances and reflects light well, though it is far less attractive than white paint. Bituminous paint must never be put on any heating apparatus as it gives off injurious fumes when heated.

A softwood that does not require painting has become popular for greenhouse construction in recent years. This is Western Red Cedar, the magnificent tree of western Canada which is known here mainly as the hedging plant *Thuja plicata*. This is a very durable wood but is not as strong as the hardwoods for large structures. While it is sometimes suggested that Western Red Cedar should be treated with a waterproofing preservative, the best method of keeping it in perfect condition seems to be to treat it yearly with a thin penetrating mineral oil that allows the wood to breathe. Linseed oil tends to turn the wood black, which is unattractive. As the cedar expands and contracts a good deal, there is sometimes trouble with slipping glass.

Oak is a strong and durable wood, and its tendency to warp is counteracted by metal bracing. Teak is very good but expensive. Agba is a cheaper tropical hardwood that is sometimes used.

Most of the recent advances in design and construction have been made with metal greenhouses. Here, at a price, you can virtually eliminate maintenance as well as getting the maximum amount of light. They do not have the cosiness of wood and you cannot so easily fix up extra shelves or temporary shading. The aluminium alloy and stove-enamelled metal greenhouses are the most expensive, trouble free and long-lasting structures. There are also galvanised steel houses. These are less costly but will need painting in time.

Reinforced concrete greenhouses are another possibility if you are not too far from a manufacturer. They have low upkeep cost and a long life. Ugliness is their main disadvantage, while heaviness of the structure blocks some light.

One of the things to look for when buying any greenhouse, particularly a metal one, is the arrangement that has been made for carrying away the moisture which will condense on the glass and the metal inside the house; one cannot have water dripping on the plants.

When buying a greenhouse that is going to be heated, it is particularly important that it should be of draught-proof construction; puttyless glass is to be avoided, unless there is an alternative soft material sealing the cracks. The method of replacing broken glass should be studied. It is worth knowing both whether the glass is of a standard size and also whether it can be obtained in small quantities.

Metal greenhouses are slightly colder than wooden ones, while those with glass down to ground level are colder in winter and hotter in summer. The latter do, however, allow tall plants to be grown and are essential if you are going to grow plants in beds of soil at ground level. It is possible to grow shade-loving plants under the staging and some greenhouses are made with glass to the ground on one side only. There is no doubt that your heating bill will be considerably reduced if the greenhouse rests on a brick wall. The inside temperature will also fluctuate less violently.

At the time of writing it is not necessary to get planning permission to erect a greenhouse that is not used for business, so long as it does not infringe the building-line of the dwelling-house. There are, however, regulations which affect the construction of a lean-to against a house wall and one cannot be sure from year to year what alterations may be made in the law. If you are a tenant, it is advisable to obtain your landlord's agreement in writing before putting up a greenhouse, and if you are a council tenant it is necessary to get the permission of the local authority. If any structure is to be put up against a boundary wall, it is, of course, essential to make sure that the wall is yours. A fact which may affect your choice of greenhouse is that it ceases to be a tenant's fixture if it is firmly fixed to a permanent brick or concrete foundation.

THE STRUCTURE

At present there is no effective substitute for glass in a heated greenhouse. Useful shelters for plants may be constructed of plastic; although it has the advantages of being light and cheap, glass has virtues that plastics do not share. A plastic greenhouse is much colder than a glass one, because plastic does not have the ability to hold in the radiated sun heat, which is one of the virtues of glass. In some circumstances it can be colder inside a plastic greenhouse than outside. Another disadvantage of plastic is that in winter in our climate the interior of a plastic or a plastic-lined greenhouse is covered with droplets of condensation most of the time. This reduces light transmission in a season when all possible light is needed. Although many people claim that an important saving in fuel cost is achieved by lining a greenhouse with plastic film, I do not recommend it. The humidity is increased at a time when it is undesirable, and unless the insulation is very well done the plastic lining is either ineffective or impedes ventilation. A great many people will not agree with me, but I would not line a greenhouse with plastic sheeting unless I were growing only shade-loving plants and keeping the greenhouse at a high temperature. The saving in heating cost might then be worth the risks of other troubles.

Another possible method of saving heating costs is double-glazing. This also reduces the light in the greenhouse, and there may be trouble with condensation and dirt between the panes. Nevertheless, the day may come when there is a perfect double-glazing unit which lasts well in greenhouse conditions. At present it is of doubtful advantage, though double-glazed side walls are quite a good idea in an orchid house. Double-glazing the roof doubles its weight and needs special construction. There is a double-glazed greenhouse on the market.

Some types of greenhouse are designed so that extra sections can be added at a later date. This can be a good idea. Many greenhouses are sold in so called 'easy to erect' sections. I have been through this nightmare twice. In both cases the greenhouse was quite satisfactory, but the instructions deplorably inadequate. This method does save money and is often unavoidable. It also greatly increases the sense of pride in possession.

One cannot take too much trouble over the foundations for any permanent greenhouse. There is also the question of the floor. For a conservatory attached to the house a tiled or concrete floor is undoubtedly the most practical. You may like to have at least one bed for climbing plants. If you are not going to grow plants in the ground, there is a great deal to be said for a concrete floor in all kinds of greenhouse. It is the easiest to keep clean and free from such things as weeds and slugs. Rammed earth or ash with a path of duck-boarding has been a traditional arrangement which helped to keep the atmosphere moist. Today, a central path of concrete blocks seems better, with the rest of the ground covered with shingle.

If a greenhouse is put up on a wet site, a concrete floor is necessary. If the soil is to be cultivated, it must be really well drained. The draining of the area will need to be done before putting up the greenhouse if there is any danger of the ground becoming waterlogged.

The soil in the greenhouse border is managed much as it would be out of doors, bearing in mind that no rain reaches it. A heavy soaking is advisable before starting a fresh crop. If a new greenhouse is put on lawn or other grass, the turf is removed with about an inch of topsoil. Then the remaining soil is dug over and some well-rotted manure or peat, bone meal and fish manure incorporated. If you are going to start using a greenhouse border that has been left in a neglected condition, it is advisable to replace at least the top six inches of soil. A good friable loamy soil with plenty of organic matter is what is needed. Neither heavy clay nor a light sandy soil will do without improvement of their structure by the addition of peat and sharp sand to the clay. Light soils also benefit from peat. Where there is really well-made garden compost it is useful on all soils, and so is well-rotted farmyard manure or dried seaweed.

All organic manures are good in greenhouses where sickness caused by a build-up of salts from excessive use of chemical fertilisers is a real hazard. Indeed, after a time all greenhouse soils tend to become sick or infected with harmful organisms, particularly where tomatoes and chrysanthemums are grown. Unfortunately, the greenhouse border cannot easily be sterilised by the amateur except by chemical means, and this can be done only when the greenhouse is empty and will remain so until the poisonous fumes have dispersed. The soil cannot safely be used for at least a month afterwards. The materials usually used are formaldehyde or cresylic acid, which are available as proprietary liquid fumigants, or dazomet, obtainable in powder form.

Greenhouse staging—the supports on which the plants are stood—is often sold with the greenhouse and is then usually made of wooden slats, though some makers of metal houses sell metal staging. Opinions differ about the best type of staging, but all are agreed that there must be a gap between the glass and any solid staging for the warm air to circulate. It is also essential that the staging should be strong enough to bear the weight of pots and soil. If the pots are going to stand in trays of shingle, the weight will be increased. With a capillary watering system the bench must also bear the weight of wet sand and remain precisely level under the strain. If you are going to grow plants in plastic pots with soilless compost, the weight will be negligible; but the six inches of wet sand on a mist-propagation bench is very heavy indeed.

Either flat or corrugated asbestos sheeting is often laid on top of either slatted wooden or metal staging. This is an excellent material so long as it is strongly supported. It can be covered with aggregate, gravel or stone chippings to hold moisture and improve its appearance. Corrugated iron and corrugated aluminium sheeting are other possible materials, and metal trays are sometimes also used. Some people believe in standing pots on wire mesh so as to allow the warm air to circulate all round them. This seems to me a short-lived and ugly arrangement. It is true, however, that in the winter a free circulation of air round the plants is very desirable, and some people remove the covering of the staging and place the pots on the open slats.

The ideal working height for a greenhouse bench is not a standard measurement, nor is the stretch of a gardener's arm. I find 2 ft. 6 in. a good working height, and a 3-ft. wide bench the widest that I can reach over from one side. The average height of cool greenhouse owners is not available; but a survey proved my own height of 5 ft. 4½ in. to be the average height of women readers of *Time* magazine, which is one of the statistics we can do without!

If you already have a greenhouse that seems to have more faults than virtues, do not despair. I have had very great pleasure out of a conservatory facing north with only a door for ventilation. Indeed, it is arguable that, for a conservatory which is supported by another greenhouse, a shady position is the best. There are also many greenhouse plants that flourish in shade.

3
Automation in the Greenhouse

EVERYONE WHO installs electrically controlled automation in a greenhouse must realise that they are embarking on a revolution in thought as well as in action. This realisation did not come to me until my automatic greenhouse was actually working. The moment when thermostats and time-switches take over from you as the decision-makers is rather like that when children grow up and can no longer be prevented from making their own mistakes. Neither your children nor your automation will necessarily make a better job of it than their predecessors. Indeed, you may not even worry any less than you did. But you will no longer be tied to the daily needs of your dependent children or of your plants.

As greenhouse automation is by no means perfected and is largely made up of equipment designed for use in totally different conditions, it is still very difficult for the amateur to know what equipment is best in any particular circumstances. The people interested in greenhouse automation at the present time are research establishments, large-scale commercial growers, the Electrical Development Council of the Electricity Boards, some of their horticultural advisers and the salesmen of some of the equipment used.

The average amateur will not be able to find an electrician who has ever fixed any equipment in a greenhouse before. Therefore the first essential is to employ only a well-qualified electrician from a good firm of some size. He will, at least, be unlikely to install unsuitable equipment in a manner that might prove dangerous in the special conditions of the greenhouse. He will not, however, have much knowledge about how it is best fitted up from a practical horticultural point of view, or have any conception of the problems that may arise in its use.

A first step for everyone is to read the helpful free booklet *Electricity in Your Garden*, obtainable from the Electricity Boards or from the Electricity Council, E.D.A. Division, Trafalgar Buildings, 1 Charing Cross, London, S.W.1. Unfortunately this is not compulsory reading for the electricians.

If you live in an area where there is a considerable amount of commercial horticulture under glass, it is likely that useful advice is obtainable from your Electricity Board. Their local agricultural adviser who also covers horticulture should have experience of greenhouse automation. It is, however, essential for the greenhouse owner to have the clearest possible idea of what he or she wants automated and how much can be spent on the job.

Unfortunately, the fully automated greenhouse requires both water and electricity. Both need to be handled with technical expertise, but electricians will not touch water, and plumbers will not touch electricity. In a complicated installation they must work to a concerted plan if the efforts of the one are not to frustrate the efforts of the other.

Until the private gardener's electrical needs are of economic importance to the industry, I fear that both second-rate equipment and doubtful advice will continue to be available. The horticultural press, who have the gardener's interests at heart, depend heavily on advertisement revenue and can rarely do much more than edit publicity material on technical subjects. They cannot have facilities for testing equipment. The Electricity Boards seem the best placed for gaining the necessary knowledge and experience of electrical devices, and I would approach them for advice about a complicated installation of any size.

Where there is a demand for a service you can be sure that it will be met in time—the important thing is to demand it. I believe, too, that it is up to us to add something to the sum of knowledge. The amateur gardeners of Britain are second to none in enthusiasm and know-how where plant growing is concerned. Unless we are just to accept the by-products of commercial advance, which may not be suited to our needs, we must experiment and think for ourselves. No new greenhouse owner can afford to ignore the new materials and techniques of recent years. There has never been a more interesting time to take up greenhouse gardening.

The attitude of the technician to automatic controls is that they should be set by him for all time and should neither be touched nor understood by the user. In a greenhouse this cannot work. It is essential to be able to make alterations to temperature settings, ventilation control and automatic watering requirements with the changing seasons. Indeed, all automatic equipment should be able to be operated manually in an emergency.

It is a mistaken economy to fit the maximum number of devices on to the minimum number of switches or fuses. If something develops a fault, it is important that nothing else should be needlessly affected. One cannot assume that technical help will be quickly available.

No equipment is more reliable than its weakest link. If a small screw has to be removed regularly for making an adjustment or cleaning a part, it is essential to have spares.

When electricity is being taken to the greenhouse for the first time, it is very important to install sufficient capacity for future needs, as an increase in load may need a heavier cable and switch gear, and lead to duplication of work.

A new problem that automation brings to the busy or absent greenhouse owner is the necessity of being able to tell at a glance if all systems have been working correctly.

Heating can be checked by a maximum and minimum thermometer which needs to be re-set regularly. Even without re-setting, it will probably show heating failure; but it will not necessarily reveal more complicated troubles. For instance, if thermostats are wrongly set, the heating coming on in the night may cause ventilators to open, which in turn keeps the heating on at full blast. Ventilation must be set higher than heating to avoid this danger.

Most watering devices can be monitored by placing a measuring jug at some strategic point, which will soon show how often or how much water has been released. Fortunately, the human nose is a first-rate instrument for judging whether the ventilation and humidity are satisfactory. It only needs training! There are, however, hygrometers which are helpful.

If automation is going to be installed in a greenhouse which is tended by a professional gardener, it is unreasonable to expect a smooth and immediate transition from traditional methods to automated ones. An old gardener with a poor education may find it difficult to adjust either his thinking or his actions to new gadgets. He may also deeply resent what he feels is a threat to and disregard of his skill and craftsmanship. A considerable part of the skill of a well-trained gardener is in the timing of results. He can raise plants to bloom in a planned succession and needs to organise the work for a year ahead. Mist propagation and capillary bench watering are wonderful tools but, as they speed growth and alter the response of plants to different soils and feeding régimes, they will alter every calculation. It is bound to take time to learn how to use the equipment to the best advantage for any particular purpose. The fact must also be faced that many of us unconsciously want technology to fail. I do not doubt that automation in greenhouses will become universal in time, but at present we all have to learn by trial and error.

Although there has been a good deal of research on the main commercial crops, such as tomatoes, cucumbers, chrysanthemums and carnations, there is no store of knowledge on the reactions of the immense diversity of plants the amateur may want to grow. Even the most skilled commercial growers are having to develop a new expertise, which they are unlikely to share with us or their rivals for many years to come.

Automation is in many ways easier for amateurs who can concentrate on the plants they can grow well rather than those for which there is a profitable market.

It is difficult to determine what amount it is sensible to spend on automating a greenhouse, and other people's opinions, although freely given, are almost valueless. The spending limit on other leisure activities, like sailing or golf, is not usually limited by the salesmen of the equipment, as sometimes happens in horticulture. 'This equipment is quite uneconomic for the amateur' is a phrase which needs to be killed stone dead. It means either 'We

AUTOMATION IN THE GREENHOUSE

are only interested in sales to large-scale growers', or 'No one I know could afford to spend so much on a greenhouse'. We will not get Rolls Royce service while this attitude persists! An automated greenhouse is a less expensive and no less reasonable hobby in this crowded island than a garden large enough to need professional upkeep. However, this fact is not yet socially accepted.

Camplex combined soil steriliser and greenhouse heater is manufactured by Simplex of Cambridge Ltd., which is a G.E.C. company

The Metomatic, 'Para' boiler burns paraffin and heats water-pipes. It is manufactured by The Metallic Construction Co. Ltd., of Derby

The burner is silent and needs little attention

The Aladdin paraffin oil greenhouse heater is available in two sizes to supply approximately 2,790 and 5,580 Btu's per hour. Heat distributors spread the warmth

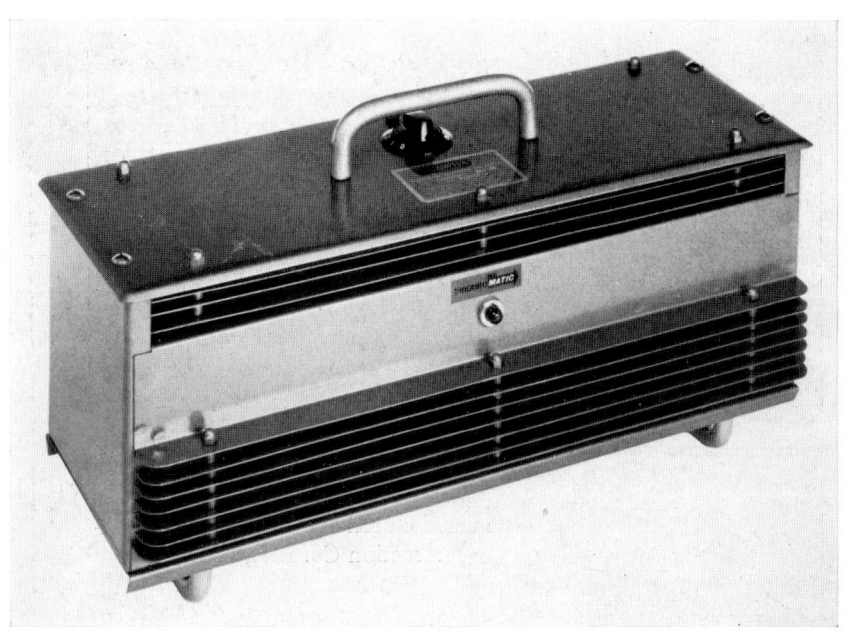

Camplex 3 kW. floor standing fan heater

The Lo-heat convector heater is available in several electrical loadings

Humex capillary trays supplied by a tank and ball-valve provide neat automatic watering

Horticultural tubular electric heaters adaptable and trouble-free. These are Ecko Hawkins Thermotubes

The Bayliss Autovent Mark III provides simple automatic ventilation in the small greenhouse

4
Heating

THERE ARE heating experts and gardening experts and perhaps somewhere there is a practical expert on heating, ventilation *and* plant growing under glass. Since none of us are likely to meet this paragon, I will do my best to give general information about heating as it affects the owner of a greenhouse. There are plenty of salesmen to stress the advantages of every heating method, and so, if I seem to go out of my way to point out the disadvantages, it is only to redress the balance.

I am not going to pretend to be entirely without prejudice here, as I am not personally prepared either to stoke a solid-fuel boiler or to handle paraffin daily. However, I recognise that, although I am willing and fortunately able to pay the price for convenience, this is not always possible or reasonable.

The first essential step is to decide what the minimum winter temperature in your greenhouse is going to be, and the second is to choose the heating method best suited to the particular circumstances. The temperature will be influenced by cost, as well as the needs of the plants you wish to grow, while the choice of fuel will be affected by convenience and storage facilities as well.

For many years a cheap and simple way of excluding frost from a small amateur greenhouse has been by means of a portable stove, burning paraffin. If the heater is carefully tended, the wick kept trimmed, and only the best grade of paraffin used, this can be successful. But it is not a satisfactory way of maintaining a growing temperature all through the winter, and you will have difficulty in keeping up a sufficiently high temperature in very cold weather.

Many people have paraffin oil heaters to supplement inadequate electric heating or as an emergency alternative to all other forms of heating. The dangers to guard against with paraffin heaters are that in very cold weather there may be a build-up of fumes, due to insufficient ventilation; or there may be a dangerous fall in temperature combined with excessive humidity. There should always be a chink of ventilation when an oil stove is burning.

It is not generally realised that the combustion of paraffin discharges a considerable amount of water vapour into the atmosphere. If the temperature is reasonably high, this will be absorbed by the warm air; in a heated room a paraffin heater actually reduces the humidity. In a greenhouse, however, on occasions when the heater is barely excluding frost, the extra humidity is a danger, and if there is a water tray on the heater it is a mistake to fill it. Some oil heaters have various arrangements of hot air or water pipes fixed above the flame. These give a wider distribution of the heat but make no difference to the amount of heat produced.

The makers of the best heaters state the maximum number of British Thermal Units (Btu) produced per hour by their heaters, and also the number of hours they will run on one filling. It is sometimes difficult to assess what temperature-lift an oil heater will give, though the rate of oil consumption is a considerable guide. An oil heater in a greenhouse can be counted on to produce at least 72,000 Btu's of heat from half a gallon of paraffin. Therefore, if a heater with a tank holding half a gallon of oil is guaranteed to burn for 100 hours on one filling, it cannot be producing more than approximately 720 Btu's per hour. Since 1 Btu per hour is equivalent to 0·293 watts this is only some 211 watts, and is too little to be useful in a greenhouse.

Most small oil heaters have a tank capacity that only lasts for one or two days. It is possible to have a larger tank outside the greenhouse with a self-filling arrangement, though it will still be necessary to check the burner frequently. A smoking burner can do considerable damage to plants.

A recent development which overcomes most of the objections to paraffin burners is the boiler specially designed for burning paraffin. This has a chimney through the roof of the greenhouse to remove fumes and water vapour, and a burner that does not require frequent attention. It is supplied from a tank outside the greenhouse and heats aluminium water pipes by means of a heat exchanger. Paraffin is a more expensive fuel than domestic fuel oil, but it can be burnt without the complicated equipment and electrical controls necessary for the most efficient combustion of the heavier fuel oils. Although the cost of a 'Para' boiler installation is greater than that of a solid-fuel boiler, it does need less frequent attention. The degree of heat is manually controlled but can be automated to some degree by a water thermostat.

For nearly a century the traditional method of heating greenhouses of any size has been by means of 4-inch cast-iron water pipes heated by a solid-fuel boiler. This is still the cheapest method. The standard cast-iron type of horseshoe boiler can now be replaced by more efficient modern types with easier cleaning and stoking methods and some thermostatic control by water thermostat. They do not, however, give the precision of heat control that electricity does and they still need regular attention.

I realise that the solid-fuel boiler will have its devotees for many years to come. The pride taken in keeping a recalcitrant boiler burning in difficult weather conditions can be a powerful human emotion that must be reckoned a pleasure for some. For others, it may be a painful necessity so long as solid fuel is the cheapest form of heating. It is not necessary to have either water or electricity on the site for solid-fuel boilers. A boiler which stands outside the greenhouse will be hard to control in a high wind and may burn out in the night. A great deal of heat will be lost from a freestanding boiler if it is not efficiently lagged. Boilers built into the brick wall of a greenhouse also lose some heat to the outside air. A water jacket helps to make a boiler more efficient, but this does not really constitute lagging. Do not forget the fuel store when assessing the cost.

The conversion of existing 4-inch piping to electric heating by means of an immersion heater is possible but not recommended, as one suffers both the slow response to changing temperatures of 4-inch piping as well as the high cost of electricity. To give a reasonable degree of temperature control by this method, both a water and an air thermostat would be needed. It is usually better to remove old piping systems if electricity is to be your fuel.

It is also possible to convert solid-fuel boilers to burn either domestic fuel oil or paraffin, but this is expensive on a small scale, and they do not use the fuel so efficiently as boilers designed for oil fuel.

There are, of course, oil-fired boilers with electric controls and with forced draught of the type used for domestic central heating. These are likely to be too costly for a small installation, particularly when you remember the cost of the fuel tank and the essential maintenance of such boilers as well as the installation and fuel.

For a large greenhouse of more than 20 feet by 10 feet oil-fired ducted air is a system worth investigating. Ducted air can be gas-fired; large electric fan heaters, too, can also be ducted. It is simply a matter of blowing warmed air through plastic or metal tubes so that it is widely distributed where it is needed. Ducted air is used industrially and also on commercial nurseries, and there are a number of different types of equipment.

So long as the source of electric power is not too far from the greenhouse, the one serious disadvantage of electric heating is the cost. The possibility of a power failure is always quoted against electricity, as though no other forms of heating failed. They can all fail, and so can the people who look after them. Fortunately power failures are rarely both lengthy enough and in cold enough weather to cause the loss of plants.

With electric heating controlled by a good-quality thermostat, no fuel is wasted and you have complete and instant control of greenhouse temperature. This is worth a great deal. There are also no fuel storage problems, dirt, trouble or dangerous fumes. There is, however, the question of safety. In the damp and rigorous conditions of a greenhouse it is vitally important not only that suitable materials and equipment should be used correctly and carefully earthed, but it is only reasonable to have the installation checked for safety from time to time. This is no place for the amateur electrician. There are many homes in Britain where all the electrical installations are not properly earthed or adequately maintained, and this situation is doubly dangerous in the damp conditions of a greenhouse. Now that suitable equipment exists, there is no excuse for making do with fittings that are not waterproof or with wiring that might corrode with greenhouse sprays.

If you decide to choose electricity as your fuel, there are a variety of different ways of using it. The horticultural tubular heater is a well tried and reliable system with no moving parts. The aluminium tubes are 2 inches in diameter with a loading of 60 watts per foot. They are versatile, as they come in lengths of from 2–12 feet. For good air circulation they should be banked in tiers at the sides of the greenhouse, starting 9 inches from the ground, and 4 inches from the outer walls. They should not be put at the ends of the greenhouse as well, since this confuses the air circulation. Personally, I have found them very satisfactory, although other methods are cheaper to buy and to install.

A method of heating which has the minimum of installation cost is a free-standing heater of either the convection or fan type. In the very small greenhouse where one of these is enough it is a very popular form of heating.

Horticultural convector heaters are available in three sizes (1 kW., 2 kW. and 3 kW.). It pays to choose the larger sizes which can be used either at full strength or with one kilowatt of power switched off. They cost little more, and the extra reserve of power is valuable even if it is only used in very cold weather. A domestic convector is neither suitable nor safe in a greenhouse and the same is true of domestic tubular heaters. Naturally, a convector will not give such a good distribution of heat as tubular heaters; but it is a reasonably priced and effective way of heating the smaller greenhouse. It is also silent. Convectors should be placed centrally and not under the bench.

Fan heaters have increased in popularity with the growing appreciation of the value of buoyant air. There are models which blow air in one direction or in two directions. They can also be used without the heating element to circulate the air in the warmer months. The heating element should be encased in a metal tube, as in the cooking rings of electric cookers. Although some of these heaters have built-in thermostats, it is always better to control air temperature with a good-quality thermostat strategically placed. All fans make a slight whirring noise when running, which is irritating to some people.

Another possible form of space-heating is by means of mineral insulated cables, fixed round the sides of the greenhouse on ceramic cleats. If corrosive sprays are going to be used, the cable should be PVC covered. The cable is specially prepared by the makers in one piece of the necessary loading and length. Even with the cost of fixing it, the total cost is likely to be something like half that of tubular heaters. The cost of electricity used is, of course, always the same for a given amount of heat produced.

The heating of a lean-to conservatory attached to a dwelling-house is a rather different proposition from the free-standing greenhouse. The heat-loss from the house into the conservatory may be considerable and will greatly reduce the heating cost of the latter. This situation is apt to make electric heating particularly worth while. Sometimes a radiator connected to the central-heating system of the home is put in the conservatory, although this does not really help with temperature control unless it has a separate thermostat. Domestic heating is often switched off at night, which is the time when most heating is needed in a greenhouse. The heating may also be off in May and September, when night frosts can be damaging under glass if there is no other form of heating.

Unfortunately domestic night-storage heaters do not work in uninsulated buildings, and so it is difficult to use off-peak electricity rates to advantage under glass. There is as yet no really satisfactory way of using off-peak electricity in greenhouses except for soil-heating, which can be controlled by a time clock rather than a thermostat.

With all forms of electric greenhouse heating a thermostat is essential and saves a great deal of money in the long run. Unfortunately the most efficient thermostats are invariably the most expensive. The rod type is best in damp conditions and should be 24 inches long for controlling the greenhouse heating. Thermostats do not last for ever and they may become sluggish with age and waste current.

HEATING

The placing of the thermostat is both difficult and important. The object is always to choose a generally representative position. It is the temperature round the plants that concerns you. For this reason thermostats built into heaters are only a rough guide. In practice the thermostat must be fixed to something solid in a convenient place where it will not get damaged. Sun shining on it is undesirable, but almost unavoidable, since, if it is shaded, the shade itself heats up and distorts the temperature.

At the time of writing aspirated thermostats are popular, with fans blowing the greenhouse air past the thermostat, which is housed in an insulated tube. Those put on the market for the amateur contain a cheaper type of thermostat than the recommended 24-inch rod type, and I have doubts as to whether this will be an advance in the long run.

The general advice is to have the heating thermostat above the plants, about a third of the way along the greenhouse and neither immediately under a ventilator, nor over a heater, nor against the roof glass. If it can be shaded by something which is not close to it, so much the better. If you keep a thermometer amongst the plants, you will soon find out if you are getting the temperature you want in the place you need it. The variations in temperature in different positions in a greenhouse are considerable and well worth knowing if you are growing a variety of plants.

Greenhouse electrical heating calculations are often based on a minimum outside temperature of $-6.7°$ C. ($20°$ F.). This means that when the outside temperature falls to $-6.7°$ C. ($20°$ F.) the inside temperature will still be kept up to the minimum winter temperature you have decided on and at which your thermostat is set. But if the outside temperature falls below $-6.7°$ C. ($20°$ F.) the inside temperature will fall correspondingly. How far it falls will depend on how much temperature lift your installation is designed to give.

Suppose that you have electrical heating sufficient to maintain $7°$ C. ($45°$ F.) in your greenhouse when the outside temperature is $-6.7°$ C. ($20°$ F.). This will mean that you have an electrical loading to give you a $25°$ F. temperature lift. If there is a cold spell and the outside temperature drops to $-10°$ C. ($14°$ F.) the temperature in your greenhouse is likely to fall to $3°$ C. ($39°$ F.). Since this is well above freezing point and the temperature is unlikely to remain as low as this for long it is a reasonable risk in most circumstances. Plants do not usually suffer visibly from short failures of heating, so long as they do not freeze; but a long period is damaging. If your greenhouse is in an exposed and windy position or in a cold part of the country, you need to allow for this.

With the memory of the quite exceptionally cold winter of 1962/3 still in our minds, most of us will have our own ideas as to the minimum outside temperature it is reasonable to guard against in our district.

I have found that, in the South Midlands at an elevation of 500 feet on an exposed site, the temperature falls to —9° C. (16° F.) often enough to be included in my calculations. With a desired minimum winter temperature of 7° C. (45° F.) and a 25° F. temperature lift my greenhouse temperature should in fact only fall to 5° C. (41° F.) when the outside temperature falls to —9° C. (16° F.). With an icy wind and an overloaded electricity supply, however, it has been known to drop a little below this figure. With only a 20° F. temperature lift which some people feel to be a fair risk I would have been in real trouble. Of course, if I was aiming at a minimum winter temperature of 10° C. (50° F.) I would need a 30° F. temperature lift.

One cannot say too often that setting a thermostat at a temperature, which the heating equipment is not designed to maintain, is a mistake. It will cause unnecessary electricity consumption in mild weather, and may keep plants in active growth only to be stricken by sudden unduly low temperatures in a cold spell. One had far better face facts and grow plants in steady conditions to which they can adapt themselves.

As the amount of electricity used and therefore its cost virtually doubles with every extra 2·8° C. (5° F.) of heat maintained in the greenhouse, few of us will aim above a minimum winter temperature of 7° C. (45° F.) when heating by electricity.

The lower the outside temperature allowed for, the greater the cost of the equipment, although the running cost will be no greater, except in the unusually cold spells when the extra heating capacity is needed to maintain a safe temperature.

HEATING

Having made your decisions about temperature you will need to work out the electrical heating requirements of your greenhouse.

To sum up, the first step is to decide what the minimum winter temperature is going to be in your greenhouse and what outside temperature it is reasonable to guard against in your district. The difference between these two figures is the temperature lift you need.

The amount of heat needed to maintain the required temperature depends not only on the power of the heater, but also on the amount of heat lost through the glass and the fabric of the greenhouse itself. As the thermal conductivity of the various materials is known, this can be worked out quite accurately. Calculations based merely on the cubic capacity of the greenhouse are hit or miss.

Listed below are the thermal factors of the various materials of which greenhouses are constructed expressed in 'U' value. (This is the heat leakage of a structure measured in terms of British Thermal Units per square foot of the surface area, per hour, per degree F. difference between the internal and external air temperature.) Fortunately these figures can be used without being understood too closely.

Thermal Factors of Material

Material	'U' Value
Horticultural glass	1·0
Asbestos sheet	1·0
Wood 1 in. thick	0·5
Wood 1½ in. thick	0·4
Brick 4½ in. thick	0·6
Brick 9 in. thick	0·5
Brick 13½ in. thick	0·4
Concrete 4 in. thick	0·6
Concrete 6 in. thick	0·5
Greenhouse floor (soil or concrete)	0·33

To work out the heat loss of the structure and to calculate the loading of electric heaters:

1. (a) Measure all the area of glass including the sash bars in square feet; (b) do the same for the brick, concrete or wooden walls; (c) measure the floor.

2. Multiply totals a, b and c by their appropriate 'U' values from the above table and add the three results together.

3. Multiply this last figure by 0·39. This allows for chance losses of heat through cracks etc., and also for the fact that there are 3·412 Btu's in a watt of electricity (1·33 — 3·412 = 0·39).

4. The final calculation is to multiply your result by the temperature lift you require.

In the following example, as given by the Electricity Council in their booklet, the temperature lift chosen is 25° F. in a greenhouse to be kept at 7° C. (45° F.). In this greenhouse the temperature will start to fall below the chosen temperature of 7° C. (45° F.) only when the outside temperature falls below —6·7° C. (20° F.). The point at which the inside of the greenhouse might reach 0° C. (32° F.) would only be when the outside temperature dropped to —14° C. (7° F.). This is very unlikely to happen, but it could do so even in Southern England in an occasional freak winter like 1962/3.

Example

To maintain a temperature of 45° F. (7° C.) inside against 20° F. (—6·7° C.) outside in a span roof house with a 4½-in. brick wall (as in diagram).

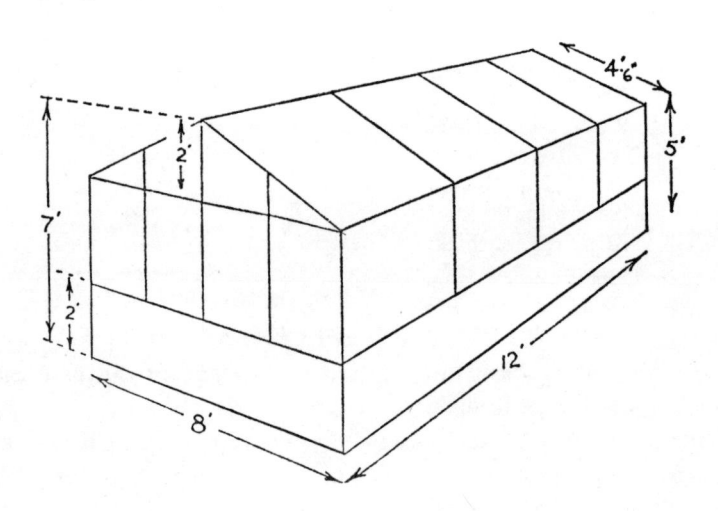

HEATING

	Area (sq. ft.)	'U' value from table	Heat loss Btu/ Hr./° F.
Glass roof 12 ft. × 4 ft. 6 in. × 2	108	× 1	108
Glass sides 12 ft. × 3 ft. × 2	72	× 1	72
Glass ends 8 ft. × 3 ft. × 2	48	× 1	48
4 ft. × 2 ft. × 2	16		16
Brick sides 12 ft. × 2 ft. × 2	48	× 0·6	29
Brick ends (including door) 8 ft. × 2 ft. × 2	32	× 0·6	19
Soil 8 ft. × 12 ft.	96	× 0·33	32
			324

Multiply 324 × 0·39 = 126 watts per ° F. rise.
Multiply by 'temperature lift' 25° F. (13·9° C.) = 126 × 25 = 3,160 watts.
Choose the next largest standard size of heater above 3,160 watts.

The Electricity Council booklet *Electricity in your Garden*, quoted above, gives an interesting guide to likely average electricity consumption in greenhouses kept at various temperatures in different parts of the country. Unfortunately, as no year is average and few greenhouse sites are average either, one can only get a very general picture of likely consumption over a period of years. The good and the bad winters do average out in the end, but the greenhouse owner's ambitions and the price of electricity are almost certain to increase meanwhile and upset the calculations. Nevertheless, electricity has such tremendous advantages in the small greenhouse that it should always be considered.

Soil warming is an aspect of heating that can be indulged in even without a greenhouse. For warming areas of soil, electric soil-warming cable is used. This is of two types—mains-voltage cable and low-voltage cable. The former is a wire with a thick protective sheathing which plugs directly into the mains; the latter is a PVC-covered galvanised wire, together with a transformer which brings down the voltage in the wires to a level that is not dangerous even if the wire is damaged. The low-voltage cable is more expensive to install because of the cost of the transformer; but the running costs are the same. The low-voltage wires are specially chosen with electrical characteristics to tie up with the transformer and must not be replaced with ordinary wire.

Where there is going to be cultivation of the soil, as in a bed on the floor of a greenhouse, low-voltage cable must be used. It should in any case be the rule, where soil-warming cable is in use, that the electricity is turned off before cultivation of any kind takes place. Mains-voltage cable is safe to touch, so long as the protective sheathing is not damaged. If there is damage, the whole wire has to be renewed. The metal-screened type of mains cable is to be preferred. This blows the fuse immediately it is damaged.

Both kinds of soil-warming cable are laid evenly in parallel lines with gentle curves at the ends, so that the wires never come close to each other and overheat. They should never be sharply bent anywhere. How closely the wires are laid, and how deeply they are buried, will depend on the purpose of the soil warming. The width between the lines of wire depends on how many watts per square foot of heating are required, and the depth at which the wires are buried depends on the cultivations required and the crop grown. The most even temperature of the whole surface area of the soil is achieved when the spaces between the lines of wire is either equal to, or less than, the depth at which they are buried. If they are deeper than the width between them there will be greater warmth directly over the wires than in the rest of the ground.

When soil-warming wires are used in an outdoor frame to replace the now outmoded hotbed of fermenting manure, a loading of 6–7 watts per square foot is advisable. Early vegetable and salad crops are grown in this way, and, since cultivation is necessary, the low-voltage type of cable is suitable. The wires are laid about 6 inches deep and parallel with the surface of the soil, even if this is built up to follow the angle of the frame light. For this type of frame off-peak electricity can be used, as the dosage method of applying the heat is adequate. This means that the electricity is switched on each night for long enough to give a dosage of 62 watts per square foot in the south of England and 72 watts in the north of England. This can be controlled by a time-switch.

HEATING

For a propagating frame a loading of not less than 8 watts per square foot should be provided and it is highly desirable that the temperature should be controlled by a thermostat. Mains cable can be used for propagation. In this type of frame, whether it is within the greenhouse or outside, 2 inches of fine clayey builders' sand is put under the cable, and another 2 inches on top. The heating wires will soon dry this, and as dry sand is not a good conductor of heat it must be kept moist. On this moist sand the boxes, pots or pans of seeds and cuttings are placed as close as possible, and the gaps between them are plugged with damp peat to keep in the warmth. If cuttings are rooted directly in a warmed propagating bed, this is made up on top of the builders' sand. A half-and-half mixture of really sharp sand and horticultural peat is often used for this and a depth of 2 inches is suitable.

A warmed bench in the greenhouse, which is not enclosed by a frame, is made up in exactly the same way. The thermostat controlling the soil temperature needs to be of the rod type and 18 inches long. It is inserted in the side of the frame or bench, so that the rod runs across the heating wires and just below the surface of the builders' sand.

If a heated frame is to be an alternative to a greenhouse for over-wintering tender plants, and also for raising early seedlings, it needs to be provided with an electrical loading sufficient to give enough temperature lift to maintain your chosen temperature in all weathers. To give a temperature lift of 12·5° C. (25° F.), a loading of 3 watts per square foot of glass for each 2·5° C. (5° F.) temperature rise is required. This kind of frame will need air heating as well as soil heating.

Warming cables can be used to heat the air in a frame either with or without warming the soil. A frost-free frame is a useful addition to the greenhouse for hardening off tender plants for the garden and for many other purposes. An outdoor frame does, of course, use considerably more electricity than an indoor one, but it is not unduly expensive to run.

Some people like to grow a few plants which need a higher winter temperature than that maintained in the greenhouse, and choose to do this in a frame within the greenhouse, rather than partitioning off a small section of the greenhouse itself and keeping this at a higher temperature.

It is possible to buy a fully fitted propagating case with enough headroom for pot plants if you do not want to construct your own.

With all soil heating a soil thermometer is a good idea to check soil temperatures at the rooting point. Propagation is usually most successful with a root temperature between 21° C. (70° F.) and 24° C. (75° F.). For propagating under mist a loading of 15–18 watts per square foot is necessary because of the cooling action of the mist.

For the busy or absent gardener a frame is apt to be more difficult to run than the greenhouse itself, as it needs more frequent attention unless it has automatic ventilation and watering. This is only just beginning to be thought of in connection with frames. At the time of writing only one firm provides such a frame, and it is a large, glass-sided, metal frame best suited for growing early vegetables.

Some of those who want to sterilise their own potting soil may find it worth considering a combined soil steriliser and greenhouse heater. This has a loading of 1·5 kilowatts and can be used as the only source of heat in a very small greenhouse or to provide additional heating capacity in exceptionally cold weather.

5
Ventilation and Humidity

FORTUNATELY PLANTS are adaptable or few would survive for long in the average greenhouse. Before I installed automatic ventilation, atmospheric conditions that would not be surprising in the Sahara sometimes alternated with the steamy heat of the Amazon, when I could not be there to watch over the greenhouse in hot weather. For many amateurs automatic ventilation seems an impossible and pointless expense. If you rarely go away from home or cannot afford any luxuries, this may well be true. But it is also true that much of the lack of success in greenhouses is due to failure to control the climate in which the plants are growing. Unfortunately, the day has not yet come when there is a single control for heating and ventilation, linked with humidity to give predetermined day and night temperatures. Perhaps this is an engineer's dream that will never reach the amateur, but it is by no means a fanciful idea.

With practical experience and observation, the control of both ventilation and humidity become virtually instinctive, and perhaps this is why these two most tricky subjects are so hard to explain adequately on paper.

For the beginner a maximum and minimum thermometer is a necessity. It is always highly desirable, if only to give an indication of what happened when you were not there.

Ventilation has three purposes: to provide the plants with fresh air, which is essential for growth; to control the temperature, and to help in the control of atmospheric moisture. The aim must always be to maintain a steady temperature, only moderately cooler at night than during the daytime, while the air should never be stagnant, nor should there be a draught.

I believe that in the kind of greenhouse this book is about you can hardly have too much air in summer. The first necessity is that there should be enough ventilation to keep the temperature down to reasonable levels in hot weather. I have discussed this problem in an earlier chapter. Unfortunately, since many greenhouses are poorly equipped, I strongly advise you to experiment a little before filling a greenhouse with valuable plants. Ventilation, like every other horticultural subject, is controversial. I have met gardeners who risk very high temperatures and believe in damping everything down and shutting all ventilators if they are unable to give enough attention to the greenhouse in hot weather.

The rate of growth of plants can be greatly accelerated by warm, close, damp conditions. Nevertheless, the amateur with a mixed collection of ornamental plants has nothing to gain from rapid, soft growth. This is particularly undesirable for perennial and woody plants, if they are to experience minimum winter temperatures later in the year. Secondly, it is not only the plants that grow rapidly in tropical conditions but also insect pests and diseases. Even the good growing atmosphere of the nurserymen's greenhouse is not always desirable except for seedlings and young cuttings, and these are best started in a propagating frame or mist unit.

At present, in practice, ventilation can only be controlled automatically by temperature, and this is not always as good as the judgment of the gardener if a wind is blowing. At the same time a thermostat is always on duty and does not forget.

The simplest and cheapest form of automatic ventilation does not even require electricity. It can, however, only lift a small ventilator which must not weigh more than 15 lb. This ingenious device is activated by a cylinder filled with a composition which expands when a certain temperature is reached and contracts when the temperature falls. It is adjustable within limits and not expensive. With ingenuity one device can even be made to operate two small ventilators.

There is another system for slightly larger ventilators, whereby

An amateur's mist unit used for seeds and cuttings

A capillary bench watered by a trickle-line in the author's greenhouse

VENTILATION AND HUMIDITY

a thermostatically controlled small electric motor opens and shuts the ventilators by means of cords and pulleys. With this method you must not forget to watch for wear on the cords, as overhead lights might crash if a cord snapped.

For larger greenhouses there are various methods of raising and lowering ventilators, either singly or severally, by means of electric motors or hydraulic rams. These are all liable to cost as much as the greenhouse itself unless it is a large one. I myself have a hydraulic ram electrically controlled, which has given me infinite satisfaction although it is one of those things that are 'not economic for amateurs', and therefore treated as morally reprehensible by everyone connected with horticulture. Oddly enough, this attitude does not apply to the ownership of such things as mink coats at thirty times the cost!

At present the most popular form of automatic ventilation is the extractor fan. This is a boon in the inadequately ventilated house because it is used with the ventilators closed. In most circumstances it can draw in enough fresh air through the cracks in the otherwise closed greenhouse; if a roof ventilator were open, the air would be drawn directly from it and the air circulation would not be effective. Extractor fans need to have louvres which close automatically when the fan is not operating. This is to keep out the wind and to avoid losing heat in cold weather. To me the main objection to fans is the whirring noise they make. Some people say that they desiccate the atmosphere more than the manually operated ventilator, but this is presupposing close personal attention to ventilation.

An extractor fan controlled by a thermostat, set at least $2 \cdot 5°$ C. ($5°$ F.) above the heating thermostat, is a great blessing even if you do not always use it. For a large part of the year greenhouses need ventilation far earlier in the day than many people attend to it. I suppose it would be possible to have a greenhouse with fan ventilation only and no possibility of opening ventilators, but it would be alarming to be so utterly dependent both on the electricity supply and the fan itself. Fans are in fact very reliable, though of course anything with moving parts may suffer from wear in time.

So far, for 95 per cent of the time all electrically controlled ventilation available to the amateur is either fully open or completely shut. The gardeners' ideal of a crack of air on the leeward side on a winter morning can only be provided manually. With all forms of automatic ventilation the possibility of manual control needs to be retained for emergencies.

Ventilation is measured in air changes per hour. The commercial grower with a large area of fast-growing crops aims at 60 air changes per hour. We are told that 30 air changes per hour are enough for amateurs. Although I do not feel competent to judge, I feel fairly sure that you want as much ventilation as anyone can be persuaded to provide. Since both equipment and ideas are changing all the time, it is essential to get the latest advice.

As a rough guide on the basis of 30 changes per hour the following sizes of fan are recommended as adequate:

$7\frac{1}{2}$-inch diameter impellor for up to 280 cubic feet
9 -inch diameter impellor for up to 500 cubic feet
12 -inch diameter impellor for up to 1,000 cubic feet

In cool or cold conditions too much humidity in stagnant air is a menace, which soon leads to botrytis and other fungal troubles. It also leads to excessive condensation on the glass and the plants, if there is more moisture than the cold air can absorb. This is one of the reasons why we were told for so long that 13° C. (55° F.) was the minimum winter temperature for many of the plants we now grow at 7° C. (45° F.). There is more margin for error with higher temperatures in winter, because warm air absorbs more moisture and heating also dries the air. The moment when the solid-fuel enthusiast is glad of his wasteful but constantly warm pipes is when the ventilators are closed and the temperature has not yet fallen enough to turn on the heat in the electrically heated greenhouse. Warm pipes keep the air circulating, and so do extractor fans and fan heaters while they are working.

Some people believe in having a small air-circulating fan. Ideally this should come on when the ventilation closes or stops. In fact, it is often linked with the heating so as not to use yet another thermostat. With fan heating this would be pointless, but with other forms of heating a fan placed high at one end of the house and pointing slightly downwards does help to keep the air moving, and also to prevent warm air settling up near the roof. Indeed, the possible permutations of automatic ventilation and heating are only limited by the cost.

In summer the main function of ventilation is to keep down the temperature. It is fair to say that all temperatures above 24° C. (75° F.) are undesirable, though they cannot be avoided all the time.

A low-built greenhouse needs more ventilation than a high one, and a small one relatively more than a large one. If a greenhouse is ventilated mainly by ridge ventilators, it is believed that these should open up an area of not less than one-sixth of the floor area. Although the maximum ventilation is needed in the hottest weather, this tends to produce a desiccated atmosphere within the greenhouse.

The three weapons with which to fight excessive temperatures in a greenhouse are ventilation, shading and extra humidity. All these are limited to some extent. Ventilation cannot be perfect on the hottest day since the greenhouse will inevitably be hotter than the outside air, and it would be preferable to have no glass at all.

Shading has a cooling effect but is limited by the amount the plants can stand without suffering from lack of light. In practice if the shading is of a permanent kind it is limited by the amount of shade the plants can stand on the dull days. Ideally all shading should be adjusted to the actual sunshine. For this reason wooden lath blinds on the outside of the greenhouse are considered a luxury form of shading. These have the maximum cooling effect and can also be controlled automatically, but they are very costly.

Translucent PVC roller blinds within the greenhouse are another possibility. They are available in various standard sizes and easily fixed to wooden greenhouses. There is also green plastic sheeting by the yard, and fine plastic netting specially designed for shading greenhouses.

Perhaps the easiest and cheapest way of shading is to apply a thin coat of either a patent shading material or a home-made brew of whiting mixed with milk or flour and water. These materials should be kept clear of the paintwork. All permanent shading should be removed as soon as possible. From the beginning of May until the end of August should be long enough, though seedlings may need shade in March, and some plants in April and September. I usually put shade on the sunny side first.

Except for shade-loving plants, greenhouse shading is merely a means of preventing their tissues from scorching or heating unduly in the artificial conditions of a greenhouse. In really well-controlled conditions with ample ventilation, tomatoes, for instance, need no shading, although many amateurs have found that shading is desirable in their own particular greenhouse.

The question of humidity depends to some extent on the plants grown and the way they are grown. If you intend to specialise in orchids, this subject should be considered even before buying the greenhouse.

I myself have grown a mixed collection of plants, on irrigated benches, which drip on to the floor every time they are watered automatically. I also have capillary benches which help to create a moist atmosphere, but do not drip on to the floor. Many people stand their pots in gravel trays in summer, removing these in winter and standing the pots directly on slatted staging. This achieves the best of both worlds, as the gravel trays can be kept moist in summer and warm air circulates all round the plants in winter. Another plan is to spread aggregate on solid staging, keeping this moist in summer and dry in winter. It would, of course, be possible to spray the floor automatically if you felt the cost to be justified. A few people feel that air circulation is so important that they make staging out of some kind of metal mesh, but this does not have a long life.

In the United States, where the summers are hotter than ours and the air often drier, the system known as fan and pad ventilation is much used; but it seems less successful in our climate. With this method air is drawn into the greenhouse through a porous pad in the side wall which is kept constantly moist.

The traditional method of keeping greenhouses sufficiently humid is by damping down the floor and staging, when watering in warm and sunny weather. This could be done every hour on a really hot day, but it would be impractical. From April a damping down in the morning and through the summer two or three times a day in sunny weather is the usual arrangement.

There is now a reasonably priced hygrometer, which shows the humidity on a dial if it is kept in a shady spot. A reading around 60 is the aim.

6

Pots, Soil and Feeding

I AM SURE that more plants are killed by over-watering than by any other means. Yet this killing by kindness is easily avoided if the principles of plant growth are understood.

With the aid of the energy derived from light, plants absorb carbon dioxide (CO_2) from the air through the pores in their leaves. There it is converted into oxygen and sugar from which the materials needed for building the plant structure are manufactured. At the same time the roots of the plant not only anchor it in the soil, but absorb water in which many nutrients are dissolved. Plants are dependent on the root hairs (at the tips of their roots) for absorbing water and nutrients.

If the soil becomes too dry the whole life process of the plant comes to a halt and the leaves droop. By the time this happens damage to the root hairs has already taken place. Plants have great powers of recovery and can overcome temporary dryness, but it is always a setback to their growth that renders them doubly susceptible to too much water until they have made new root hairs to absorb it. One of the greatest dangers to pot plants is that the soil will become sour, and this process is greatly hastened by waterlogging. The modern composts are designed to keep the soil friable and well-aerated in spite of constant overhead watering.

The moisture needs of plants vary greatly, not only between one plant and another, but also with the seasons and the health and activity of the plant. How often water is needed depends, too, on the temperature and dryness of the atmosphere and the degree

POTS, SOIL AND FEEDING

of evaporation from the pot itself. Another factor is the type of compost used.

All these variables make it impossible to give simple general instructions, like 'water twice a week'. The general idea is that the roots of a growing plant must never be either dry or in a waterlogged condition in which all air is excluded from the soil. In all fertile soil there are air spaces between the soil particles. That is why drainage must be free. The usual advice is to water thoroughly so that all the soil in the pot is moistened and then to wait until it is approaching dryness before repeating the process. Nevertheless every experienced gardener has been baffled by those who give a little dribble of water every day and still grow good plants.

It may seem illogical that plants should grow well in pots that are kept constantly moist by capillary attraction while standing on automatically watered benches of wet sand. The explanation here is that the soil is never compressed and saturated. The air is not wholly excluded and only the water that is absorbed by the plant or the atmosphere is replaced.

Until recent years clay pots and soil-based composts were the inevitable choice. Today, the new greenhouse owner not only needs to choose between clay and plastic pots, and soil-based or loamless composts, but also has to decide on the watering method. All these will affect the basic activity of growing plants in pots and keeping them watered which is what the greenhouse is mainly about.

To many the plastic pot seems a retrograde step, but it is now clear that it has come to stay. Its advantages are that it is light, relatively unbreakable, easy to clean and well suited for use on capillary benches. Its disadvantages are that over-watering is slower to right itself than in the clay pot, and it has no charm of appearance. Hand-watered plants in plastic pots do, however, require less frequent watering which makes life easier in hot weather. A new hazard on the other hand is that a heavy plant in a plastic pot of light, soil-less compost is liable to be top-heavy and blow over.

For generations we have been saying that the porosity of the clay pot is essential for the healthy growth of plants, so naturally there is a certain amount of controversy before everyone is ready to say that plastic pots are better. Nevertheless, I do not feel that I could recommend anyone today to buy a new supply of clay pots unless they are for orchids or alpine plants or large specimen plants. The use of plastic pots for cacti is also controversial but widely practised. The fact is that the plastic pot makes life easier, both for the gardener and the plants, so long as they are correctly watered. There is a much reduced danger of a set-back due to dryness and a slightly increased danger of excessive wet. After all, the Japanese have been keeping miniature trees healthy in glazed pots for hundreds of years. A porous pot is not essential to plant health.

The receptacles needed for greenhouse plants are to some degree a matter of preference. The traditional arrangement is to sow seeds either in wooden boxes or clay pans. Today, many amateurs are likely to choose plastic seed trays that take less space to store and are easy to clean. They can also be induced to water themselves on a capillary bench, which is important in the automated greenhouse. Trays come in various sizes including a small one, $8\frac{3}{4} \times 6\frac{1}{3} \times 2$ inches deep, and another 10 inches square and 3 inches deep. For pricking out young seedlings, a pan $2\frac{1}{2}$ inches deep is needed.

Pots come in many sizes from 2 inches in diameter upwards. The most often used in the average greenhouse are probably the $2\frac{1}{2}$-, $3\frac{1}{2}$- and 5-inch sizes. There are also dwarf pots with a depth three-quarters of their diameter, and round seed pans half the depth of their diameter.

When putting a plant into a pot, the aim is to accommodate the roots comfortably with sufficient room for new growth and some drainage material, while leaving room for watering. Pieces of broken clay flower pot have long been used for drainage and are known as 'crocks'. They are placed concave side downwards over the drainage holes. For plants that are to remain in the same pot for a long time, free drainage that does not get silted up is important. This is achieved by putting several crocks at the bottom, covered by small gravel or rough peat to prevent fine soil from washing through. Crocks are not necessary in small pots except for cacti. All this presupposes overhead watering which you may not be going to indulge in.

The modern plastic pots have a number of small holes in the base rather than one large one and do not need crocks.

In the past a multitude of different soil mixtures have been used successfully for pot plants. There is indeed no limit to the possible variations for particular plants. Today the cost and scarcity of labour as well as increased knowledge of plant growth have led to a more scientific assessment of potting composts. It is remarkable that it is only in the present century that controlled scientific testing of the traditional gardening practices has been carried out.

The basis of all traditional composts is the topsoil of good pasture together with the grass sod. This is dug and stacked for a year to rot down, before being mixed with other ingredients to improve the texture or nutrition of the compost. This is a time-honoured and excellent plan, provided that high-quality materials and the necessary labour are available. I fear that it will not be long before this practice comes to have the nostalgia of some of Mrs. Beeton's excellent recipes. It will soon seem as fanciful as making cakes with two dozen eggs and the best brandy, that are kept for a year before eating.

It is now more than thirty years since the introduction of the John Innes composts did so much to simplify and standardise the traditional type of soil mixtures. With these the vast majority of plants can be grown in one set of composts of varying nutritional strengths. For the amateur the invention of the John Innes composts was a breakthrough of major importance. Here for the first time was a compost that equalled the mysterious and laborious concoctions of the experts, and yet could be bought ready-mixed in a bag. It also had a clear recipe which could be made up at home by those who were willing to take the necessary trouble.

Unfortunately this happy state of affairs was too good to last indefinitely. J.I.P., as it came to be called, is based on a particular quality of stacked matured loam which is increasingly scarce and costly. Also, many people cannot tell if the compost is of good quality. In the course of time any old loam has come to be used in some of the compost sold, and few of us can now find the best-quality ingredients to prepare it for ourselves. Although good J.I.P. is still as good as ever, the conditions in which we live today make it unlikely that it will be the potting compost of the future.

Having said all this, I must admit that I have not personally found anything which gives better results than John Innes composts from a good source or home-made with good ingredients and careful sterilisation. Only two basic composts are needed, one for seeds and one for potting. For mature plants, shrubs and such long-growing plants as chrysanthemums that need a richer compost, more of the fertilisers may be added, but only in the proportions recommended below.

Here for those who have the facilities to make them are the formulae for these traditional and well-proved composts.

John Innes Seed Compost (J.I.S.)
2 parts by bulk of medium loam (sterilised and sifted) through $\frac{3}{8}$-inch sieve
1 part by bulk of horticultural grade of moss peat
1 part by bulk of coarse sand
To each bushel of this mixture add $1\frac{1}{2}$ oz. of superphosphate (18 per cent phosphoric acid) and $\frac{3}{4}$ oz. of chalk.
The chalk can be either ground chalk, ground limestone, limestone flour or whiting.

John Innes Potting Compost (J.I.P. 1)
7 parts by bulk of medium loam (sterilised and sifted through $\frac{3}{8}$-inch sieve)
3 parts by bulk of horticultural grade of moss peat
2 parts by bulk of coarse sand
To each bushel of this mixture add 4 oz. of the John Innes Base fertiliser and $\frac{3}{4}$ oz. of chalk.

The base fertiliser can be bought ready mixed or made up as follows:

John Innes Base
2 parts by weight of hoof and horn meal $\frac{1}{8}$-inch grist (13 per cent nitrogen)

2 parts by weight of superphosphate of lime (18 per cent phosphoric acid)

1 part by weight of sulphate of potash (48 per cent potash)

Four ounces of John Innes Base fertiliser and ¾ oz. of chalk forms one 'dose' for a bushel of the peat, loam and sand mixture. This makes John Innes potting compost No. 1, and this is used for the first potting of young plants. Two 'doses', or double the amount of fertiliser and chalk per bushel produces J.I.P. 2 for plants in 5-inch pots and most established pot plants. For shrubs in large pots or tubs, for chrysanthemums in their flowering pots, and on other occasions when a rich and lasting soil is needed three measures of John Innes Base and chalk are added to produce J.I.P. 3. All these composts are sold ready mixed and, unless large quantities are needed, it is much easier to buy them by the bag. The saving in money by mixing your own is slight, unless you prepare your own loam.

Loam consists of the topsoil and grass of pasture, rotted down with animal manure. Ideally turves should be cut from April to June when the grass is lush. They should be 4–5 inches thick and a foot square. These are stacked, grass side downwards and not quite touching, so that air penetrates the heap. Two inches of strawy manure should go on top of the second layer of turves, and a sprinkling of ground chalk or limestone on the fourth layer and so on until the heap is completed. For the best results it should not be larger than 7 feet wide or 6 feet high. Make sure that it is thoroughly wet right through and then cover it with a piece of corrugated iron to keep off the rain. Six months later it should be both matured and dry. For use, cut the stack like a loaf of bread and mix the different layers together before sieving it through a ⅜-inch sieve. It is then ready to be sterilised.

The sterilisation of loam for potting composts consists of heating it as quickly as possible to 82–93° C. (180–200° F.) and maintaining this temperature for 10–20 minutes. Slow heating, high temperatures or over-long sterilisation are all dangers to be avoided. Various methods can be employed to sterilise soil on a small scale from special electric sterilisers to an old saucepan.

The loam used for John Innes composts should be what is

known as medium loam. This is neither very light and sandy, nor a sticky clay. Very chalky soils are unsuitable, and a slightly acid loam is preferred.

It is possible to make up the composts without sterilising the loam, and no doubt many gardeners do, but sterilisation does undoubtedly produce a more reliable result. Weed seeds are killed, and also some harmful organisms, so that what comes up is what you sowed. The fact that some beneficial bacteria may also be destroyed need not worry the grower of ornamental plants in pots. Certain chemical changes take place during sterilisation and the formulae are devised to produce a balanced result after sterilisation. It is, however, pointless to use sterilised compost if it is kept uncovered in the vicinity of dead plants and old soil. An almost clinical cleanliness is a great help in greenhouse gardening.

For those who are still determined to use unsterilised garden soil for pot plants I suggest that a mixture of 2 parts sifted garden soil, 1 part sharp sand, 1 part peat or leafmould and 2 parts Powlings compost or really well-made garden compost is a possible general mixture. Powlings compost is a proprietary compost made of organic materials that will improve both the texture and the nutrition of home-made mixtures. It can also be used as a topdressing for established pot plants and for improving the fertility of greenhouse soil.

In the United States where supplies of suitable loam were always scarce in some parts of the country, serious development of loamless composts took place twenty years ago at the University of California. The various peat and sand composts devised there and known as U.C. composts have been available here for some years but have not made the same impact as in the United States. Croxden Soil-less, U.C.E.E. and Garford U.C. are composts that are on the market at the present time, based on University of California formulae.

Further developments of soil-less composts adapted to our conditions have been put on the market in recent years. The J. Arthur Bowers compost, the Eclipse Peat composts and 'EFF' soil-less composts are all examples which have their adherents. The last-named is particularly successful with ferns.

In 1966 a new style of all-peat compost became generally available after years of research. It is too early to say if any soil-less compost will have as much long-term success as the John Innes composts, but the front-runner of these composts has proved more popular with commercial growers than any since the introduction of J.I.P. Levington Compost, launched with massive advertising, consists of a standardised form of milled peat with added fertilisers, and is supplied in two grades, one for seedlings and cuttings, and the other for all potting. It is not, however, recommended for rhododendrons, azaleas, ericas and other acid-loving plants. It already has at least one competitor.

A feature of all-peat composts is that plants grow very rapidly in the early stages and that seed germination is good. A disadvantage of lightweight composts, particularly when used in plastic pots, is that large plants become top-heavy. I think that a large specimen plant is easier to manage in a traditional soil-based compost, particularly if it needs staking. All potting composts that are largely composed of peat tend to dry out more slowly in dull weather and yet seem to lose moisture more quickly in sunny weather. They need to be rather wetter than soil for the plants to be able to draw the moisture out of them. They need a different watering technique, and I believe that this has delayed their acceptance by gardeners. Many people have failures at first which put them off. If peat dries completely it is difficult to moisten again and the whole pot needs to be soaked.

Looking into the future it is clear that a standard, sterile, factory-made compost that is light to transport is virtually a necessity in this crowded island. It was bound to come and is likely to remain popular. For lightness, both soil and sand have to be eliminated as they have been in the most recent soil-less composts.

Those who come fresh to greenhouse gardening may well wonder what all the fuss has been about as they put a standard material as clean and light as bulb fibre into their plastic pots, and they are indeed very fortunate to start at a time when seed and potting composts are so easy to buy, to use and to store. It is also far easier for the old and disabled to take up gardening as a hobby in the age of lightweight compost, plastic pots and automation.

A feature of the soil-less composts is that they must not be rammed hard. One must avoid leaving empty pockets round the root ball, but a tap on the bench and an absolute minimum of pressure with the fingers should be enough. The idea is to grow plants in a well-aerated mixture which will encourage vigorous root action, and to feed them regularly. Young plants grow away very fast, and even seedlings have to be pricked out early so as to avoid damaging their tangled roots. Several makes of all-peat compost have a lime-free version for lime-hating plants.

One of the complications of the proliferation of new composts is that the supplementary feeding needed by plants growing in them differs from one to another. On the whole the John Innes composts provide nutriment over a longer period than the more modern composts which tend to give an early spurt to growth, and to need extra feeding sooner, though this is not always the case. The makers and distributors can and should be asked for their recommendations if they are not provided with the compost. Feeding usually needs to start after six to eight weeks.

When growing lime-hating plants (technically described as calcifuge) there is a fair measure of disagreement as to what composts to grow them in today. In order to adapt the John Innes composts for lime-hating plants, the chalk is replaced by an equal quantity of flowers of sulphur. Although this acid type of John Innes compost is sold ready mixed, it is not widely available. On the whole, lime-free composts of any kind have to be specially ordered. Some of these plants have long been grown in various mixtures of peat, sand and leafmould, and in the encyclopaedia of plants at the end of the book I suggest various alternatives which are not, however, exclusive. It is, of course, pointless to take a lot of trouble over a lime-free compost and then water the plants with a very alkaline tap water.

It is usual for plants suffering from an excess of lime to show signs of what is known as chlorosis. They cannot get the nutriment, usually iron, which they need from the soil because the lime prevents its release to the plant roots. This makes the plants look yellowish and off-colour. A dose of sequestrene will often put them right for quite a time even in adverse circumstances, but it will have to be repeated eventually.

The John Innes composts are not used for growing plants in the greenhouse border. In this the soil is managed much as it would be out of doors, bearing in mind that it does not have the beneficial effects of rain or frost upon it. If you are going to start using a greenhouse border that has been left in a neglected condition for any length of time, it is very much better to start off with fresh soil. A good friable, loamy soil with plenty of organic matter and, above all, really good drainage, is what is needed.

The soil in the greenhouse border cannot easily be sterilised by the amateur except by chemical means. This can be done only when the greenhouse is empty and going to remain so for a time. The chemical most often used is formaldehyde, and it will give off fumes that are poisonous to plants for a month after fumigation. One pint of commercial formalin (40–42 per cent formaldehyde) is diluted with 49 pints (approximately 6 gallons) of water. Soak the soil with a rose can, and then cover with sacks for 48 hours to keep in the fumes. Planting should not take place for about four weeks or until all smell of formaldehyde has completely gone. This process is used for diseased or doubtful soil.

When renewing or manuring the soil in greenhouse borders, it is not wise to use animal or green manure unless it is in a thoroughly decomposed state. Really well-made and matured material from a garden compost heap is an excellent dressing for the soil, but do not try this until you are satisfied that you are a reliable compost maker, or all sorts of weeds and bugs may be introduced into the greenhouse. Both bonemeal and fishmeal are valuable organic fertilisers and can safely be used in a greenhouse border.

The composts for cacti and succulents are described in a later chapter. Orchids have special requirements both as to compost materials and the method of potting. This needs to be demonstrated. The nurserymen who supply the plants are very indulgent to beginners and also sell the necessary sphagnum moss and osmunda fibre. Fortunately the purchased plants can usually remain as they are for the first year. An alternative substance in which to grow orchids and other epiphytic plants is specially prepared fir bark.

Another interesting material sometimes used in potting is vermiculite. This is a substance, allied to mica, which has been expanded by heat into an extremely absorbent granular material. It is very light in weight and has a phenomenal capacity for holding water without becoming sodden. Vermiculite, like sand, contains no nutriment but some people have great belief in it for the germination of seeds and the rooting of cuttings. All plants started in it must be transplanted as soon as possible into a more nutritious compost. Choose a horticultural grade of vermiculite, as that sold for the insulation of buildings is not suitable.

Charcoal is a material I would never be without. A little crushed charcoal is a soil sweetener which is helpful with plants that suffer easily from over-watering.

There are many grades of sand and grit, and crushed brick is an absorbent gritty material. Aggregate is another inert absorbent substance that keeps composts open and is much used to hold moisture on greenhouse benches. It is essential to have a supply of sharp sand always available for propagation—the coarse river kind, never builders' sand. When mixing composts it is most satisfactory to have the sand dry and peat moist. The fertiliser is best mixed with the sand before you add it to other ingredients.

Horticultural peat is a much used but rather loose term. The grades available do not remain constant and it is advisable to ask for a type suitable for making John Innes composts if you are going to use it for potting.

Leafmould is a potting material that suffered a decline in popularity when it was excluded from J.I.P. Nevertheless keen gardeners have never abandoned it and prefer it for some plants instead of peat, while for others peat and leafmould can be used together. Leafmould in areas with very alkaline soil will itself be alkaline, and unsuitable for lime-hating plants.

Once plants are established and growing the question of extra feeding arises. The feeding of pot plants is not an exact science as the precise needs of most of them are not even known. Most of us will use a ready-mixed general fertiliser in liquid or powder form. The secret of feeding pot plants is 'little and often'. There are many different proprietary liquid feeds to be applied diluted with water, not to mention fertiliser pills and chemical compounds to be used dry or dissolved in water. Never feed pot plants when they are dry at the roots, very recently re-potted, dormant or sickly. With the John Innes or other well-balanced composts, the plants do not need any supplementary feeding until the pots are full of roots. Some people wait until they see the first signs of flowering but this is often too late.

In a rough and ready way we say that nitrates encourage active leafy growth, while phosphates and potash are helpful in the production of flowers and fruit. These three (often referred to as N, P and K) are the major plant nutrients although calcium, iron, sulphur, magnesium, manganese, boron and traces of still other elements known and unknown all play their part in plant growth.

Personally I am a great believer in organic fertilisers and I usually use liquid manures made of seaweed that contain nitrogen, phosphates and potash as well as essential trace elements. These can also be used for foliar feeding when a fine mist sprayer is used to distribute the diluted liquid on the leaves.

A special chemical feed devised for use with the John Innes composts can be bought as ready-mixed crystals to be dissolved in water. There is also a proprietary carnation feed and a number for tomatoes. These are rich in potash and can be used occasionally on other plants.

7
Automatic Watering and Capillary Benches

AUTOMATIC WATERING, as I see it, is any system which enables plants to receive the water they need when they need it, without the gardener being present at the time.

In this book I am mainly concerned with the watering of pot plants in the amateur's greenhouse. If the greenhouse or conservatory is in a shady position and the owner rarely away from home automatic watering is entirely unnecessary. In the sunny greenhouse, however, small pots may dry out several times a day in hot weather unless effective steps are taken to control shading, ventilation and humidity. This means both being at home and not forgetting the greenhouse. Plunging all the pots in damp peat is a possible solution. Nevertheless, automatic watering is a great boon that is likely to influence the amateur's greenhouse increasingly as it is developed.

Automatic watering can be applied to pot plants in a number of ways. The first thought was to imitate rain, and water can be applied from above in the form of a spray, a trickle or a drip. Water can come from below in the form of a periodic flooding when the pots stand in water for a short time or through the medium of a capillary bench. With the latter the moisture is drawn up into the pots by capillary attraction from the bench of wet sand on which they are standing.

The first question to settle is the source of the water. In most districts rain water is preferable to mains water for watering pot plants, although it needs to be pure. The water collected from a roof in a town is unlikely to be preferable to mains water, while the slimy contents of many greenhouse water tanks have been described by one gardening writer as 'disease soup'! Nurserymen tend to have bore holes and wells to save the cost of large quantities of mains water as well as to avoid the toxic chemicals that are put into it for human protection. It is not particularly easy to discover how suitable the water is for plants except by trial and error.

Both excessive lime and excessive iron are liable to cause trouble with sophisticated automatic watering equipment. Hard and chalky water leaves a white deposit on the plants if they are regularly sprayed with it. It is also unsuitable for lime-hating plants. I have used mains water with a very high lime content, and although I would not recommend it for anyone who had to make their living growing plants I would certainly not give up the idea of automatic watering because there was no alternative.

For the more sophisticated systems and controls a considerable mains water pressure is needed, and if it is lacking this can be overcome by an electric pump. A pump also enables rain water to be used if enough can be collected in a large tank. This can be worth doing even if the tank does have to be topped up with mains water in dry spells. All this applies to large-scale use.

On a small scale the source of water can be a 1-gallon glug bottle or even a plastic detergent bottle that is kept filled by hand. There is no limit to the ingenuity which can be used.

As anyone who has kept a greenhouse knows, even the position of a pot on the bench will affect the amount of watering it needs, not to mention the varying sizes and types of plant and pot as well as the stage of growth. For this reason, watering systems which depend on water trickling or dripping into individual pots are extremely difficult to regulate effectively for a mixed collection of plants as the sole source of water. A trickle-line with adjustable nozzles is, however, a very useful piece of equipment. I use mine to supply water to an irrigated capillary bench.

In 1962 the National Institute of Agricultural Engineering devised a method of making a capillary bench that has been widely adopted since then, and is described in detail in the Ministry of Agriculture Horticultural Machinery leaflet No. 10.

Although such a bench can in fact be constructed in various ways, the principles remain the same. As everyone knows, water rises through soil or sand by capillary attraction above the level of standing water. In practice, it has been found that if the water level is 2 inches below the surface of a sand bench on which pots are standing this produces a suitable degree of moisture at the base of the pots for capillary watering.

The automatic provision of such a supply of water by capillary attraction through moist sand and with the water supply controlled by a float-valve is the present definition of capillary watering. This does not need electricity to control it. There are commercially produced kits for fixing up such an arrangement designed for amateur use.

It has also been found that 5 inches of soil can be put directly on top of the sand of a capillary bench and it will function as an automatically watered capillary bed if it is not desired to grow plants in pots.

There is a limit to the height of pots used on capillary benches that can be relied on to draw up sufficient water in all conditions. This means that one begins to run into trouble with 6-inch pots. In fact there seems to be no problem except in hot sunny weather when an occasional overhead watering by hand keeps them going. Some people use a shallow type of pot for this reason.

The amount of water saturating the bench and the amount of water held in the soil in the pots varies to some degree with the nature of the sand on the bench and the soil in the pots. Fine particles of either sand or soil have smaller pores between the particles than coarser sand or soil. The water rises farther the finer the materials while more air is held in soil that has coarse particles. We could all spend the rest of our lives experimenting and arguing about the ideal compost for each species of plant on a capillary bench.

I approached the whole subject very tentatively, expecting it to need greater scientific exactitude than is likely to be practical in the average greenhouse. I found in fact that most plants grew as well or better than previously on all the capillary benches I rigged up whether by well-tried or hand-to-mouth methods. So long as the plants received enough water and were not seriously too wet all was well, as indeed it is in any amateur greenhouse with any form of watering. It would need far more extensive experiments than mine to determine the ideal composts for all subjects, but the normal composts available and used by amateurs are reasonably successful, so long as none is pressed down or allowed to solidify with a great deal of overhead watering.

The perfectionist will say that the mature, perfectly balanced specimen plant needs very firm potting and individual attention when watering. It is an undoubted fact that the skilled professional can grow a better plant of this kind than I can. There is still much to be learnt about growing plants with all the automatic watering methods. I am sure too that we have not heard the final word on composts or how to handle them. All I do say is that most people can grow plants which will delight them on capillary benches. They can also care for many more plants at a time with less effort.

Capillary watering can be carried out on benches or at ground level, and there are a number of devices on the market for regulating the watering of such benches. The true capillary bench needs to be extremely level ($\pm \frac{1}{8}$ inch) if it is to work perfectly and this is not always possible. A simpler variant is the irrigated bench. This has no standing water level and water is merely applied to the surface of the sand, the surplus being allowed to drip off. I have such a bench which is watered by a trickle line controlled by a time-switch and a solenoid valve. I can adjust the number of waterings and their duration according to the season. As a weekend gardener I have found this very efficient because the dripping incidentally damps down the floor. For this also the bench should be level but, if there is a slope in a long bench, you can divide it into short sections with plastic sheeting which will even out the water supply.

The Macpenney system, using a ceramic block and a solenoid valve, can be used to control watering systems more precisely according to the weather conditions, but this is less foolproof when not attended to, as its various parts are liable to block up with algae or to lime-up. Both these systems require electricity. An irrigated bench could be watered by hand by turning a tap if one wished. Rigid PVC tubing drilled with holes is an alternative to a trickle-line. Plastic sheeting and piping have opened up a new field for 'do it yourself' control of water. The 500-gauge plastic sheeting is best for the base of capillary benches.

There are several small-scale water control systems using either an ingenious syphon arrangement or various kinds of float valve, which either distribute water through a trickle-line or maintain a water level in a capillary bench. These are usually designed for mains water though some can be run off a header tank. None, however, require electricity.

One firm markets a ready-made system of capillary trays made of glass-fibre that fit on top of the benches in small greenhouses. No electricity is needed, and water is supplied either through a small tank with a ball-cock or by a glug bottle which needs frequent re-filling by hand in hot weather. This system is an easy and very neat way of applying the N.I.A.E. system at fairly high cost but with a minimum of 'do it yourself' or things that can go wrong.

The capillary bench need not be expensive to construct, but it must be strong as well as level. Corrugated asbestos, with 6-inch corrugations, running along the length of the bench, can be used as the base if it is well supported. The edges of the bench should be 1 inch higher than the top of the corrugations. All but the middle corrugation are filled with some material that does not compress under weight, such as pea gravel. The central channel is then covered with a strip of polythene sheeting and the whole bench is covered with 500-gauge polythene. For the N.I.A.E. and similar systems the water supply will come by plastic pipe to this central corrugation, and when the piping is completed the whole will be covered with 2 inches of sand which will draw up the water from below, the wetness depending on the water level. The method of control of this water level is the important part and new methods are being developed all the time. I think one must look around and apply common sense. This is a rapidly developing field of activity, with every nursery and garden centre in the country needing to water plants without employing unnecessary labour.

For those who wish to stand plants in the open during the

summer months, it is possible to buy a valve which enables a sand bed to be kept watered at the same time adjusting to heavy rain that might otherwise flood it. This system is equally suitable on a large greenhouse bench.

The easiest way to grow pot plants on capillary benches, whether irrigated or not, is in plastic pots. The method could not be simpler. The pots are lightly filled with soil or other compost, which is not pressed hard down, and no drainage material is used. Plants in clay pots can also be put on capillary benches, so long as any drainage material in the bottom of the pot is removed, and so long as a small plug of glass wool (as used in roof insulation) is inserted through the drainage hole to make contact between the soil in the pot and the sand on the bench.

To establish capillarity, the pot is pressed firmly on to the sand bench with a slight screwing action. One initial watering with a watering can is usually enough to ensure that capillarity is established but it is as well to keep an eye on pots newly put on the bench as some may need a second watering to get them started. This is particularly true of the larger pots or in hot weather. After this no further attention should be needed unless the pots are moved. Normally one can move the pots around without any hand watering, provided that they are firmly replaced by means of the screwing action I have described. This becomes an entirely automatic action when moving pots. Every now and then some pots do fail to regain or retain capillarity, particularly in very hot weather.

If an irrigated bench is consistently too dry, the plants will root through the drainage hole into the sand. Some plants are much more inclined to do this than others, but it is not a problem if conditions are right.

The sand on capillary benches does need renewing from time to time. In the bright warm summer months the growth of algae and moss is a problem, as it is unsightly. One can scrape off the surface of the sand and add a little fresh sand when rearranging the plants. The used sand is useful in the garden and could be re-used in the greenhouse once it has weathered out of doors. I find that the birds pick it over and do a thorough cleaning job in my garden.

One very important point about capillary watering is that newly potted plants, as well as seedlings and cuttings potted up for the first time, will suffer a set-back if watered in this way immediately. They can stand on the bench; but do not screw them in to establish capillarity for a couple of days. Broken roots need to heal before being subjected to the continuous moisture of the capillary bench.

8

Lighting

ON THE WHOLE, the amateur owner of a cool greenhouse is not seeking to encourage active plant growth in the darkest winter months. Nevertheless, from October through February lack of light will be the limiting factor on plant growth so long as adequate heat is available. Heat without sufficient light for balanced growth is not helpful, except for plants that grow naturally in shade.

Artificial light undoubtedly helps in raising seedlings and rooting cuttings early in the year. Properly controlled, it produces sturdy growth when daylight is inadequate. For a plant with a high light requirement, like the tomato, this is particularly valuable. But in January and February the kind of greenhouse described in this book does not provide sufficient heat for many tender young plants to grow well, unless soil warming and extra lighting are used together.

In the confined conditions of the average greenhouse the necessary lamps tend to obstruct the natural light and may not be used enough to justify their cost. However, suitable lamps are now available and could transform the activities of someone who specialises in plants that need to be started early in the year. Some bedding plants are raised commercially with a rapid and predictable result in 'growth rooms' that are artificially illuminated 24 hours a day.

In theory it is possible to cover and insulate the whole greenhouse in something like a giant tea-cosy and to use nothing but artificial lighting in the coldest months of the year. The idea is that so much heating cost would be saved that lighting and insulating would be economically reasonable.

If plants are to be grown entirely by artificial light, it is really more sensible to do so in a well-insulated building or cabinet rather than a greenhouse. Growth cabinets have been used in research for many years and are now being used by some commercial growers. Plant growing under lights indoors has been done more in the United States than in Britain, and there are several American books on the subject intended for amateurs.

Artificial Light in Horticulture by A. E. Canham of the Electrical Research Station, University of Reading, is the standard work here. It is essential reading for anyone who is seriously interested in using artificial light in horticulture, but it is fairly technical.

The initiation of buds and therefore the flowering time of many plants is influenced by day length. The manipulation of day length, both by lighting and by blackout, is much used commercially in the production of chrysanthemums; its use is slowly spreading to other plants. Although this procedure is not practical in the small mixed greenhouse, the fact that such favourite plants as fuchsias and regal pelargoniums can be induced to flower in winter, by giving them two hours of artificial light in the middle of the night, should be enough to arouse the interest of some amateurs.

Lighting has long been used for flower forcing, as ordinary tungsten lamps are adequate for forcing early bulbs if used for 12 hours a day in a warm cellar.

Most of the plants in which we are interested prefer 14-16 hours of daylight and need powerful illumination if they are not to make unbalanced growth. 'Warm white' fluorescent tubes provide the most effective and practical source of light for growing plants wholly by artificial light. Unfortunately, they require reflectors and special switchgear, and they take up space. It is desirable, too, to be able to raise or lower the lights according to the growth of the plants. That is, unless the plants themselves can be raised or lowered.

For small-scale amateur experiments and seed-raising, there is a small plant irradiator which does not take up much room or obscure natural light or need special switchgear. It has a 160-watt mercury-fluorescent lamp and is made for horticultural use.

LIGHTING

Briefly, lighting can be used in horticulture in four main ways:
1. To increase day length, by extended hours of light.
2. To break the night and thereby create a long day effect on some plants.
3. To provide a brighter light on dark days.
4. To replace daylight altogether.

Also, one must not forget the ordinary moisture-proof lamp to light your way in the darkness and the movable spotlights now made for outdoor use for floodlighting special features in the garden or greenhouse.

Knowledge of the light needs of plants, both in the type of light and its intensity, is increasing all the time. Equipment is also improving and becoming more readily available to the amateur. Fortunately this is one field where the cost has fallen through the years in spite of inflation.

The lighting needed to maintain grown plants for display in the home is less than that needed to grow plants to maturity, so that fixtures with only a single fluorescent tube are possible. A double-tube fixture is better than a single tube and a reflector over the light is needed for both practical and aesthetic reasons. In a very dry atmosphere there is a great deal to be said for a mini-greenhouse or plant cabinet, that is enclosed in glass and artificially lighted. American 'Grow-Lux' fluorescent tubes can be used in the home. They are not necessarily better than the 'warm white' coloured tubes, but they are tinted in a way which has a dramatic visual effect. The red colours in the plants are enhanced and their texture appears to be more richly revealed.

I have only been able to hint at the possible wonders of lighting in horticulture, as every individual lighting problem will be different and most will need expert advice.

As the cost of heating rises, it is certainly worth remembering that the cellar may become the most practical place in which to grow the least hardy plants. It is also an interesting thought that in an indoor growth room day and night are when you decide they shall be.

9
Buying Greenhouse Plants

GREENHOUSE PLANTS are acquired in a multitude of ways. In looking round my own greenhouse I see a jacaranda grown from a seed pod that fell at my feet in the main street of Bulawayo, together with the oleander whose only claim to a place is that its parent shaded a wonderful picnic in Morocco, while the loquat was grown from seed of fruit I would have been wiser not to eat, in Turkey. Sentiment can be carried to absurd extremes, and I have seen a conservatory entirely filled by the tree that grew from a chestnut which fell on a courting couple!

Greenhouses are often homes for stray plants that are received by chance and kept in sickness and in health until death mercifully intervenes. Strong men are unable to throw away a living plant and some plant nurseries have no doubt been founded on this human failing. With skill and experience all plants are potential sources of more of their kind. The mind boggles at the number of plants that could be produced in one small greenhouse by a dedicated maniac. Nevertheless, if the contents of a greenhouse are to make an attractive picture or a balanced and interesting collection, a majority of plants should be deliberately chosen. These may be raised from seed, bought as plants or begged from friends, but choice is important.

I have described how to care for plants in other chapters; here I would like to make a few observations about buying plants.

For the beginner the first problem is to know what plants exist, what they look like and what their names are. I have done my best to include enough plants which can be grown in cool greenhouses to satisfy any non-specialist. If you want to concentrate on one particular plant or group of plants, it is worth joining their specialist society at an early stage.

The Royal Horticultural Society's Shows in London, for those who can reach them, give a valuable insight into what is available. The growers of most greenhouse plants have exhibits at various times, and catalogues can be obtained and plants ordered. To me, plant catalogues have always been a source of pleasure and interest. They are no longer free for the asking but some are more valuable to the plant enthusiast than many gardening books.

Some people value rarity above all other qualities and want to grow plants their friends have never seen. Seeds and cuttings from botanical gardens and private collectors feature in this field, though here, too, nurserymen can help. Some of them are plantsmen first, and salesmen of necessity, and almost all stock small quantities of the less usual plants which are not included in their catalogues.

Although nurserymen have many fine qualities, communicativeness on paper is not one of them. They are always busy, normally under-staffed and their work is heavily seasonal. The besetting sin of the gardening public is wasting nurserymen's time. It is not fair to use them as a free plant health service, and they cannot afford to listen to the life histories either of plants they sold long ago or of their customers. They rightly think us crazy when we order plants singly or in very small numbers to be sent by rail. The carriage and packing may cost more than the plants. Nurserymen usually refuse to dispatch plants at once or on any particular day and I expect they are justified. Clearly, the larger firms at the height of the season must work to an orderly system. The normal practice is to dispatch the plants in rotation in the sequence in which the orders were received. Whether this maddening practice is always necessary or not, the effort needed to cause any deviation from it is rarely worth while. It is, however, one of the reasons for the growing popularity of the Garden Centres with container-grown plants that can be bought and taken home at once. Nevertheless, many of the less common plants are still likely to have to be ordered from a distant nursery.

The moral is to look ahead, to order well in advance with instructions of crystal clarity, and to avoid ordering single plants or expecting greenhouse plants to travel in either the dead of winter or the heat of full summer. The packing is so skilled that hardy plants are safe in their wrappings for some time in winter but, as most greenhouse plants have no really dormant season and are sensitive to cold, a minimum of travel time is always important.

It does not pay to buy cheap plants, although money can sometimes be saved by buying smaller, younger plants if you have the skill and patience to bring them to maturity.

You may not realise that a large nursery will have several thousand copies of its catalogue in circulation at one time. So, however big the stocks, all plants cannot possibly always be available in the numbers that might be asked for. An article in the gardening press or a mention on television or radio can cause a run on one variety which could not be foreseen. Besides, turnover may be rapid and reprinting is slow and expensive.

Garden Centres have sprung up all over the country and vary enormously in quality. Although they are largely concerned with hardy plants, some of them are good sources of greenhouse and indoor plants. Beware of shade-loving, tender plants which have been exposed for sale in hot dry surroundings or on cold pavements outside florists' shops in winter. The so-called house-plants can be ordered by name nearly everywhere from florists, and some of the raisers have shops at their nurseries which are the ideal source of tropical plants.

In my cultural notes I have tried always to name the best planting time, and this will help when ordering, although pot plants are more adjustable in this than those lifted from the ground or grown in boxes. On the whole, nurseries send out plants at suitable planting times, but, if you order a mixed lot, it is not unknown for half the order to arrive next week and the other half next year without a word of warning or explanation. This probably means either that it is the wrong planting season for part of the order, or that the available plants are still too small to send out. Nowadays, most catalogues give very explicit instructions about ordering, and these should be studied as closely as the fine print in an insurance policy. It is, for instance, a practice with some firms to file the order for the plant that is out of stock and to supply it later (often a year later) when fresh stock is available. This will be done automatically unless contrary instructions are given and you will have only yourself to blame if you have not read the rules. Another frequent practice is to send the nearest substitute to a plant that is out of stock unless specifically told not to.

Buying bulbous plants is fairly simple, as the great majority are sold in a dormant state; on the whole those that flower in late summer or autumn are dispatched in spring and the winter, and spring-flowering plants are sold in the autumn. Lilies are mostly planted in the late autumn and they should arrive packed in damp peat with roots attached. It is a mistake to buy lilies as dry bulbs exposed to the desiccating atmosphere of a department store, when they cost no more if bought from a nursery specialising in lilies.

Geraniums are best bought in April or early May for the greenhouse, though they are available all the year. Cacti and succulent plants are very adaptable, but they, too, are probably best purchased in spring and re-potted at once if necessary.

When plants are transferred from the commercial greenhouse to your own, they are likely to find a different climate altogether. This is as it should be, since the nurseryman's aim is different; he needs his plants to make growth as swiftly as possible, without their becoming soft and drawn, while the atmosphere in your greenhouse is likely to be drier and cooler. On the whole, most plants will receive less check in their growth if they are bought in spring, when the weather is warm but not yet hot. As this is also the re-potting time for the majority of the more permanent greenhouse plants, it is convenient in every way.

Timelessness is one of the most valuable qualities of gardening in the rushed life of today. If you are able to await the changing seasons, the vagaries of the climate, British Rail and the horticultural trade with unruffled calm, you have the ideal gardening temperament. But do not be so far removed from mundane worries that you forget to sign 'unexamined', when goods arrive by rail that may be liable for a damages claim after being unpacked.

10

Plants from Cuttings

THE UGLY WORD 'propagation' covers all the methods by which we raise new plants. Without either propagation or the purchase of young plants, gardening soon becomes an exercise in tidiness and the garden a museum of plants. Sooner or later all gardeners want to raise their own plants. Some will say that all they need is a green thumb, or a plastic bag, or even a glass of water! Many rely on the numerous variations of traditional methods with varying success. Yet others have such frequent failures that they give the whole thing up.

The amount of propagation actually done by an amateur does not necessarily reflect any assessable need. If it is an agreeable and fascinating occupation, the need for new plants seems to multiply exceedingly. If it is often a failure little will, in fact, be done. In propagation for the amateur the one really important point is that the methods used should be successful and suited to the special circumstances and interests of the individual.

There are few more satisfying occupations than raising new plants, and it is also something that everyone can do. Unfortunately today the rising cost of labour and the increase in mass selling methods are reducing the variety of plants stocked by nurserymen every year. We must not blame the nurserymen, who often continue stocking rare plants at a financial loss to themselves. We must blame ourselves for the fact that so few of us take the trouble to buy anything but the commonest and most hackneyed plants. The rapid spread of enthusiasm for flower arrangement has opened the eyes of women, at least, to the potential riches of plant form. I hope that this will help to keep some of the more interesting plants in circulation. Nevertheless, those who want to grow unusual plants and rare shrubs are likely to have to do more of their own propagation and exchange in years to come.

The quickest way to increase the numbers of many greenhouse plants, particularly shrubs and climbers, is by taking cuttings. It is also wise to take a few cuttings of tender shrubs in the garden to replace losses in a harsh winter. Propagation by cuttings means that every child is identical with its parent; in gardening this is considered an advantage. Seed-raised plants sometimes hark back to distant and less desirable ancestors. The cutting, on the other hand, will vary in quality only with how well or how badly the shoot for the cutting is chosen, and with the health and vigour of the parent plant. Of course, the progress of the new young root system will depend on the way in which you care for it.

In general it is the vigorous young shoot which has not reached ripeness or flowering that roots most readily. Many people who are said to have green fingers have in reality either an instinctive or an informed ability to choose a likely cutting, and a firm thumb when inserting it in the soil. Nowadays with mist propagation even the firm thumb is no longer desirable.

Cuttings should be severed with a sharp knife or razor blade, preferably in the morning when crisp and fresh. If they cannot be used immediately, a plastic bag will help to keep them fresh.

From the moment a cutting is separated from the parent plant it is in a race against death. It will certainly die unless conditions are propitious for it to grow roots before the supply of food and moisture in its tissues is exhausted. Warmth, moisture and light encourage growth; so, ideally, all three should be provided. But cuttings have no roots to absorb moisture, and they soon flag in sunlight or a dry atmosphere. The answer to this for leafy cuttings has always been either a close atmosphere with shade or a frame of pure sand, which is not shaded but frequently sprayed with water. This last combination of warmth, moisture and light led to the idea of automatic misting. At first, constant mist was tried. It was soon found that this was neither necessary or desirable. All that is needed is a constant film of moisture protecting the leaves from desiccation so that advantage can be taken of the encouragement of full light to growth. Too much wetting leaches nutrients from the leaves and also cools the rooting medium. It is, however, safer to have too much than too little misting.

For rooting cuttings a high air temperature is not necessary; it is warmth below the soil that makes the process much more swift and sure. The time-honoured phrase 'bottom heat' has been superceded in our affluent society by the 'warmed propagating bed'. Today, electric heating wires controlled by a thermostat are the complete answer to controlled warmth at the roots, and the running cost is small. If electricity does not reach as far as the greenhouse, an electrically warmed frame or propagator can be used near to the source of power. However, in the truly automatic greenhouse there is the new thrill of mist propagation.

Mist propagation is of special interest to the gardener who has not previously been very successful in the propagation of plants, as well as to the enthusiast who does a great deal of propagation. The continuous moisture of mist seems to prevent rotting, which is just the opposite of what one might expect. Mist is also of special value to the busy or absent gardener. The main advantage of a mist unit is that it creates and maintains ideal rooting conditions automatically until the cuttings are rooted. Also, additional cuttings may be inserted at any moment without further preparations. An important point often overlooked is that seed raising under mist is a simple procedure requiring no attention until the seedlings are pricked out. For the weekend gardener this is the first complete answer to propagation without regular attention.

The main objection to mist propagation is the cost of the equipment. In the eyes of the expert my amateur dabbling under mist would not be worth it. For years it was not considered 'worth it' to heat even the smallest greenhouse by electricity, although this is now generally accepted as the best way to heat a small amateur greenhouse. Each one of us must make our own decisions about expenditure on convenience, pleasure and leisure. It is not a matter for the experts. You will find detailed information about mist propagation in the next chapter.

Cuttings are often described as soft or half-ripe. A soft cutting is where there is no woody stem at all, and for these a close, moist atmosphere or mist is absolutely essential. Warmth is also desirable for most of them, as they have little stamina and need to develop roots as quickly as possible. Half-ripe, or soft-wood, cuttings are made from the tips of the current year's growth of woody plants, when it is firm but not yet fully ripened. Many shrub cuttings are of this type.

Many succulent plants may be increased by leaf cuttings. In nature they sometimes drop their leaves which then start an independent existence; so we encourage this means of increase by detaching leaves and inserting them in a sandy compost. Many succulents with a rosette of leaves will root quite easily if the whole of the top of the plant is used as a cutting. Echeverias that have become leggy are re-rooted in this way. A few tropical greenhouse plants can also be raised from leaf cuttings. Begonias, saintpaulias, sinningias, and streptocarpus are plants that can be raised in this way. The big leaves of Rex begonias can produce several plants if notches are made in the veins at the back of the leaf, which is then pinned down on moist compost. Mature but not old leaves are used for cuttings, and it is from the stalk and the back of the leaf that new roots may emerge.

There are also hard-wood cuttings and root cuttings, but they are not likely to be used for greenhouse plants.

Opinions vary as to the ideal compost for cuttings, the essentials being that it should both hold moisture and yet drain freely. The compost recommended by the John Innes Institute for general use consists of 1 part loam, 2 parts granulated peat and 3 parts coarse sand, all measured in bulk. If the cuttings are not to be potted up separately soon after rooting some people use equal parts of loam, peat and sand, and they also spread sand on the surface so that some of it runs down into the holes made for the cuttings.

Where there is a warm propagating frame, this is often filled with a fine pure sand in which the cuttings are inserted. This is good for quick rooting but contains no nutriment. Vermiculite is another possible rooting medium which provides good conditions for rooting, so long as the cuttings are transplanted as soon as they are rooted.

Many people use a mixture of sand and peat. This is also sterile and has no nutriment, but it holds more moisture than sand alone. Opinions vary as to the proportions of sand and peat to use, from equal quantities to 75 per cent peat and 25 per cent sand.

In the summer months most cuttings are quite willing to root without artificial heat in the greenhouse, so long as they are kept shaded and enclosed in a damp atmosphere. Enclosing a pot in a plastic bag is a simple way to root cuttings in warm weather. As soon as they are rooted the bag can be opened and then removed when they are fully established. The small plastic domes which fit individual pots are also useful. These are slightly ventilated. In all propagators, frames or glass-covered boxes, condensation will collect on the glass. This should be wiped clear once a day, when the opportunity can be taken to air the cuttings for a few minutes.

All cuttings need to be handled with care when just rooted. They are potted up singly and shaded for a few days. A humid atmosphere is desirable, but over-watering must be avoided.

There are a few exceptions to the rule of keeping cuttings in a close atmosphere. Woolly leaved plants are sometimes liable to rot, and zonal pelargoniums are best left uncovered, as also are cacti and succulent plants.

Plants to grow from cuttings

I have listed plants that you may wish to increase by cuttings in the cool greenhouse, together with the type of shoot to choose and the time of year to take the cutting. For full cultural details see the alphabetical encyclopaedia in Chapter 17.

Abutilon   Firm young shoots in autumn.
Acacia   Half-ripe wood with a heel in late summer.
Azalea   Half-ripe shoots in summer.
Baura   Half-ripe shoots in spring.
Boronia   Young shoots in August.
Bougainvillea   Firm young shoots with a heel in spring.
Cacti   Stem cuttings in summer.
Calceolaria   Young non-flowering shoots in August or September.

Callistemon Matured wood in late spring.
Camellia Half-ripe shoots in August or September. Difficult without mist.
Campanula (*C. isophylla*) Non-flowering shoots in spring or summer.
Cantua Young shoots in spring or summer.
Carnation Non-flowering side shoots in August, September or February.
Cassia Tips of shoots in spring.
Celsia Soft cuttings in spring.
Cestrum Half-ripe shoots in late summer.
Chrysanthemum Young shoots round base of plant in early spring.
Citrus Firm young shoots in spring.
Clianthus Firm young shoots in summer.
Coronilla Firm short-jointed shoots in late summer.
Crassula Stem or leaf cuttings in summer.
Cuphea (*C. ignea*) Tips of shoots in spring or summer.
Cytisus Firm young shoots in August.
Datura Young shoots in spring.
Echeveria Young rosettes or single leaves will root in spring or summer.
Erica Tips of side shoots in June or July.
Erythrina Cuttings removed with a heel of old wood in spring.
Eucalyptus Side shoots in June.
Euphorbia (*E. pulcherrima*) Tips of shoots in spring.
Fatshedera Firm young growth in spring.
Fatsia Tip of main stem in spring.
Felicia Half-ripe shoots in autumn.
Fuchsia Soft cuttings in spring or half-ripe in autumn.
Grevillea Half-ripe shoots in summer.
Heliotropium Young shoots in spring or autumn.
Hoya Firm young shoots in spring.
Hydrangea Side growths in May or non-flowering shoots in August.
Impatiens Tips of shoots in water at any time.
Jacobinia Short-jointed growth in spring.

Jasminum Soft cuttings in spring.
Kalanchoe Non-flowering shoots in July.
Leptospermum Side shoots in May.
Lippia Cuttings with a heel in early summer.
Lotus Young shoots in late spring.
Luculia Shoots with a heel in autumn.
Mandevilla Firm side shoots in late spring.
Mesembryanthemum (shrubby) Firm young shoots in late summer.
Mimulus (*M. glutinosus*) Firm young shoots in spring or summer.
Mitraria Young shoots in summer.
Nandina Ripe shoots in early autumn.
Nerium Well-ripened shoots root in water in summer.
Nierembergia Non-flowering shoots in August.
Passiflora Young shoots with a heel in spring.
Pelargonium (zonal and ivy-leaved) Short-jointed shoots preferably in August and September or March and April.
Pelargonium (regal) March to September but June and July are the best months.
Pimelea Firm young shoots with a heel in spring.
Plumbago Half-ripe shoots in spring or summer.
Polygala Young shoots in spring.
Prostanthera Firm side shoots in summer.
Punica Half-ripe shoots in July.
Rochea Firm tips of shoots in March to flower second summer.
Schlumbergera Cuttings two joints long in spring.
Sedum Stem or leaf cuttings in summer.
Sollya Firm young shoots with a heel in spring.
Sparmannia Tips of shoots in spring.
Streptosolen Young side shoots in spring or summer.
Tibouchina Firm young shoots in spring.
Trachelospermum Non-flowering side shoots in summer.
Tradescantia Short-jointed shoots at any time.

11
Mist Propagation

ALTHOUGH MIST PROPAGATION has been available for a decade, very few amateur gardeners have used it. There are a number of different systems on the market. It is even possible to have mist propagation operated by a battery, or, alternatively, without electricity at all. Nevertheless the systems that have revolutionised the nursery industry require mains electricity and a source of water under mains or pumped pressure.

While mist propagation can be done in a frame, the cool greenhouse owner is likely to want a small mist propagation unit within the greenhouse. For this it is essential to have a strong and level bench that will support the weight of six inches of wet sand. There should also be a source of electricity and water at normal mains pressure. Three or four square feet is the minimum size for a one-nozzle unit. In a larger installation there is often a weaning unit, where rooted cuttings are gradually weaned from dependence on the constant damp and warmth of a mist unit to the ordinary conditions of the greenhouse. In the average greenhouse there is no room for this and I have not personally found any need for it for small-scale propagation. It is, however, worth considering, if you can devote a special greenhouse to propagation.

The equipment usually consists of an electric control box, a solenoid valve (sometimes called a magnetic valve) which turns the water supply on and off, and also an electronic leaf or sensing element (a pair of electrodes) which regulates the frequency of the misting. It is placed amongst the cuttings and so subjected to the same conditions of sunlight, temperature and humidity as the cuttings themselves.

MIST PROPAGATION

The object of the exercise is to keep a constant film of moisture on the leaves of the cuttings without using more than the minimum amount of water, so as to avoid leaching the nutriments from the leaves. There is, however, a fairly wide tolerance of different conditions in most cuttings, and in America much use is made of mechanical timing devices. Alternatively, in our weather a device sensitive to light can be used to control mist.

When the mist falls on the electronic leaf, a film of water builds up. This connects the two electrodes of which it is made and so creates a circuit with the controller; the controller then breaks the electric connection with the solenoid valve and thus turns off the water. When the moisture on the electronic leaf has evaporated the circuit is broken and once again the solenoid valve is energised and turns on the water. The equipment is designed for use in full sunlight and normal well-ventilated greenhouse conditions. In this way the misting is regulated by the actual conditions surrounding the cuttings. You will, of course, need one or more misting nozzles and connecting piping and filters.

For taking cuttings of greenhouse plants under mist it is necessary to heat the rooting medium. This can be done either by mains voltage or by low voltage heating cable of sufficient capacity to maintain a temperature of $21°$ C. ($70°$ F.) to $24°$ C. ($75°$ F.). To run this efficiently a rod-type thermostat is also needed.

What is known as a twin control box is often recommended for the amateur. It enables both a mist unit and automatic watering for a bench to be run off the same control box. Although this may save money, I have not personally found it to be a good idea. My own choice is to use the equipment designed for nurserymen which has stood up to rough use and exacting requirements for years. This equipment is never advertised where amateurs might see it. It is, however, available on demand. The control box is a more complicated one and used to be much more expensive than the simpler amateur version; this is no longer the case.

For very little extra cost you can get a control box that will operate the commercial type of electronic leaf, which is much more foolproof than the amateur type. The electrodes are buried in plastic and can be kept clean with an occasional wipe over with fine sandpaper, while the amateur type are very brittle and best cleaned by immersion for a minute in a 50/50 solution of spirits of salt and water. This can need doing as much as once a week in a district with very chalky water. In any case, spirits of salt is not a substance one wants to have in a house where there are children. The amateur type of controller will not operate the commercial type of electrode.

The controller is a sealed unit which normally has to be returned to the makers if it gives trouble. With all electrical equipment in greenhouses it is vital to know just exactly what the arrangements for servicing are in your area. Such facilities as exist are not evenly spread over the country. This is something which is likely to improve with the rapid spread of this type of equipment; but at the time of writing it is certainly worth paying more for the most trouble-free equipment you can find. I have never yet encountered an electrician who had an electronic leaf in stock, and with the amateur type it is absolutely essential to keep a spare. It is a weakness of the system that it needs an electrician to connect it, though this can be done in a moment if both the electrician and the electrode are to hand. The cost and delay involved in getting professional help encourages the amateur electrician who is an absolute menace in the greenhouse.

Solenoid valves must be installed truly vertically and need occasional servicing; but they seem reliable so long as the piping starts clean and the correct filters are fitted.

The misting nozzles are fitted with replaceable filters that need very occasional cleaning, though just at first they may block up with sediment in new piping. The actual jet can be adjusted by a screw at the top or turned off altogether by screwing down the striking pin. If this is done a piece of rubber should be inserted to protect the tip of the striking pin. In this type of nozzle, which is the most widely used, the distance between the hole the jet of water comes out of and the striking pin which breaks it up into mist droplets is most accurately adjusted with a feeler gauge. This can be obtained for a few pence from any garage, and a setting between 8 and 12 thou. is recommended. All this sounds complicated but is perfectly simple to do.

MIST PROPAGATION

Excessive lime in the water can be a source of trouble in a mist unit. Excessive iron can also cause trouble. If there is a source of clean rain water, this can be used with a booster pump in districts where the water is unsuitable. Lime in the water is apt to clog up the misting jet in time together with any very fine tubing or tiny holes in automatic equipment. In time it forms a deposit on the leaves of cuttings and a crust on the surface of the sand in which they are rooting. Such water is unsuitable for propagating lime-hating plants and is said to inhibit rooting generally. I have not myself found this a trouble. I do not, however, grow many lime-hating plants. Acid peat in the rooting medium helps to counter-act the effects of alkaline water. The effect of a build up of lime deposit on the electrode will eventually be to prevent the electrical contact being made and lead to continuous misting if it is not cleaned.

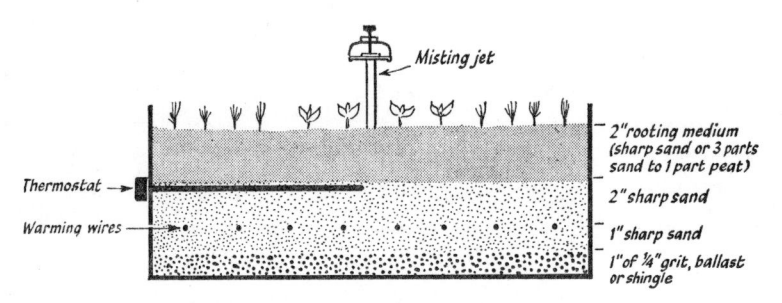

Typical make-up of mist propagating bench

The sand should be free of lime and if boxes or pots are used for cuttings or seeds they are placed just above the level of the thermostat rod surrounded by moist peat.

In order to set up mist propagation you must have a strong level bench which will support 6 inches of wet sand. There should also be a source of electricity as well as water at a steady mains pressure. It is possible to have battery-operated misting equipment and there is a system which only needs water; but most mist propagation is done with equipment that needs both.

Three or four square feet is the minimum size for a one-jet unit. Corrugated asbestos is usually used for the base and flat asbestos sheeting for the sides. Whatever material is used there must be free drainage.

On top of the base goes 1 inch of ¼-inch grit, balast or shingle. Above this another inch is filled with sharp sand. On this is laid the soil heating cable with a loading of 15 watts per square foot. This is covered by another 2 inches of sharp sand. After this it is usual to put a 2- or 3-inch depth of the rooting medium for the cuttings. This may in fact be another 2 inches of the same sharp sand.

The heating cable is controlled by a rod thermostat set at from 21° C. (70° F.) to 24° C. (75° F.). This is let into the side of the unit with the rod running across the line of the heating wires and immediately below the rooting layer. It is quite a good idea to put a layer of wire mesh over the heating cable to prevent it being damaged by tools.

The electrode stands among the cuttings, supported on a bamboo cane. It is there to sense conditions in the area where the cuttings are. Obviously, the nearer it is to the misting jet, the more quickly it will react to the mist and the shorter will be the duration of each burst of mist. So the placing of the electrode affords additional possibilities of adjustment of the exact amount of mist. If the electrode is correctly placed, there should be little or no surplus water dripping from the bench. The cuttings should always have a slight film of damp on them. If the rooting medium is too dry, the cuttings will tend to grow a big callus but put out roots only very slowly. The mist replaces evaporated moisture, but it does not actually add water to the rooting medium, which must be thoroughly moist to start with. It may need additional watering occasionally in hot weather. As there are heating cables below, it is quite possible to find that you have a rooting medium which is bone dry beneath the surface. If, on the other hand, the mist is too heavy, it tends to cool the rooting medium and to leach nutriment from the leaves of the cuttings.

Air should be able to circulate freely round the cuttings; so one does not want to box them in. It will probably be necessary to protect some of the woodwork or glass of the greenhouse from the mist with clear plastic sheeting. If the water is hard, a limy deposit settles on the glass which is difficult to remove.

MIST PROPAGATION

Those who object to a sudden burst of mist in the face are urged to take precautions. It is almost impossible for the proud owner of a new mist unit to remember not to lean over his precious cuttings for minutes at a time!

There are several suppliers of equipment and the various parts are not necessarily interchangeable. One firm replaces the usual electrode with what it calls an electro-mechanical detector. This is a sensitive balance which is moved by the weight changes caused by the wetting and drying of a piece of foam plastic under the mist. The important thing is to have a clear idea of what you want the equipment to do for you. Then you can ask the right questions at the outset. It is always wise to take up-to-date advice before embarking on any electrical equipment.

The actual use to which you put your mist unit may affect its position in the greenhouse. The prevailing wind and the position of the ventilators is worth considering, as wind will lead to uneven misting. It is valuable to be able to put the rooted cuttings that have been potted up adjacent to the mist unit for a few days. The slight mist that reaches them makes their transition from mist to the ordinary bench easier without the added expense of a weaning unit. Very soft cuttings may benefit from a plastic cloche or bag or other forms of a close atmosphere for a few days after coming out of the mist.

Seeds can also be raised under mist and I will go into this in the next chapter.

12

Plants from Seed

RAISING PLANTS from seed is the nearest we get to something for nothing in the greenhouse. So long as you do not think of time as money, it is very near indeed. Many unusual plants are only obtainable as seed while every plant is more interesting if one has watched it develop from the very beginning.

All plants that are true species can be raised from seed, and there are reliable strains of many cultivars. For anyone with the patience to do so, the great majority of the plants included in this book can be raised in this way. For the average amateur, however, quick results are wanted, and the plants most often raised from seed flower in their first season.

As far as decoration under glass is concerned it is the half-hardy annuals that are most popular. They all come from the warmer parts of the world and, although many of them are often raised under glass and planted outdoors when all danger of frost is over, few give of their best in the average British summer. In the greenhouse where their fragile grace is not spoilt by heavy rain and chilly winds, they grow more luxuriantly. Under glass one does not want too many very tall annuals, and brilliant orange flowers are sometimes hard to place; but there are so many to choose from that we can grow new kinds every year. A few hardy annuals are also of value because they can be sown in the autumn to flower very early in the year. These include clarkia, iberis, linaria, lychnis, nemophila and phacelia.

Amongst the half-hardy annuals, I think schizanthus deserves a special note, as it has every virtue as a cool greenhouse plant. It is easily grown from seed to produce an endless profusion of delicate and beautiful flowers throughout March, April and May. As if this was not enough, it can also be grown to flower in summer, pests do not seem to care for it and the cut flowers last exceptionally well in water. There are both very tall and dwarf kinds. Some other attractive half-hardy annuals are brachycome, eucnide, limonium, nemesia, salpiglossis and torenia.

Many of the plants we think of as tender annuals are really perennials that are grown as annuals. These include alonsoa, antirrhinum, cuphea, heliotropium, nierembergia, petunia and trachelium.

Another group are the so-called climbing annuals. These are of great value in quickly furnishing a large conservatory at small cost. It will be found, however, that in their native homes in tropical and sub-tropical parts of Africa and South America they are perennials. Nevertheless we treat them as annuals, as they grow with great speed and flower in their first season. Cobaea, eccremocarpus, ipomoea, and quamoclit are members of this group. My favourite is still the Morning Glory (*Ipomoea rubrocaerulea*) which gives a magnificent display even when confined to a 5-inch pot.

Some favourite greenhouse plants are perennials which are sown in late spring to flower in the winter and spring of the following year. These include calceolaria, cineraria and the winter-flowering primulas. They need some skill in cultivation to bring them to perfection but provide an effective way of filling a greenhouse with flowers from November to June.

Biennial plants which take a full year to reach flowering size have lost popularity in recent years although many people raise cyclamen from seed. They are usually sown in August to flower around Christmas sixteen months later. Where there is room for it *Campanula pyramidalis* is still a worthy plant when well grown.

Some foliage plants can be raised from seed in a single season such as *Grevillea robusta* and *Jacaranda mimosaefolia*. Although these are tropical trees they are attractive as small plants and the jacaranda will flower eventually in a large conservatory if it is kept within bounds by judicious pruning.

Warmth has an important bearing on propagation of all kinds and below a certain temperature seeds do not germinate. The temperature at which they start to grow depends to some degree on the climate of their native homes and so varies considerably. It is said that the best temperature for germination is 10° F. higher than the optimum growing temperature of the plant. This is an interesting thought, but not of much practical use to most of us!

As most greenhouse plants come from warm climates the most favourable temperature for their seeds to germinate will be above that at which we normally keep our greenhouses. We cannot give each seed a different temperature but 21° C. (70° F.) is desirable for the germination of many seeds. This means that it is a great advantage to have a propagating frame or heated mist unit within the greenhouse, as it would be wasteful to heat the whole greenhouse to this temperature, even if it were possible. This frame can be anything from a home-made box fixed above a heater, to a specially built propagating frame fitted with soil-warming cable and another cable for heating the air. If you are going in for propagation seriously this is well worth having, but it is far from essential. Many tropical plants have started life in a linen cupboard, although this is not the ideal place.

In an electrically heated frame it is possible to set the thermostat at a higher temperature until germination has taken place and then to lower it gradually. Even so it is a mistake to sow seeds too early in the year, for the time will soon come when they are ready to be put on the open benches. In February the light is poor, and the temperature in the slightly heated greenhouse is too low for young plants to make much progress. Although it is possible with supplementary lighting and heating to grow virtually anything at any time I do not personally think it pays most of us to sow seeds before early March. By this time the general temperature of the greenhouse can be prevented from falling below 10° C. (50° F.) without too much expenditure, and good growing conditions maintained. The weather varies so much at this time of year that each season will have its problems; but, however you manage it, sudden changes of temperature must be avoided for tender seedlings.

Perhaps I should give a warning about small electric propagators that are arranged so as to give a certain temperature lift. The actual temperature inside them will vary according to the temperature of their surroundings. If the sun shines on such a seed-raiser it will not switch off. On the other hand if it is kept in a very cold place it may never be warm enough. Temperature can only be accurately controlled with a good-quality thermostat.

The principles of growing plants from seed are the same indoors and out, no matter what method is used. A steady degree of moisture and sufficient warmth for germination must be maintained until the seedlings appear. Most failures are probably due to a period of acute dryness after the seed has started to grow but before the seedlings are noticed. Even an hour's desiccation in bright sunshine can kill them in the early stages.

For seed sowing there are standard-sized wooden or plastic trays 14 × 8 × 2 inches or useful plastic ones half this size. Small pots and pans often hold all the seedlings needed of one kind and little square plastic pots that can stand close together are convenient. If the traditional shallow clay seed pan is used it must be well scrubbed and allowed to soak for 24 hours if new, or it will absorb moisture from the soil.

John Innes seed compost can be used for fine seeds, although most are quite happy in J.I.P. 1 which can also be used for pricking out. A mixture of 4 parts peat and 1 part sand can be used for the real lime-haters such as ericas. The modern all-peat seed composts (which do contain lime) are successful with most things.

The compost used must be moist to start with. Opinions differ as to whether to give a light watering with a fine rose after the seeds are sown or whether to water from below either before or after sowing the seeds. In any case moist soil and a moist atmosphere need to be maintained either in a propagating case or by covering the receptacles with glass or plastic until germination takes place.

Very tiny seeds do not need covering with soil and larger seeds should only be covered with their own depth of sand or compost. The impulse to sow too thickly is very strong and leads to nothing but trouble.

If conditions are right nearly every seed will germinate and it will be difficult to separate the tiny plants without damaging their roots when pricking out. This is when they are lifted and replanted, well spaced out in a deeper receptacle. It is an operation better done too soon than too late. The traditional time was when the seedlings developed their first true leaf, but the shock often seems less when they are still at the seed-leaf stage. This is particularly true in all-peat composts which encourage very fast growth in the early stages. The spacing at pricking out depends on the rate of growth of the particular plants and how long they will remain in the box. A 1½- to 2-inch spacing each way is usual in a box 3 inches deep. Pricking out into boxes is mainly done to save space, and the larger container is easier to keep uniformly moist than small pots. However, on a capillary bench tiny pots are no trouble and better plants are usually grown in individual containers.

Personally, I raise seeds under mist, and germination appears to be 100 per cent. I use small plastic pots and pans with extra drainage holes. A very porous compost is desirable for seed sowing under mist. A satisfactory mixture can be made of equal quantities of peat and horticultural vermiculite. The pots stand directly on the warmed sand base of the mist unit an inch above the warming wires. I also pack moist peat round the pots. They remain under the mist until they are pricked out. There is no trouble with damping off, and no covering or shading of the pots is needed. This is the answer to prayer for the weekend gardener. The young plants will need light shading for a day or two after leaving the mist, but then I grow them on my capillary benches in the usual way.

Young plants when potted for the first time are usually put in 2½- or 3-inch pots. The soil used should be damp but not soggy; it can then be trickled in round the roots of the plant, while the latter is held so that its neck is just below the rim of the pot. Seedlings are potted so that the seed leaves are just clear of the soil. Leave half an inch at the top for watering.

The plants you are most likely to raise from seed are listed below. Annuals are marked A, biennials B and perennials P; then follow the sowing dates most appropriate to the slightly heated greenhouse and the approximate time taken from seed to flowering. The full cultural details for the different varieties of each plant will be found in Chapter 17.

Ageratum P, grown as A. March to May. About 18 weeks.
Alonsoa P, grown as A. March to May. About 16 weeks.
Antirrhinum P. August or September for spring flowering.
Begonia (fibrous rooted) P. February or March. Nearly 6 months.
Brachycome A. March. About 13 weeks.
Browallia P. March and April. About 6 months.
Calceolaria A and P. June, for flowering the following May.
Calendula A. Autumn for spring flowering.
Campanula B and P. May. Approximately 14 months.
Celsia B. Can be flowered in about 20 weeks from March sowing. Autumn sowing produces larger plants.
Cineraria B. May to July for flowering November to March.
Clarkia A. August or September for spring flowering.
Cobaea P, grown as A. March or April. About 16 weeks.
Cuphea A and P. March. About 16 weeks.
Cyclamen P. August for flowering 16 months later.
Diascia A. Spring. About 14 weeks.
Didiscus A. Spring. About 18 weeks.
Dimorphotheca A. Spring. Mostly about 8 weeks.
Eccremocarpus P. February for late summer flowering.
Eucalyptus P. March or August. Quick-growing foliage plant.
Eucnide A. March or April. About 15 weeks.
Felicia P. March for winter flowering.
Freesia P. Early spring. About 7 months.
Gerbera P. March or when new seed available. About 15 months.
Grevillea (*G. robusta*) P. March. Foliage plant from late summer.
Heliotropium P. March. About 15 weeks.
Impatiens A and P grown as A. April or May. About 11 weeks.
Ipomoea A. April for late summer.
Kalanchoe P. March to flower the following year.

Lilium   P. *L. formosanum* and *L. philippinnse* should flower the second year.
Limonium   A. March or April. About 14 weeks.
Linaria   A. September for April flowering.
Lobelia   P and A. Spring for summer and autumn for spring.
Lychnis   A. Spring for summer and autumn for spring.
Martynia   A. March. About 18 weeks.
Matthiola   B and A. There are kinds to sow at various times of the year.
Nemesia   A. March to June. About 13 weeks, or September for spring.
Nemophila   A. September for March flowering.
Nierembergia   P. March and April for July onwards.
Petunia   P, grown as A. April. About 14 weeks.
Phacelia   A. Spring. About 12 weeks, or September for March.
Primula   A and P. March to June for winter and early spring.
Quamoclit   P, grown as A. March for late summer.
Rehmannia   P. May for flowering in summer of the following year.
Rosa   P. The Fairy rose, sown in March, will flower in 10 weeks.
Salpiglossis   A. March and April, about 20 weeks. August for May.
Schizanthus   A. August for March and April, spring for late summer.
Streptocarpus   P. February and March for late summer.
Thunbergia   A. Late March. About 15 weeks.
Torenia   A. March and April. Approximately 15 weeks.
Trachelium   P. Early spring, about 23 weeks, or June for next year.
Tropaeolum   A. September for spring or March for summer.

13

Bulbous Plants

IN THIS COUNTRY, when bulbous plants are mentioned, our first thoughts are for the hardy spring-flowering bulbs such as hyacinth and narcissus. They flower at a welcome time of year and the cool greenhouse is, of course, perfectly suited to their culture. But it is the tender bulbs that must not be forgotten. Some forty different kinds are included in this book; though not all of them are ideal pot plants, all are worth consideration.

From the point of view of the beginner bulbous plants have many virtues. They are in general singularly free from insect pests; they survive occasional neglect better than most things, and many have beautiful, waxy and long-lasting flowers. Some bulbous plants can be kept in the same pots for several years, and many have a dormant season when they can be ignored and yet live to bloom another day. Most bulbs, too, have next season's flower already formed inside them when purchased; so they are sure to bloom at least once unless you positively murder them!

There are, however, some of the rarer and more exotic bulbs which may take a year to settle down and flower satisfactorily. Imported plants which have been collected in their natural habitat may have been uprooted while recognisable, that is, when in full growth, and these suffer a setback. Nursery-raised stock is the most satisfactory. It is always worth buying the best bulbs from a reliable source; bargains in bulbs, or indeed in plants of any kind, are a very poor gamble.

Perhaps I should explain that among bulbous plants I include all those with thick fleshy roots, even if they are botanically called corms, rhizomes or tubers.

The cultural routine of the majority of greenhouse bulbs is simple. They are potted up when received and kept only just moist until it is clear that they are growing. Then they are watered in the ordinary way and given an occasional feed until the flowers appear. The commonest mistake is to give them far too much water when they are just starting to grow and before the young roots are able to absorb it. Then the soil goes sour and the base of the bulb may rot. However, it is when the flowers are over that the most dangerous time comes, for that is when they get neglected. It must be remembered that next year's flowers are manufactured by this year's leaves. These must have full light and attention until they die down.

Only three bulbous plants included in this book are evergreen. They are clivia, vallota and zantedeschia, although the last is often dried off and forced to rest. Vallotas are often sold as dry bulbs and can be very unwilling to start growing again. It is best to buy pot-grown plants when possible. These evergreen plants are kept watered all the year, though they need much less water when they are not growing actively.

As I have said, most greenhouse bulbs have a resting season when they need to be kept either dry or nearly so, and it is a help if the numbers of their resting months are marked on their labels or pots. You will find the details for the treatment of each plant at the end of the book, but the principle needs to be understood. The rest period is usually emulating a dry season of hot sunshine, and to push the pots into the darkest corner and to douse them with water because their leaves are limp, is certain death. This is the treatment meted out to hundreds of thousands of cyclamen sold in bloom each year. I doubt if any greenhouse owner has escaped the gift of their sodden remains.

It is generally agreed that the best cyclamen are freshly raised from seed. This is usually sown in August or September to flower about sixteen months later, although some varieties will make a small flowering plant in a single season if sown early in the year. The newcomer to gardening is unlikely to raise very good plants from seed at the first attempt. Many cyclamen are worth keeping for a second year, and some people keep them healthy and free-flowering for many years. These old warriors are most often found on the window-sill above the kitchen sink and they are usually white. As soon as the flowers are over, cyclamen should be encouraged to rest by gradually reducing their water supply while keeping them in a strong light. The leaves will die off with perhaps one or two remaining through the summer. Personally I put the pots in the plunge bed, sunk to the rim, at the beginning of June but do not water them. Although this is not ideal in a very wet summer, they always survive. Towards the end of July I re-pot them in new soil and start them into growth—though sometimes they have already started of their own accord—bringing them into the greenhouse at the end of September.

Although it may sound complicated, I assure you that in practice the cultivation of bulbous plants is simple when they are grown in soil in the traditional way. They do not lend themselves so well to modern forms of automatic watering. I have, however, grown good cyclamen on capillary benches.

Fortunately the more expensive bulbous plants, like clivia, nerine and vallota, improve from year to year with reasonable care, while some that are cheaply replaced may not be worth keeping for more than one season. Hyacinths, narcissi, scillas, tulips and bulbous irises should be planted out in the garden after being grown in pots. That is, unless you are specialising in growing rare species in pots in an alpine house. Freesias, hybrid gladioli, polianthes and tigridias are best replaced each year. Indeed, the modern freesias can be raised from seed in seven months. *Lachenalia pendula* is a very attractive Christmas-flowering plant, which is distinctly less good the second year, as the bulbs tend to divide into a number of small ones too young to flower. This is also true of tigridias and bulbous irises. Lachenalias are, however, worth keeping.

Most gardening writers, possibly because of their skilled professional experience, do not seem to deem it a disadvantage if a plant must be constantly renewed from seed or cuttings, with many re-pottings and pinchings and sprayings and tyings up all the year round. It is true that as expertise increases one wants to be applying the hard-earned skills. But I am all for a quiet life; a big fat bulb which positively prefers to be left sitting in the same pot for years endears itself to me far more than the most showy chrysanthemum. But here I am on dangerous ground, for in gardening circles one simply does not criticise the chrysanthemum, the lily or the rose! Individuals may be scorned, but their families have to be loved if you are not to be regarded as an eccentric species yourself.

Rechsteinerias, sinningias (formerly gloxinia) and smithianthas are interesting plants for the warmest of cool greenhouses. There are also begonia species with rhizomatous roots for shady conditions.

If you are a beginner, the hardy spring bulbs, cyclamen grown from corms, freesia, ixia, lachenalia, nerine and vallota are worth trying early in your career.

Although it is perhaps the better-known bulbous and tuberous rooted plants that are the most rewarding in size of bloom and reliability, there is great satisfaction in growing a rare species and waiting for a flower you have either never seen before, or only known in some wild and distant land.

In the following list I give approximate flowering and resting times for bulbous plants; for full cultural details please turn to the end of the book.

Achimenes Late summer. Quite dry by November. Start in April.
Agapanthus Midsummer. All but dry end of September until April.
Amaryllis Autumn. Reduce watering spring to August.
Babiana Summer. Quite dry from September to January.
Begonia (tuberous hybrids) Late summer. Quite dry November to March.
Bessera Summer. Let die down. Keep dry until growth starts in spring.
Chlidanthus May or June. Almost dry through winter.
Cyclamen Winter. Rest after flowering until July.
Freesia Early spring. Quite dry June to September.
Gladiolus (*nanus* hybrids) April or May. Quite dry August to November.

Gloriosa   Summer. Quite dry November to March.
Haemanthus   Treatment varies. See end of book.
Hedychium   Late summer. All but dry October to March.
Hippeastrum   March to June. All but dry October to February.
Hymenocallis   Spring. All but dry through winter resting period.
Iris   Various. See end of book.
Ixia   May. Allow to die down, then quite dry until October.
Lachenalia   Winter. Keep watered until they die down. Then keep dry in sun until re-potting in August.
Leucocoryne   Spring. Treat as freesias.
Lilium   Summer. Allow to die down naturally. Keep just moist. Seedlings are kept growing through first winter.
Lycoris   Late summer. After leaves die keep dry until growth starts.
Milla   Late summer. Dry off gradually after flowering. Keep quite dry in temperature of 13° C. (55° F.) through winter.
Nerine   Late summer and autumn. Dry off gradually in May. Keep quite dry until August.
Ornithogalum   Various. Keep dry when leaves turn yellow until growth starts.
Sparaxis   April and May. Treat as ixias.
Streptanthera   June. Treat as ixias.
Tecophilaea   Spring. After leaves die down keep dry until August.
Tigridia   June and July. Quite dry November to April.
Tritonia   May. Dry off gradually, then quite dry until November.
Veltheimia   February or March. Dry off gradually and keep dry until August.
Zephyranthes   Various. Keep just moist even when resting.

14
Cacti and Succulents

ALL SUCCULENT PLANTS are not cacti, but all cacti *are* succulents, for it is the plants that have adapted themselves to very harsh conditions by storing moisture in thick succulent stems or leaves, which are known as succulents. Cacti are the members of a single botanical family called *Cactaceae*, which have almost entirely dispensed with leaves.

Although conditions in the cool greenhouse are not (or should not be) harsh from the plant's point of view, they are controlled conditions in which almost all cacti and other succulent plants can be grown to perfection. They require little artificial heat and less attention than most plants. As they will survive periods of neglect that would kill many things, they are good plants for the weekend gardener. They are tolerant of the dry heat of the small greenhouse, so long as it is well ventilated. They are not, however, suitable for an automatic greenhouse with capillary bench watering. While it is quite possible to grow some succulents on capillary benches, the conditions are unsuitable for anyone who wishes to specialise in these plants.

My purpose here is to select interesting and decorative succulent plants for the cool greenhouse out of the many hundreds that are available from the specialist growers. As there are so many to choose from and this is not a book for the specialist, I have made a personal selection of those I have found decorative and interesting. I think that the contrasting forms and textures of many succulents add variety and interest to any mixed collection of ornamental plants. They are also good in sunny windows, conservatories and garden rooms. I have chosen cacti that are free-flowering or of interesting shape and colour. The succulent plants are often of most value for their unusual form and leaf colour, and for the important fact that they are equally decorative all the year round. Indeed, many succulent plants flower between Christmas and Easter.

In recent years the sale of cacti and succulents has become quite an industry, encouraged partly by human failings. Thousands of people buy small cacti and then kill them by kindness (over-watering) or believe they can survive without any water at all. Hundreds of others are attracted by the charming bowl gardens of cacti and succulents. Although these survive much longer in the home than the average pot plant, they also have a high mortality rate as there is no proper drainage. However, the mainstay of the industry is the successful amateur who becomes an enthusiast and starts to collect whole families of different species, like postage stamps. You will find that the appreciation of these curious plants does grow on one to an amazing degree, and the cactus enthusiast is soon short of space for his collection. As with all specialisation it is worth joining one of the cactus and succulent societies if you are going to grow many of these plants.

Personally, I feel that in the conservatory a few, fairly large succulent plants, or collections of them in large pans or troughs, are more effective than a large number of small specimens. Very striking effects can be achieved by planting an indoor rock garden with cacti and succulents. Until you have seen them growing naturally with free root room, as in the magnificent 'Jardin Exotique' at Monte Carlo, you can hardly imagine the full decorative potentialities of these plants.

It is quite wrong to think that they should be kept permanently in tiny pots. It is true that they will survive in a stunted condition for longer than any other kind of plant, but for handsome healthy specimens, re-potting at least every other year is advisable. This can be done at any time, but is best done shortly before growth starts in early spring.

In nature cacti develop extensive root systems in their search for moisture, and the small pot is a compromise on our part. It helps to avoid stagnant moisture at the roots that is soon fatal to cacti.

In the native homes of the majority of these plants the rainfall is sometimes heavy but infrequent, and there is a dry resting season. Fortunately the great majority of desert plants adapt themselves quite well to resting in our winters and growing in the summer. This means that they are kept dry or nearly so through the cold months. So long as they are dry, they are resistant to temperatures far below those of their native homes. It is not, however, possible to raise cacti from seed in low temperatures and young plants should be kept moist and growing through their first winter. All cacti that are kept in warm rooms or greenhouses heated above 4° C. (40° F.) need occasional water in winter to prevent shrivelling.

The best time of year to make a start with succulent plants in the greenhouse is in the spring. The first thing you will want to know is what soil to use. There is no hard and fast rule about this and many soil mixtures have been advocated and used with success. The most important points are that the compost should be very porous and should contain some coarse particles so that it is well aerated. In their struggle to conserve moisture in the desert regions in which they live, cacti and succulents are adapted so as not to transpire freely through their green parts as other plants do, thereby losing vital moisture. This makes it all the more essential that some air reaches their roots, and that is why waterlogging so quickly kills them. At the same time complete dryness at the roots when they are growing is a threat to their existence even if they are able to survive it.

Because desert soils are often rich in minerals, a seed compost is not rich enough. There is no magic formula for these undemanding plants. Personally, for most desert plants I use 3 parts of J.I.P. 2 with the addition of 1 part of coarse sand or other gritty material, such as crushed flint as used in chicken food. I believe in mixing a little crushed charcoal with the soil and I also add a little bonemeal if I am not expecting to re-pot the plant for some time. In general a mixture of 2 parts loam, 2 parts sharp sand and 1 part peat is a satisfactory consistency for these plants. It is better to re-pot yearly than to feed cacti and succulents, but they can be given occasional weak doses of the feeds you give to your other plants.

Tiny pots get too hot in summer and dry out too rapidly so that the tips of the roots get burnt. It is usually wise to re-pot bought plants in a slightly larger size of pot that will hold their roots comfortably. It is equally undesirable to over-pot them. Always use soil that is thoroughly damp all through; then do not water for several days and keep the plants shaded until they have had time to start growing again.

Until recently cacti and succulents have been grown in well-crocked clay pots. Today, they are sometimes grown and sold in plastic pots. Opinion is divided as to whether clay or plastic pots are best, but, as plastic pots are not porous, the plants in them require much less frequent watering than in clay pots, and the consequences of over-watering are more likely to prove fatal. They do, however, grow faster if well managed. Epiphytic cacti do well in plastic pots.

The next problem is watering. A few plants need special treatment and this is described in the details of their cultivation at the end of the book. But in general cacti and succulents show the first signs of renewed life in February or, more often, March each year. This is the signal for regular watering to start, although it must be only very moderate for the first few weeks. In summer cacti in small pots need watering nearly as often as other plants if the atmosphere in the greenhouse is dry. I know it would be much simpler if I could say: 'Water them twice a week from May to September'; but conditions vary far too much. If you are in doubt as to whether to water a cactus the thing to remember is *don't*.

At the end of September watering must be reduced in preparation for the winter. From the end of October until growth starts in spring, the intention must be only just to prevent the soil from becoming bone dry right through the pot. If they are grown in small pots, they are happier when the pots are plunged in coarse sand or stones. This keeps the roots cooler in summer, and in winter it is easier to keep them slightly damp without watering. Indeed, only the surrounding sand need be watered a few times during the winter.

Re-potting is usually done in March and April. Remove the old crocks and exterior soil and cut back any dead roots before re-potting in a slightly larger pot. Plant them at the same depth as before, using damp soil. Firm potting is not desirable for these plants. It is important not to overwater until the roots are established once more.

Some people complain that their cacti do not flower. This is often because they have bought seedling plants which are still too young to flower. Another reason for not flowering may be starvation for many years in the same pot. Often, however, I think it is because the plants have not been given a resting period. Apart from being kept dry in winter, the temperature should not be above 7° C. (45° F.) if they are not to be excited into growth. Many amateurs who specialise in cacti set their thermostats at 4° C. (40° F.) through the winter. Because of the high winter temperatures cacti grown indoors flower much less well than those in the greenhouse.

Epiphytic cacti from the tropical forests of South America naturally prefer higher temperatures and different composts from the majority of cacti. These are given at the end of the book in the description of each plant concerned. Epiphytic cacti included in this book will be found under aporocactus and schlumbergera.

Many commonly grown cacti can be raised from seed quite easily with steady moisture and a constant temperature of from 21° C. (70° F.) to 27° C. (80° F.). The baby plants must be kept growing through their first winter and are happiest above 10° C. (50° F.). Many cacti produce offsets which can be carefully separated and rooted as cuttings. The pads of opuntias and the tips of columnar cacti will usually root easily in summer, if cut off with a sharp knife and allowed to dry for several days. It is wise to dust the cut ends with flowers of sulphur. Coarse sand or vermiculite are good rooting materials, and the cutting can be very lightly inserted, or tied to a stick so that it is held just clear of the damp surface into which it will soon send roots.

If the roots or the base of a cactus rot, its life can usually be saved by cutting off the roots or base and re-rooting the whole plant as if it was a cutting.

In summer most succulent plants are easily increased by leaf or stem cuttings, and some, like echeverias, produce offsets that can be cut off and used as cuttings or the whole top of the plant can be re-rooted. Many succulent plants are raised from seed commercially, and this often produces the best-shaped plants, but takes considerably longer. It would require another book to go into all the possible methods of raising and growing some of these strange plants enough to satisfy the specialist. For most of us who only want a few attractive succulents it is simpler to buy them as young plants. For the specialist there are several societies and a wealth of literature devoted to desert plants. The cacti in the following list should flower freely every year even when young. Aporocactus, Echinocereus and Echinopsis may take longer than the others to reach flowering size, but they are particularly worth waiting for.

Aporocactus flagelliformis, brilliant pink or red.
Chamacereus silvestrii, orange-scarlet.
Echinocereus species with variously coloured flowers.
Echinopsis eyriesii, white.
Mammillaria bocasana, pink, **M. elegans**, carmine, **M. elongata**, white and **M. prolifera multiceps**, yellow.
Notocactus apricus, N. ottonis and **N. tabularis,** all with yellow flowers.
Parodia aureispina, yellow and **P. sanguiniflora**, blood-red.
Rebutia minuscula, scarlet, **R. violaciflora** and various hybrids.
Schlumbergera × **buckleyi** (syn. **Zygocactus truncatus**) commonly known as the Christmas Cactus, scarlet.

15
Pests and Diseases

THERE ARE a fearsome number of pests and diseases known to science that may attack plant life, just as there are multitudes that may attack man. However, your own greenhouse is an isolated community over which you have a great deal of control. For healthy plants kept in clean conditions with well-regulated ventilation are not prone to disease, and with pests the first thing to remember is that prevention is infinitely better than cure.

I have come to the conclusion that the introduction of the more serious pests into my greenhouse is almost always the direct result of adding new plants to my collection. It is essential to examine every new plant very closely, and wise to spray it with a general insecticide before putting it into the greenhouse. If it can spend the first two weeks isolated from the rest of the plants, so much the better. Nurserymen have far greater pest-control problems than the average gardener and have to take effective measures. Nevertheless, while bought plants rarely show active signs of trouble, like children returning from the best-regulated schools they may be incubating something that will show itself in a few days.

Many troubles with plants are due to faults in cultivation rather than to pests, diseases or fungal attack. Plants crowded together and making soft weak growth are attractive to biting insects and provide cover for their depredations. Brown edges to the leaves, although occasionally due to a mineral deficiency in the soil are usually the result of too dry an atmosphere.

The sudden dropping of buds may have the same cause, though

it is often due to temporary dryness at the roots, followed by conscience-stricken heavy watering which the shrivelled root-tips cannot absorb. It is certainly the result of adverse growing conditions, which may only be a sudden change in environment. People often move plants into a conspicuous but draughty spot just as they are coming into flower.

It is often natural for old leaves to turn yellow and fall but, if this is excessive and the plant has not been allowed to dry out, it is probably being kept too wet. If a whole plant, or a number of plants, take on an unhealthy yellowish tinge but have not stopped growing, they may need feeding. If they are lime-hating plants, they may be suffering from lack of iron due to the effects of an alkaline soil or water supply. In this case a dose of iron sequestrene is likely to be the quickest cure. If it is only one plant, you can, of course, re-pot it in lime-free soil and water only with rain-water.

Great attention is focused today on the ever-changing and ever more lethal chemicals which destroy an ever wider variety of pests at the touch of a button. It is vitally important to read the instructions carefully and follow them to the letter. If there is a warning that the makers do not accept responsibility even if the directions are followed, you cannot say you have not been warned.

Personally I prefer to burn the occasional plant rather than introduce powerful poisons into my greenhouse or my home. Pyrethrum and derris preparations and white oil insecticides are not poisonous or otherwise dangerous, and they control most greenhouse pests if you are vigilant and do not let things get out of hand. Sometimes they are sold mixed with more lethal ingredients, but this will be stated on the container.

A useful booklet is available from the Henry Doubleday Research Association called *Pest control without poisons*. If you are determined to use the whole armoury that modern science has produced, *Gardening Chemicals* compiled by the Royal Horticultural Society's Laboratory lists those that are available for amateur use and what they in fact contain, as well as whether they have Ministry of Agriculture approval.

In spite of all the chemicals available, the pests are still with us and some of them have developed immunity to substances which were formerly lethal to them. Today, biological control of greenhouse pests is being actively studied for commercial use. It is already possible to control red spider and whitefly by introducing their natural predators, which have been specially bred for the purpose. This eliminates losses from damage from powerful chemicals and does not build up resistance in the pest population. Biological controls are not easily available for amateurs.

The sheltered conditions of a greenhouse are favourable to insect as well as plant life, and the pests most likely to try to share your greenhouse with you are listed below.

ANTS
These should be controlled because they transport aphides from plant to plant and so spread virus and other diseases. Both derris and pyrethrum discourage ants but many ant killers contain BHC or chlordane.

APHIDES
Greenfly and similar creatures of varying colours are the most unavoidable pest of all. They weaken and disfigure plants by sucking the sap; they spread virus diseases, and multiply in numbers with incredible speed. As they continue their depredations all the year round in the heated greenhouse, you can never relax your vigilance in searching them out. Fortunately almost every insecticide on the market destroys them. I use a combination of pyrethrum and derris; but there are countless alternatives, including systemic insecticides which are absorbed into the sap of the plant and so kill anything that tries to eat the plant either above or below ground. These are undesirable for food crops.

CAPSID BUGS
These usually appear in the autumn and attack chrysanthemums and other composite flowers, deforming the flowers and producing pin-point holes on the leaves. The adult bugs are $\frac{1}{4}$ inch long and usually a pale yellowish-green with reddish-brown mottling. The young are green, wingless and active. Both the plants and the surrounding soil should be sprayed. Pyrethrum can be used,

though the chrysanthemum specialist may wish to fumigate with something stronger.

CARNATION TORTRIX MOTH

The moths have greyish-brown fore wings and bright orange hind wings. They lay large patches of eggs on the upper surfaces of leaves. Their yellowish-green caterpillars with dark heads damage a number of ornamental plants. Fortunately, the caterpillars roll up leaf tips and spin themselves a home, in which they can be squashed between finger and thumb if you are on the alert. They feed on the buds and flowers of carnations as well as the leaves. If things get out of hand, you may have to resort to DDT.

EARWIGS

These can be troublesome in a hot dry summer. They emerge at night and damage the blooms of chrysanthemums and other plants; they also make ugly punctured holes in the leaves of some succulents. They take refuge in the daytime in various objects such as hollow bamboos and matchboxes, which can be left as traps. If you are plagued with earwigs, there is probably some cavity in wood where they congregate, and it is worth finding and destroying the occupants each morning. Ant killers also deter earwigs.

EELWORMS

Eelworms are only destroyed by sterilising the soil. Chrysanthemums attacked by eelworm have light green patches, on the lower leaves, which to start with are limited by the main veins. They later turn brown and black and spread to the whole leaf. The bottom leaves are affected first. Immersion in water at 46° C. (115° F.) for precisely 5 minutes is known as the hot water treatment, and it is essential if the plants are to be kept or any cuttings taken from them. The whole plant is freed from soil and treated in winter before boxing up to produce cuttings. This must be very accurately done and the temperature maintained exactly if it is to be effective without damaging the plant.

LEAFMINER

This maggot makes white channels in the leaves of cinerarias and chrysanthemums. When found at the end of their channels, they should be pinched. Malathion spray and most greenhouse fumigants deal with this pest.

MEALY BUG

This creature looks like a tiny whitish woodlouse. Its eggs are protected with a white wool that will probably be the first thing you notice. This is an extremely persistent pest and it is important not to let it get established. It is the only pest I have ever had on my cacti, and it is likely to arrive either on a cactus or a hard-wooded plant. Fortunately it does not spread rapidly in the early stages, but it is hard to kill and will need two or more applications of insecticide. In a small private greenhouse it pays to pick off and destroy each bug with the point of a pin, or to dab them and their eggs with a paintbrush dipped in methylated spirits. One can spray with white oil. Malathion is often recommended, but it cannot be used on the Crassula family or ferns.

RED SPIDER MITE

This is one of the most serious greenhouse pests and rather hard to spot, as the individual insects can barely be seen. Their attack is first noticed by results, as the affected leaves take on a pale lifeless tone due to quantities of tiny bleached spots on the leaves; these occur where the mites are feeding on the under-surface. The mites are pale straw-coloured, turning in autumn to red, and they weave minute webs over the lower surfaces of the leaves. The reason for their rapid spread is too dry an atmosphere, and the plants most likely to be attacked are shrubs and carnations. To keep red spider under control, syringe the under surfaces of the leaves of woody plants with water in warm weather. There are proprietary sprays, aerosols and fumigating smokes to tackle this pest, and instructions should be followed carefully, since more than one application will probably be necessary.

SCALE

Scale insects sometimes get introduced into the greenhouse on shrubby plants and are easily overlooked. They are most likely to be found on the backs of the leaves of evergreen shrubs. The females attach themselves to the leaves and stems, which they frequently match in colour, before covering themselves with a leathery covering. They harm the plants by sucking the sap. Scrubbing them off the leaves and stems with soapy water is an old-fashioned remedy, which keeps their numbers under control. Systemic insecticides and liquid malathion kill this tiresome pest.

THRIPS

Healthy plants in a reasonably moist atmosphere are not much attacked by thrips. They are minute blackish grey-winged insects, and the damage they cause is very similar in appearance to that of red spider. There will, however, be no webs under the leaves and probably no visible insects. Syringing the undersides of the leaves with clear water discourages thrips, and derris and pyrethrum are effective remedies.

WHITEFLY

These live up to their name, being tiny, snow-white flies. They would be charming if their larvae were not sucking insects. Fortunately, they are interested only in a minority of plants, but they are hard to eradicate. Regal pelargoniums, fuchsias and tomatoes are the plants most likely to be attacked. There is no non-poisonous remedy and several applications of any proprietary whitefly killer or greenhouse fumigant are necessary. Do not let nettles grow under the staging, as whiteflies are partial to them.

WOODLICE

These may become established in a greenhouse. They feed at night, mostly on decaying organic matter, but sometimes they attack plants. Some people say that the remedy is to keep a toad. I do have a toad and I have never been bothered by woodlice, but I do not claim that this proves anything. Ant powders can be used.

If your greenhouse or conservatory does not connect with the dwelling-house, fumigating smokes are a possible method of keeping it free from insect pests or clearing up a severe outbreak. At least one does not have to be there with the noxious fumes—although they do leave a slight deposit. Most fumigants work best at a fairly high temperature, and the smoking is best done at sundown on a warm, windless day. The greenhouse should then be left closed overnight. Before starting, seal up all cracks and follow the instructions closely. Make sure, too, that none of the plants is dry at the roots.

Apart from insect pests, the most usual troubles in a greenhouse are various forms of mould and mildew, due largely to overcrowding or faulty ventilation.

DAMPING OFF

Seedlings sometimes rot at soil level, and in a warm muggy atmosphere the trouble may spread rapidly. The use of sterilised composts and thin sowings make this trouble unlikely, but the remedy is watering with Cheshunt Compound.

GREY MOULD (*Botrytis cinerea*)

In damp weather, particularly in autumn, a grey fluffy mould may appear on plants. The first line of defence is to try to alter the conditions which caused it—a damp stuffiness. Grey mould is less of a problem above 10° C. (50° F.), though saturated, static air always encourages moulds. Dead and damaged flowers and foliage are the first to go mouldy and should be removed. Sulphur spray is one remedy. Colloidal copper and sulphur preparations are the safest fungicides.

If you grow Zonal pelargoniums, you may have trouble with black-leg. This is a blackening of the stem which usually starts at ground level and eventually kills the plant. Cuttings are often affected and should be burnt. It is not a frequent trouble with growing plants, but they should be destroyed if seen to be infected.

Carnation wilt is a danger if carnations are repeatedly grown in the same soil or in very damp soil. The soil should be sterilised and the affected plants not used for propagation.

Carnations, chrysanthemums and cinerarias sometimes suffer from leaf rust. If this happens, remove and burn the affected leaves. Spraying with a thiram fungicide is the usual recommendation. I burn the plant. Happy plants do not get rust.

Last, but not least, there are the virus diseases. These are varied in their visible effects. They include acute malformation of the leaves, which may be crinkled, twisted and discoloured, or of an uncharacteristic shape for the plant concerned. Some affected plants are merely small and poor doers. As there is no cure it is best to destroy any plant you feel sure has virus as it will be a source of infection to others. The prevalence of virus makes it important to get pelargoniums, carnations and chrysanthemums from a reliable virus-free source. Virus affects the whole sap of the plant and can be passed on by means of the knife when taking cuttings. No cuttings must be taken from infected plants.

In pelargoniums virus shows itself as a spotting and starring of the leaves which is most noticeable in early spring. Although plants may appear to recover in the summer, they will never in fact do so. It is wiser to burn them.

To end on a happier note, do remember that many insects are working with you and not against you in the garden. The Ministry of Agriculture publishes a bulletin called *Beneficial Insects*, with illustrations in colour, to help you to identify your friends and helpers in the insect world. These spend their lives devouring your enemies—so long as you do not destroy them by indiscriminate spraying.

16

Specialisation

IT IS ONLY by trial and error that you will discover which plants respond best to your treatment of them. Every greenhouse has its particular conditions of light, heat, ventilation and humidity, quite apart from the personal eccentricities of the owner!

In nature it is well known that some species are confined to a single tiny area, where conditions are just right to enable them to flourish and also to hold their own with other vegetation. In the greenhouse, although plants do not have competition and are in a completely artificial environment, their subtle preferences remain.

It is a fact that when I used to depend on a kind neighbour who watered my greenhouse during my absence in the middle of each week, some plants became visibly happier and others less so, while when a relative did the watering the results were different yet again. It was noticeable, too, that the plants which flourished under each person's care had points in common. The plants from Mexico liked my relative, the South Americans preferred my neighbour, and the Australians really only liked me!

Now that I grow most of my plants on capillary benches and they draw up the water they require by capillary attraction, the results are different once again. Curiously enough there are few plants that object to steady moisture so long as the compost is not compressed and airless. Now, the problem is not the hand that wields the watering can but the nature of the water. The very alkaline mains water where I live is unsuitable for a number of plants which thrive if rain water is used.

As countless amateurs have discovered for themselves there is more than one way to grow any plant. Both plants and people vary in their adaptability, and no one can predict for certain what the reactions of either will be to a given set of conditions.

The other feature of plant growing is that it is a creative activity and interests change as experience develops. Although most of us start with a mixed collection of plants, many decide after a time to concentrate their efforts in one field. Some devote all their energies to a single plant or a related group of plants. Others become interested in plants adapted to a particular region or habitat, such as desert, mountain or rain forest. Yet others collect every known member of a related group in much the same spirit as some people collect stamps. With others there is a particular purpose for which plants will be raised year after year.

Our favourite plants may be chosen because we find them beautiful, scented, rare, challenging, fashionable, saleable or even edible! A north-facing greenhouse may encourage an interest in shade-loving plants, while travel may stimulate an interest in plants seen in their natural home. Begonias, camellias, cacti, carnations, chrysanthemums, ericas, ferns, fuchsias, orchids, pelargoniums, primulas and saintpaulias all have their dedicated admirers. Most of them have a special society devoted to their interest. These societies are well worth joining. They are usually affiliated to the Royal Horticultural Society which in turn has groups concerned with camellias, rhododendrons and lilies.

The tuberous begonia with its profusion of lavish flowers has many admirers. The dry tubers can be kept warm in winter without heating a greenhouse in the coldest months of the year. In fact, if you become interested in the begonia family, you will soon want to grow the many fibrous-rooted and ornamental-leaved kinds that need a winter temperature of at least 10° C. (50° F.). It is a very large and interesting family and I have only included a selection of the very varied species.

I have already devoted a chapter to cacti and succulent plants which have a great fascination for me, though I have never been able to limit myself to any one section of plant life. The question of space is an important one when deciding what you are going to grow. Nine 3-inch pots, crammed together so that they are touching, take up 1 square foot of bench space while a single well-developed specimen plant in a 6-inch pot may take up twice as much room. It is possible to have a large collection of cacti in only a fraction of the space needed for most other plants. The feature of all established amateur greenhouses is that they are either far too full or quite empty. If air cannot circulate freely among the plants, there is bound to be trouble. Nevertheless I know of a greenhouse less than 6 feet square in which over two hundred plants spend the winter in pots. This takes skill and vigilance.

In Victorian times whole greenhouses were filled with ferns and there are signs of a revival of this interest. Ferns need shade and a moist atmosphere, but no great heat.

The flowering plant with the largest following under glass is the chrysanthemum. The growing of chrysanthemums can become a competitive passion that I do not claim to understand. This plant owes much of its popularity to its ability to play box-and-cox with the utilitarian tomato.

Although it is troublesome to grow prize chrysanthemums really well, the rewards of specialist skill are great. With manipulation of day-length it is now possible to have flowers at any time of year, and with chemical treatment their height can also be controlled. To me their constant presence in the shops discourages my own efforts, but the fact that late-rooted cuttings can now be bought from the specialist growers in late summer to produce flowers at Christmas is a great advance. This does away with the necessity to take cuttings early in the year and to tend the plants all through the summer before they do their bit in the autumn and winter. Nevertheless the chrysanthemum enthusiast positively welcomes a routine extending throughout the year. In Japan, where the control of growth by cultural methods is an art form, even greater wonders are to be seen.

A favourite plant for cool conditions is the carnation. There is perhaps no greenhouse plant that produces so many flowers for cutting in a year as the perpetual-flowering carnation, although it is not a graceful plant, even when well grown. It needs a tall house with very good ventilation to do well.

As both carnations and chrysanthemums are important commercial crops, far more is known about their every whim than about most greenhouse plants. Their ills are well documented, as the research stations have submitted them to everything short of psychoanalysis. There are many books devoted to chrysanthemums alone, and I can give only some basic and elementary information in this book.

Now we come to what I always feel is the friendliest plant in the greenhouse. It puts up with all sorts of people and their failings, and does not confine its flowering to any one season. This is the pelargonium, which includes the Zonal pelargoniums that most of us think of (wrongly) as geraniums. There are also the Regal pelargoniums with their huge velvety blooms, as well as miniature kinds and varieties grown for their ornamental or scented leaves, not to mention many rare and curious wild species.

It is a surprise to many people to discover that bedding pelargoniums are merely the toughest hybrids that are willing to overlook the frequently sodden British summer. They are, among Zonal pelargoniums, what the country dancer is to the prima ballerina. Most people have no idea of the range of colour and delicacy of marking of the really choice kinds available from specialist nurserymen. For those with little space the miniature varieties are of special interest.

If you want colour all the year round and have little time or money to lavish on your conservatory, a small collection of pelargoniums increased yearly from cuttings is a very satisfactory arrangement. We have in Great Britain an enormous range of species and a great fund of knowledge of these plants. The pelargonium, too, has its own society and literature.

The fuchsia is another favourite plant with great variety and a long flowering season. It responds to skilful cultivation, yet is easy to propagate and can be grown with very little heat.

The saintpaulia enthusiast really needs a greenhouse that is warm rather than cool. I have included this plant because so many are grown even in the most unsuitable conditions. One either loves or hates the vivid purple glow of the saintpaulia. It is one of the best plants for growing under artificial lights indoors.

The saintpaulia belongs to a group of plants that are known

SPECIALISATION

collectively as gesneriads, as they all belong to the family *Gesneriaceae*. They all have velvety leaves and rich exotic blossoms. They flourish in moist and shady conditions with a fair amount of heat. Unfortunately they have come in for more than their share of name changing in recent years. Some people like to specialise in the whole group. These are the names to look for in this book: achimenes, naegelia, reichsteineria, sinningia (gloxinia), and smithiantha.

Orchids are in a class of their own as their cultivation is different from that of most greenhouse plants. The majority of orchids are epiphytic in nature. This means that they grow on trees but do not obtain nourishment from their host. Curiously enough, they seem to interest men far more than women. Orchids do not mix well with other plants, since a moist atmosphere is essential as well as considerable shade in summer. It is not worth specialising in orchids unless you can maintain a minimum winter temperature of 10° C. (50° F.). A wise first step is to read the admirable beginner's guide of the Orchid Society of Great Britain. Although many orchids are costly, they are very long-lived plants, and it is by no means essential to be wealthy to indulge in this hobby. Nurserymen who sell orchids are particularly helpful to new customers, and are prepared to explain the special potting methods and materials.

Some people become fascinated by other epiphytic plants, of which a number can be grown in the cool greenhouse. Names to look for here are aporocactus, aechmea, bilbergia, epiphyllum, neoregelia, nidularium, platycerium, rhipsalidopsis and schlumbergera.

Another form of specialisation is growing plants for cut flowers or exotic foliage for flower arrangement.

There is no telling to what flower you may feel particularly drawn, but I hope you will find plenty to choose from in this book. It has often been the enthusiasm of amateurs that has led to the transformation of a flowering plant from a neglected species to a favourite plant with many hybrids in a variety of colours.

Many greenhouses are bought with the idea of raising plants for the garden. It is certainly true that the only way to have a display

SPECIALISATION

of unusual bedding plants is to raise them from seed, but this only occupies the greenhouse for a few months of the year. For me the greatest pleasure is to have flowers in the greenhouse all the year round and to know that it is a pleasant refuge for myself from the elements and the telephone.

17
Encyclopaedia of Cool Greenhouse Plants

IN THIS chapter you will find cultural details for growing all the plants described so far and many more besides. I have endeavoured to give all the names by which each plant may be described in catalogues. I believe that all are commercially available in the United Kingdom at the time of writing, at least in the form of seed. If there is difficulty in obtaining unusual plants, the advisory departments of the gardening papers are most helpful and the Horticultural Trades Association runs a service to put customers in touch with suppliers.

I have tried to describe each plant and to give an impression of its ultimate size, time of flowering and value in the greenhouse. The cultivation is based on the John Innes composts, which are referred to by initials to save space. I also suggest alternatives and sometimes say 'or similar compost', by which I mean that any potting compost in general use is likely to be satisfactory. At a time when new all-peat and other ready-mixed composts are constantly being introduced and none have been in use for nearly as long as the successful John Innes formulas, I cannot say with any confidence that any are better, although they are of a more constant standard and some are more convenient. Personally, I try them all and have not failed to grow plants with any. A point to remember is that peat-based composts need to be kept rather wetter than soil-based composts for the plant roots to be able to extract the same amount of moisture from them. I still prefer soil-based composts for most cacti, succulents and shrubby plants that are to remain in the same pot for any length of time. It is sometimes a disadvantage that compost should be light in weight and pots liable to blow over, and sometimes a great advantage. For the elderly or disabled, it may make the difference between pleasure and pain in gardening.

The phrase MWT 7° C. (45° F.) means that this temperature should be the minimum winter temperature for the plant. Where no temperature is given, the plants can be grown with MWT 4° C. (40° F.) and are worth trying so long as the greenhouse is frost-free. All the plants in the book can, of course, be grown at higher temperatures than those mentioned. One cannot be dogmatic about temperature when so much depends on other factors. In general, if the temperature is lower than it should be, it is all the more important to avoid overwatering or any unnecessary dampness in the surroundings in winter. Spare heating capacity makes the control of the atmosphere and adequate ventilation easier in cold weather.

Many people today have inadequate heating capacity to maintain the temperature at which their thermostats are set in cold spells, and all greenhouses have warmer and colder spots inside them. One cannot guarantee that any plant will thrive at any particular temperature, but I have done my best to select those most likely to flourish in cool conditions.

Abutilon *Malvaceae*
Flowering shrubs with pendant flowers. They can be trained up pillars or grown in tubs or pots. MWT 7° C. (45° F.)

CULTIVATION. Pot in March and re-pot when needed after trimming back in February. Use J.I.P. 3 with good drainage or all-peat composts. They need a lot of water in summer but little in winter. They are quickly increased by cuttings rooted at 21° C. (70° F.) or by seed sown in heat in March.

SPECIES TO GROW. Hybrids with orange, red, yellow and white flowers from August to November. *A. insigne*, rich carmine veins on white, winter (climber for border); *A. megapotamicum* (syn. *A. vexillarium*), red and yellow, summer, 6 feet; *A. milleri*, yellow flowers with carmine veins, continuous flowering; *A. striatum*.

'Thompsonii', mottled green and yellow foliage, orange flowers, used for summer bedding, 4–5 feet.

Acacia (Mimosa, Wattle) *Leguminosae*
Beautiful Australian evergreen trees and shrubs with fluffy yellow flowers in winter and spring. Easy and quick-growing but the tall kinds do not flower when young. MWT 7° C. (45° F.)

CULTIVATION. Buy in pot and re-pot firmly every two or three years in J.I.P. 2 or plant in border of large conservatory. Water freely except in winter and keep in full sun. Stand pots outdoors from June to September. All can be raised from seed (chip before sowing). Pinch when young to keep them compact. Cuttings root in summer.

SPECIES TO GROW. *A. armata*, ultimately 10 feet, yellow, early spring, and *A. drummondii*, lemon yellow, spring, are the best for pots; *A. baileyana* and *A. dealbata* (florist's mimosa) quickly become tall and flower in early spring.

Achimenes *Gesneriaceae*
South American tuberous-rooted plants with brilliant flowers over a long season in late summer. Suitable for hanging baskets.

CULTIVATION. Pot in J.I.P. 2 or other compost in spring, 1 inch deep and six to a 6-inch pot. They are usually started into growth in shallow pans of damp peat in April at 16° C. (60° F.) and transplanted when 2 inches high. They appreciate shade, warmth and moisture while growing and need supporting with twigs. Dry off gradually after flowering and store dry in their pots at MWT 10° C. (50° F.). In other words store and start indoors unless the greenhouse is kept at MWT 10° C. (50° F.).

SPECIES TO GROW. *A. coccinea*, crimson-scarlet, 1 foot, *A. longiflora*, *major*, violet-blue, 15 inches, and hybrids in many shades.

Adiantum (Maidenhair Fern) *Polypodiaceae*
Beautiful ferns with vivid green finely divided fronds.

CULTIVATION. Usually bought in small pots in spring. Re-pot in March in 2 parts peat to 1 part each of loam and silver sand with a little charcoal, or use EFF compost. Shade and plenty of water is needed through the summer. They like a moist atmosphere, but do not actually spray their fronds. See also FERNS.

SPECIES TO GROW. *A. capillus veneris* (British Isles) and its varieties, small; *A. pedatum*, deciduous, nearly hardy; *A. venustum*, fairly large, nearly hardy; all others are better with MWT 10° C. (50° F.). *A. cuneatum* and its variety 'Fritz Luthi'; *A. fragrans*, the most widely grown; *A. hispidum* (syn. *A. pubescens*) and *A. tenerum scutum ramosum*, with dark-coloured fronds, are others that are available.

Aechmea *Bromeliaceae*
Grey-leaved urn plant (bromeliad) with spectacular flower-head. Easy house-plant. MWT 10° C. (50° F.)

CULTIVATION. Preferably receive as present in bud! It is an epiphyte and the rosette of leaves must be kept filled with water (rain-water is best). The rosette with a flower will eventually die, and new shoots develop at its base. Keep the rosette filled with water in the original pot until fairly large. Then re-pot singly in warm conditions, or leave them all together, when they will make one very large plant. The offshoots will take two years to flower. Keep the roots just moist in summer but dry in winter. Give full light in winter and light shade in summer. Feed with dilute liquid feed in the rosettes when they are growing actively. A well-known house-plant firm recommends equal quantities of pine needles (*Pinus sylvestris*), leafmould and peat for young plants, and equal parts of peat, sand and osmunda fibre with some leafmould and pulverised cow-dung for mature plants. It is only necessary to re-pot if they become top-heavy.

SPECIES TO GROW. *A. rhodocyanea* (syn. *A. fasciata*). The head of pink spiny bracts and small blue flowers is attractive for several months.

Torenia Fournieri—a greenhouse annual for late summer

Thunbergia alata (Black-eyed Susan)—an annual climber from South Africa

The beautifully veined and velvety flowers of Salpiglossis

Trachelium caeruleum has dense heads of tiny blue flowers

Aeonium *Crassulaceae*
Easily grown succulent plants from the Canary Islands.

CULTIVATION. Pot in March in 3 parts J.I.P. 2 to 1 part sharp sand or in any well-drained soil mixture. Water freely in summer and sparingly from November to April. Cuttings root very easily, even large stem cuttings of the tall kinds.

SPECIES TO GROW. *A. arboreum* and its purple-leaved variety grow like small trees with rosettes of leaves at the tips of the branches and yellow flowers in spring when mature; up to 2½ feet in time. *A. domesticum* (syn. *Aichryson domesticum*) has a variagated form often sold as a house-plant, a much smaller plant. *A. haworthii*, small and shrubby with blue-grey leaves margined red. *A. undulatum*, slow-growing on a single stem. *A. tabulaeforme* is a flat rosette of pale green, woolly leaves. All may have yellow flowers when mature.

African Corn Lily *see* IXIA

African Hemp *see* SPARMANNIA

African Lily *see* AGAPANTHUS

African Violet *see* SAINTPAULIA

Agapanthus (African Lily) *Amaryllidaceae*
Half-hardy summer-flowering South African plants with fleshy roots and handsome heads of blue or white flowers. They are particularly suitable for growing in tubs.

CULTIVATION. The naming of agapanthus is confused and all kinds may be sold as *A. umbellatus* or *A. mooreanus* in addition to the names given below. All are very similar and need the same treatment. The deciduous ones are hardy outdoors in a well-drained sunny position. Pot in March, grouped in tubs, or singly in 9-inch pots of J.I.P. 3 or any rich compost. Water very freely when growing, from April to September and then sparingly. Keep them nearly dry in winter. Feed before flowering, which is around midsummer under glass. Re-pot only when extremely pot-bound. Increase by division in May. Seed sown in March should flower in the third summer.

SPECIES TO GROW. *A. africanus* and hybrids, evergreen, blue, about 2 feet; *A. campanulatus*, deciduous, blue, 3 feet, *A. praecox* evergreen, blue and white varieties, 2–4 feet.

Agathaea *see* FELICIA

Agave *Agavaceae*
Tough Mexican succulent plants with rosettes of ornamental leaves. Suitable for tubs put out of doors in summer.

CULTIVATION. Pot in spring in J.I.P. 2 with added grit. Re-pot every two or three years. Water moderately April to September and keep just moist in winter. They can stand outside in summer or be used in tropical bedding. There are dangerous spines at the tips of the leaves. *A. americana* is increased by offsets, *A. victoriae-reginae* only by seed.

SPECIES TO GROW. *A. americana*, glaucous blue leaves and varieties with leaves striped with pale yellow, ultimately too large for tubs; *A. victoriae-reginae* is a slow-growing and interesting plant, with white margins on very dark green leaves.

Ageratum *Compositae*
Easily grown half-hardy annual with very long flowering season.

CULTIVATION. Sow in March to May and pot singly in 3–5-inch pots of J.I.P. 1 or other compost. Bedding plants may be bought and potted up in spring. The dwarf kinds are best in pots.

SPECIES TO GROW. *A. houstonianum* (syn. *A. mexicanum*) 18 inches, has many dwarf hybrids 5–8 inches tall, such as 'Florists Blue', 'Blue Blazer', 'Fairy Pink' and 'Little White'.

Agrostemma *see* LYCHNIS

Aichryson *see* AEONIUM

Aloe *Liliaceae*
Evergreen succulent plants from Africa with orange and red flowers on mature plants.   MWT 7° C. (45° F.)

CULTIVATION. All aloes like a fairly rich porous soil with good drainage. J.I.P. 2 or 3 with some added grit is suitable. Water freely in summer, sparingly in winter and keep in full sunlight. They can be plunged outdoors in summer. Increase by cuttings, offsets or suckers. Allow cuttings to dry before inserting in a mixture of peat and sand. *A. variegata* (Partridge-breasted Aloe) is the most popular and increases rapidly by offsets. It has small red hot poker flowers every year.

SPECIES TO GROW. *A. arborescens*, red, winter, leaves toothed, ultimately large on tall stem; *A. aristata*, orange-red, May or June, small rosette; *A. ferox*, similar to *A. arborescens*; *A. variegata*, reddish, winter, leaves attractively mottled with white, up to 1 foot.

Alonsoa *Scrophulariaceae*
Very long-flowering tender perennials from Peru grown as half-hardy annuals.

CULTIVATION. Sow from March to May in 16° C. (60° F.) and transplant singly to flower in 5–6-inch pots in J.I.P. 2 or other compost. Pinch out the growing point for bushy plants or flower un-pinched in small pots. Support them with twigs and never allow them to dry. They flower from June onwards from an early sowing.

SPECIES TO GROW. *A. acutifolia* (syn. *A. myrtifolia*), scarlet, 2 feet; *A. mutisii*, pink, 1 foot; *A. warscewiczii compacta*, scarlet, 1 foot.

Aloysia *see* LIPPIA

Amaryllis (Belladonna Lily) *Amaryllidaceae*
Nearly hardy South African bulbs with showy flowers in autumn. Not to be confused with *hippeastrum*, sometimes called amaryllis.

CULTIVATION. These succeed best in the greenhouse border planted while dormant in summer 9 inches deep. They need rich soil and plenty of organic matter. They have leaves through the winter which die down in summer and should be cleared only when yellow. The flowers appear without leaves in September or October. Plant outdoors against the greenhouse wall in full sun in warmer localities.

SPECIES TO GROW. *A. belladonna*, silvery-rose and its varieties and hybrids, about 2 feet.

Ampelopsis *Vitaceae*
Deciduous climber with pale mottled leaves that is used as a trailing foliage plant in pots.

CULTIVATION. Pot in J.I.P. 2 or other compost in spring and re-pot yearly in 6-inch pot as it is only useful when kept small. Cut back in autumn when the leaves fall.

SPECIES TO GROW. *A. heterophylla elegans*, pink, white and green leaves.

Anigozanthus (Kangaroo Paws) *Amaryllidaceae*
Australian herbaceous perennial with iris-like foliage 1 foot high, and curious red and green woolly flowers on 3-foot stems.
MWT 7° C. (45° F.)

CULTIVATION. The plants are increased by division of the fleshy roots in spring, or by seed sown in March. The seed is very slow to germinate and needs warmth. Established plants need full sun and plenty of water in summer. A porous, peaty compost suits these plants, which should be kept quite dry for a time after flowering. Re-pot in late autumn and start into growth.

Species to grow. *A. manglesii*, summer, 3 feet.

Antirrhinum (Snapdragon) *Scrophulariaceae*
Half-hardy perennials, usually grown as annuals, that will overwinter in the cool greenhouse.

Cultivation. Sow in August or September for spring flowering, otherwise in early March. Pot the seedlings singly when large enough and grow them on to flower in 6- or 7-inch pots in J.I.P. 2 or similar compost. For one big spike of bloom pinch off sideshoots, otherwise pinch out growing point when 2 inches high to induce bushiness. Feed when flowers show. They can be grown in the greenhouse border for cutting in early spring.

Species to grow. *A. maius* hybrids in all colours but blue are available from $1\frac{1}{2}$–$3\frac{1}{2}$ feet.

Aphelandra *Acanthaceae*
Popular house plants with evergreen zebra-striped leaves and yellow bracts. MWT 10° C. (50° F.)

Cultivation. Cuttings from young shoots with a heel can be rooted in a temperature of 18° C. (65° F.) in spring, and take about a year to flower. This plant prefers a warm greenhouse but is often received as a gift and greatly benefits from a recuperative summer in the greenhouse. After flowering keep just moist but never dry. Prune back in March and re-pot in April in a compost with plenty of humus. Shade in summer and keep in a warm, moist atmosphere. It likes plenty of water when in flower.

Species to grow. *A. squarrosa louisae*, about 18 inches; *A. squarrosa* 'Brockfeld', similar but a more compact plant. Their natural flowering time is the autumn.

Aporocactus (Rat's-tail Cactus) *Cactaceae*
Epiphytic cactus from Mexico with long trailing stems and red or pink flowers in late spring. MWT 10° C. (50° F.)

Cultivation. This cactus needs a porous, peaty, lime-free soil and should not be cramped at the roots. Give plenty of water during summer and almost none in winter. Keep in full sun. Increase by seeds sown when ripe, or by cuttings placed in sand.

SPECIES TO GROW. *A. flagelliformis* (syn. *Cereus flagelliformis*).

Aralia *see* FATSIA

Araucaria (Norfolk Island Pine) *Pinaceae*
Elegant bright green conifer with tiered branches that used often to be grown indoors. MWT 7° C. (45° F.)

CULTIVATION. Re-pot only occasionally in March in J.I.P. 2 or 2 parts sandy loam to 1 part leafmould. Water freely in summer and give plenty of air and some shade. Water moderately in winter. Feed occasionally. Increase by seed in warmth or by tip cuttings in autumn.

SPECIES TO GROW. *A. excelsa*, ultimately large but slow growing.

Ardisia *Myrsinaceae*
Small evergreen shrubs with fragrant but uninteresting flowers followed by showy and very long-lasting red berries.
MWT 10° C. (50° F.)

CULTIVATION. Grow in J.I.P. 2 with added peat or equal parts of loam and peat with a little sharp sand added. Seeds from ripe berries can be sown in heat in spring but take several years to become an effective size. Sideshoots can be used as cuttings in spring. Prune in spring to keep in shape.

SPECIES TO GROW. *A. crispa* (syn. *A. crenulata*), red flowers followed by berries, ultimately 3 feet; *A. japonica*, white flowers, followed by red berries, 1 foot.

Arum Lily *see* ZANTEDESCHIA

Asclepias (Blood Flower) *Asclepiadaceae*
Slightly woody perennial, often grown as an annual, with umbels of orange and scarlet flowers from July to November.
MWT 7° C. (45° F.)

CULTIVATION. Sow in warmth in early March and pot singly. A mixture of loam and leafmould can be used, or any peaty compost. Water freely in summer and support with a stake. Keep nearly dry in winter and cut back and start into growth in early spring. New shoots can be used as cuttings but where space is limited it is not worth keeping through the winter.

SPECIES TO GROW. *A. curassavica*, 1½–3 feet.

Asparagus *Liliaceae*
Decorative foliage plants that can be grown as small pot plants or as climbers. MWT 7° C. (45° F.)

CULTIVATION. Pot in March in J.I.P. 2 or similar good compost. *A. plumosus*, when large, can be trained up strings. Increase by cuttings or seed in warmth in spring; or by division. Water freely when growing, less in winter. Shade improves the colour.

SPECIES TO GROW. *A. plumosus* (Asparagus Fern) and its dwarf variety *nanus*, feathery fronds; *A. scandens*, also climbing but coarser leaves; *A. s. deflexus*, similar but less readily available.

Aspidistra *Liliaceae*
The Victorian foliage plant with an iron constitution.

CULTIVATION. Grow in shade in any potting compost. Re-pot only occasionally and feed sometimes. Sponge leaves when dusty. Increase by division in April.

SPECIES TO GROW. *A. lurida* and its variegated form have glossy leaves and insignificant flowers.

Astilbe (Spiraea) *Saxifragaceae*
Hardy perennials with graceful plumes of flowers that can be forced to flower early under glass.

CULTIVATION. Pot the roots in autumn in J.I.P. 2 or similar compost in 6-inch pots, and plunge outdoors until January. Bring into the greenhouse and water freely always. They can stand in saucers of water when growing strongly. Feed weekly when the flower spikes show. After flowering harden off and plant in the garden. Do not lift the same plant two years running. Increase by division of the roots in spring. The warmer the greenhouse the earlier the flowers.

SPECIES TO GROW. *A.* × *arendsii* hybrids such as 'Ceres' and 'Rhineland', pink, 'Fanal' and 'Granat', crimson and 'Professor van der Weilan', tall, white. All are 2½–4 feet tall.

Astrophytum (Star Cactus) *Cactaceae*
Curious and attractive globular cacti from Mexico with pronounced ribs but few spines, and yellow flowers in summer.

CULTIVATION. Buy in spring and re-pot when necessary in cactus compost containing lime, or J.I.P. 2 with added coarse sand. Water regularly in summer but keep nearly dry in winter. Grow in full sun. They are slow-growing.

SPECIES TO GROW. *A. asterias*, *A. capricorne*, *A. myriostigma* and *A. ornatum* are all rather similar.

Australian Blue-bell Creeper *see* SOLLYA

Australian Fuchsia *see* CORREA

Australian Mint Bush *see* PROSTANTHERA

Avocado Pear *see* PERSEA GRATISSIMA

Azalea *Ericaceae*
Showy evergreen and deciduous shrubs to flower from November to May according to temperature and treatment. See also RHODODENDRON. MWT 7° C. (45° F.) for 'Indian Azaleas'.

CULTIVATION. The florist's 'Indian Azaleas' are neither Indian nor azaleas but varieties of *Rhododendron simsii*. I include here plants generally thought of as azaleas. Indian azaleas are mostly raised in Belgium, and are best bought in bud but already showing colour. They will have been grown in a mixture of peat, leafmould and pine needles and, unless they are clearly very damp, soak the pot in a bucket. Then water with care, as they are sensitive to both dryness and sodden wet. After flowering pick off dead blooms, trim straggling shoots, keep in a shady part of the greenhouse and syringe. Re-pot when necessary in April. Plunge outdoors in light shade from June to October, but never allow the roots to get dry.

All azaleas need lime-free soil; a compost of 3 parts peat, 1 part sand and 1 part lime-free loam, or lime-free J.I.P. 1 are possible potting mixtures. Water with rain water if possible in hard-water districts. Japanese and Mollis azaleas should be potted firmly in 6–10-inch pots in autumn. Mollis azaleas, being fully hardy, can be left plunged outdoors till February, but Japanese azaleas only until Christmas. Increase by cuttings of half-ripe wood in August, or by layering. Re-pot every second year and top-dress alternate years in autumn.

SPECIES TO GROW. Indian Azaleas, in a variety of colours, flowering from November to May according to temperature and treatment. Evergreen azaleas from Japan (varieties of *A. obtusum*) and many hybrids, known as Japanese and Kurume Azaleas, including the well-known *A. 'Hinodegiri'*, crimson, and *A. 'Hinomayo'*, pink. Deciduous azaleas from Asia Minor, known as Mollis Azaleas, numerous hybrids in many colours, April flowering.

Babiana (Baboon-root) *Iridaceae*
Dwarf bulbous plants with brilliant flowers in late spring.

CULTIVATION. Pot in October or November, four or five bulbs to a 5-inch pot. Plant deeply, in J.I.P. 2 or similar compost. Start watering when growth shows. After flowering dry off gradually and keep quite dry from September until January.

SPECIES TO GROW. *B. stricta rubro-cyanea*, dark blue with a red eye, May or June, 6–8 inches; or mixed hybrids of various colours.

Barberton Daisy *see* GERBERA

Bauera *Saxifragaceae*
Easily grown and neat Australian evergreen shrub flowering mainly in winter and spring.

CULTIVATION. Pot and re-pot when needed in sandy loam and peat or lime-free J.I.P. 2. Do not allow the plants to become pot-bound before their full size is reached. Increase by half-ripe cuttings in warmth in spring. Plunge out of doors in summer.

SPECIES TO GROW. *B. rubioides*, pale red, pink or white, 1–2 feet.

Begonia *Begoniaceae*
Tender perennials with very showy flowers over a long season. Only some members of this large tropical family are suitable for the cool greenhouse.

CULTIVATION (tuberous-rooted large-flowered hybrids). Start the tubers in damp peat and sand in a shallow tray indoors in a temperature of 16° C. (60° F.) from March to mid-April and pot up singly when well rooted in 4½-inch pots of J.I.P. 3. Pot on later into larger pots. Water freely in summer and shade. Remove male flowers at either side of the larger double flowers. Feed when the pots are full of roots. Dry off gradually after flowering and keep quite dry in their pots and frost-free until March.

B. semperflorens cultivars may be bought as bedding plants in spring or raised from seed sown in a temperature of 16° C. (60° F.) as early as practicable. They can also be increased from cuttings and will flower most of the year if the temperature does not fall below 10° C. (50° F.).

Rex begonias are grown for their ornamental leaves. They flourish under the staging in summer and survive MWT 10° C. (50° F.), as do many other species with attractive leaves or flowers, or both. These are increased by leaf cuttings in summer. A mature leaf is pressed flat on damp soil after making cuts in the main veins at the back of the leaf; they root well under mist. The tuberous kinds can also be increased in this way if you wish.

The winter-flowering Gloire de Lorraine and 'Optima' and similar varieties are not suitable for the cool greenhouse.

SPECIES TO GROW. Numerous hybrids of tuberous begonias with large single, double and frilled flowers in many brilliant colours; 'Multiflora' hybrids with quantities of smaller flowers and 'Pendula' hybrids with trailing habit; *B. evansiana* is a tuberous species with many pink flowers in late summer that is almost hardy; *B. rex* cultivars with variously shaped and coloured leaves need MWT 10° C. (50° F.); *B. semperflorens* (fibrous rooted) hybrids in all shades of pink, red and white, with green or red leaves, continuous flowering, 9–12 inches. If you become interested in the begonia family those listed below are all attractive plants and worth trying in the cool greenhouse with a MWT 10° C. (50° F.). *B.* × 'Abel Carriere'; *B. haageana*; *B. incarnata*; *B. maculata*; *B. metallica*; *B.* × *richmondensis*; *B. schmidtiana*; *B. sutherlandii* and *B.* × *weltonensis*.

Belladonna Lily *see* AMARYLLIS

Beloperone (Shrimp Plant) *Acanthaceae*
Small evergreen shrubby plant with small white flowers and ornamental pink bracts. Popular house-plant. MWT 10° C. (50° F.)

CULTIVATION. Re-pot in spring in J.I.P. 3 or loamless compost. Old plants can be cut back early in the year. Feed May to September, and water freely in summer but less in winter. Cuttings of young shoots root at any time with bottom heat.

SPECIES TO GROW. *B. guttata*, ultimately tall if not cut back.

Bessera (Mexican Coral Drops) *Amaryllidaceae*
Unusual and expensive bulbous plant with delicate scape of scarlet pendulous flowers with white centres.

CULTIVATION. Pot in spring in J.I.P. 2, three to a 6-inch pot. Water freely while growing but keep quite dry and free from frost during the winter resting season. Increase by removing offsets in the spring.

SPECIES TO GROW. *B. elegans*, scarlet, late summer, 1–2 feet.

Billardiera *Pittosporaceae*
Evergreen climber from Tasmania with attractive blue berries in autumn.

CULTIVATION. Plant in the greenhouse border in lime-free soil. Increase by seed or cuttings in warmth.
SPECIES TO GROW. *B. longiflora*, greenish-yellow flowers changing to purple, followed by deep blue berries.

Billbergia *Bromeliaceae*
Curious bromeliad plants from Brazil and Mexico that flower in winter or spring and have long-lasting rosy bracts.

CULTIVATION. Allow to grow into a clump and re-pot only very seldom in March. Treat like AECHMEA. Increase by snapping off a mature offset in spring. Trim off lower leaves and root in warm propagating frame. Keep them in a shady position. Water sparingly in winter.

SPECIES TO GROW. *B. nutans*, yellowish-green flowers with blue margins and large rosy bracts, 1 foot, MWT 7° C. (45° F.); *B.* × *windii*, similar but with stiffer and wider leaves, MWT 10° C. (50° F.).

Bird of Paradise Flower *see* STRELITZIA

Black-eyed Susan *see* THUNBERGIA

Bleeding Heart *see* DICENTRA

Blood Flower *see* ASCLEPIAS

Blood Lily *see* HAEMANTHUS

Blue Dawn Flower *see* PHARBITIS

Blue Gum *see* EUCALYPTUS

Blue Lace Flower *see* DIDISCUS

Blue Marguerite *see* FELICIA

Boronia *Rutaceae*
Easily grown small evergreen shrub from Australia with very fragrant flowers in winter. They are long-lasting but not showy.

CULTIVATION. Pot very firmly in lime-free J.I.P. 2 or equal quantities of peat and loam with some sand. Use 5–7-inch pots and keep the soil moist but never sodden. They like sunshine and a dry atmosphere and can stand outdoors from June to mid-September. Pinch back young plants to keep them bushy. Increase by cuttings of young shoots in summer in a close frame or under mist.

SPECIES TO GROW. *B. megastigma*, brownish-purple and yellow flowers, late winter, 2 feet.

Bottle Brush Tree *see* CALLISTEMON

Bougainvillea *Nyctaginaceae*
Showy climbing shrubs with long-lasting, brilliantly coloured bracts, that can be grown in pots.   MWT 7° C. (45° F.)

CULTIVATION. Pot or plant in February in J.I.P. 2, or very well-drained light soil in a sunny position. A prepared hole with restricted root run or a tub suits them well. Water freely from March to September, then reduce watering and keep nearly dry from December to March. Prune older plants hard back in February. Increase by cuttings of firm young shoots with a heel of older wood in a propagating frame in spring.

SPECIES TO GROW. *B. glabra*, magenta, and its cultivars 'Cypheri', 'Sanderiana' and 'Snow White'.

Brachycome (Swan River Daisy)   *Compositae*
Effective half-hardy annual with abundant daisy flowers over a long period.

CULTIVATION. Sow in March or April and pot seedlings singly in 4-inch, or three to a 6-inch pot in J.I.P. 2 or other compost. Water freely and support with twigs.

SPECIES TO GROW. *B. iberidifolia* in various forms with mauve, pink or white flowers, up to 2 feet under glass.

Bridal Wreath *see* FRANCOA

Browallia *Solanaceae*

Tender perennials grown as annuals with an immensely long flowering season. MWT 10° C. (50° F.) for winter flowers.

CULTIVATION. Sow in March or April for autumn flowering and pot either singly to flower in 4-inch pots, or three together in a larger pot. I have known this easily grown plant to flower continuously for a year. Grow in J.I.P. 2 or other compost and feed when buds are forming and from time to time. If *B. speciosa* is sown in early summer and pinched several times it will produce a bushy plant to flower the following year and can be overwintered with MWT 7° C. (45° F.).

SPECIES TO GROW. *B. speciosa major*, violet-blue, up to 2 feet; 'Silver Bells' is a white form; *B.* 'Sapphire', dark blue with white eye, 1 foot.

Brugmansia *see* DATURA

Brunsfelsia *Solanaceae*

Free-flowering semi-deciduous shrub suitable for pots.
MWT 10° C. (50° F.)

CULTIVATION. J.I.P. 3 with some added leafmould is an ideal compost. They like heat and a moist atmosphere while growing. Re-pot only every second year. Water freely while growing, but very little in winter. Prune lightly each spring. Half-ripe cuttings can be rooted in a temperature of 21° C. (70° F.).

SPECIES TO GROW. *B. calcyina floribunda*, rich violet fading to white, through spring and summer, ultimately 4 feet.

Bryophyllum *see* KALANCHOE

Busy Lizzie *see* IMPATIENS

Butterfly Flower *see* SCHIZANTHUS

Calamondin *see* CITRUS

Calceolaria (Slipper Flower) *Scrophulariaceae*
Plants of South American origin with very long-lasting and showy flowers. The herbaceous kinds have large speckled and blotched velvety flowers and the shrubby kinds smaller yellow flowers.
MWT 7° C. (45° F.)

CULTIVATION. Mix the fine seeds with sand and sow thinly in June, just pressing it into the surface of a pan of moist soil. Pot singly and keep preferably in a north-facing frame until the end of September. The dwarf hybrids will flower in 4- or 5-inch pots of J.I.P. 2 or similar compost, and the larger hybrids can take 7- or 8-inch pots, but avoid re-potting between November and March. They need light shade except in winter. Feed shortly before flowering when the pots are full of roots. Prune back old plants after flowering. The leaves are very brittle and attractive to greenfly. The shrubby kinds are raised from cuttings of young shoots which root easily in summer and early autumn.

SPECIES TO GROW. *C. multiflora nana* dwarf hybrids are easier to manage and slightly hardier than the larger ones; the flowers in various warm colours appear in spring and early summer, 6 inches upwards. Some shrubby varieties are *C.* × *burbidgei*, yellow, autumn and winter, 2–4 feet; *C.* × *profusa* (syn. *C.* × *clibranii*) lemon yellow, about 3 feet; *C. violacea*, see JOVELLANA.

Calendula (Pot Marigold) *Compositae*
Easily grown hardy annual that can be grown to flower in early spring in the cool greenhouse. MWT 7° C. (45° F.)

CULTIVATION. Sow from July to September in a cold frame and pot singly in 5- or 6-inch pots of J.I.P. 2 or other compost. Bring into the greenhouse in late October and keep near the glass. The growing point should be pinched out when the plants are 3 or 4 inches high. Dead flowers must be removed.

SPECIES TO GROW. Improved varieties of *C. officinalis*, particularly the more compact ones such as 'Golden King', 'Orange King', 'Lemon Queen' and 'Radio', 1–2 feet.

Californian Bluebell *see* NEMOPHILA

Calla Lily *see* ZANTEDESCHIA

Callistemon (Bottle Brush Tree) *Myrtaceae*
Easily grown Australian evergreen shrub with grey-green leaves and flowers like scarlet bottle brushes. Good in a tub in an airy and minimally heated conservatory.

CULTIVATION. Re-pot every other year in J.I.P. 2 or 3, or equal parts of sandy peat and loam. Keep near the glass in full sun and stand outdoors after flowering until late September. Trim fairly severely after flowering. Give plenty of water while growing and feed occasionally. Keep rather dry in winter. They like plenty of ventilation and a rather dry atmosphere. Increase by cuttings of matured wood in summer in a propagating or a cold frame.

SPECIES TO GROW. *C. citrinus splendens*, scarlet, May and June, ultimately large; *C. linearis*, crimson, July, 3–5 feet.

Camellia *Theaceae*
Hardy and slightly tender evergreen flowering shrubs sometimes grown under glass for their beautiful flowers in winter and early spring.

CULTIVATION. Pot very firmly in May in a rich, lime-free compost and re-pot every two or three years, top-dressing in other years. Never allow the roots to get dry. Harden off after flowering and

Calceolarias come in various sizes and types but none need much heat

The yellow flowers of *Primula kewensis* are welcome in winter

The Gerbera provides long-lasting cut flowers for many months of the year

Zinnias make gay pot plants in a short time

plunge outdoors in partial shade until October. They need no pruning except to keep them in shape. They grow well in the border of a large conservatory if a moist atmosphere is maintained in summer. Feed before and after flowering with fish meal or dried blood.

SPECIES TO GROW. Hybrids of *C. japonica*, single or double, crimson to white; *C. reticulata*, 'Captain Rawes', rose-crimson; *C. sasanqua*, carmine, white and pink varieties; *C.* × *williamsii* 'Donation', semi-double, pale rose-pink.

Campanula *Campanulaceae*
Biennial and perennial plants with attractive bell flowers over a long season.

CULTIVATION. *C. pyramidalis* is called the Chimney Bellflower because it was a favourite Victorian plant to put in the fireplace in August. It flowers for a long time, so long as bees cannot reach it to pollinate the flowers. Sow seed in a cold frame in April, then pot singly or plant out in the garden until autumn, when the plants are potted in 9- or 10-inch pots in J.I.P. 3. They can winter in a frost-protected frame or greenhouse and stand outdoors the following spring until the buds show. They need a lot of water, and should be fed when the flower spikes appear. Discard after flowering or trim off straggling shoots and keep for another year. Keep nearly dry in winter. *C. vidallii* can be grown in the same way. *C. isophylla* is a very attractive perennial easily raised from cuttings of non-flowering shoots in spring and summer. Cut right back in late autumn and discard after the second season. It is a good basket plant. *C. fragilis* is very similar but raised from seed sown in spring to flower the following year.

SPECIES TO GROW. *C. fragilis* (Italy) light blue, trailing, July and August; *C. isophylla* (Italy) blue and, variety *alba*, white, trailing, August and September; *C. pyramidalis* (Europe) pale blue or white, July, 4–5 feet; *C. vidallii* (Azores) white with yellow centre, late summer, up to 18 inches. There is also a pink form.

Candle Plant *see* KLEINIA

Candytuft *see* IBERIS

Cantua *Polemoniaceae*
Small evergreen shrub from Peru with cherry-red tubular flowers hanging below the branches in spring.

CULTIVATION. Pot or plant in March and re-pot or topdress yearly in J.I.P. 2 or a mixture of sandy loam and leafmould with good drainage. It is upright and good against a pillar. Water freely while growing and keep just moist in winter. Prune after flowering. Increase by cuttings of new shoots in propagating frame in spring or summer.

SPECIES TO GROW. *C. buxifolia* (syn. *C. dependens*), pink to red, April and May, 3–5 feet.

Cape Cowslip *see* LACHENALIA

Cape Heath *see* ERICA

Cape Lily *see* CRINUM

Cape Primrose *see* STREPTOCARPUS

Carnation (*Dianthus caryophyllus*) *Caryophyllaceae*
Perpetual carnations like cool airy conditions and it is often suggested that a whole greenhouse should be devoted to them alone, but this is not essential. MWT 7° C. (45° F.) for winter flowers.

CULTIVATION. The plants are grown from cuttings of short-jointed, non-flowering sideshoots 3 inches long in February. These are rooted in pure sand with mild bottom heat. They can also be taken in August and September and are best from young plants. The cuttings must be potted up as soon as rooted. J.I.P. 2 can be used, followed by J.I.P. 3 with a few limestone chippings or small pieces of charcoal. Some people prefer a compost without peat which can be made up of 4 parts good loam and 1 part sharp sand with a dusting of lime and a proprietary carnation fertiliser.

Young plants bought in spring in 3-inch pots must not be allowed to get pot-bound, but moved to 6-inch pots. Two-year-old plants will need re-potting into 8- or 9-inch pots. Good drainage, firm potting and a 3-foot bamboo stake are needed. The pots should stand on moist shingle or aggregate. In order to create bushy plants and good flowers the plants are stopped and disbudded. The growing point of rooted cuttings should be pinched out at the sixth leaf (this will already have been done to bought plants). A further stopping of the resulting sideshoots is done by degrees, the fastest growing shoots being done first. But do not do any stopping after June for flowers the following winter, or August for spring flowers. Disbud flower stems to leave terminal bud only.

The plants are best plunged outdoors or in a cold frame from June until September, and not shaded. Start feeding when first blooms are cut. Commercial carnations are often grown in the ground, the young plants being planted out from 3-inch pots 8 inches apart. The advantage of pots for the amateur is that they can be moved about. It is wise to start with healthy young plants from a specialist nursery and not with cuttings from a friend. Plants can be kept four years but are best replaced after two years.

Perpetual Malmaison carnations are treated in the same way, but stopped only once and kept in the greenhouse all the year round.

SPECIES TO GROW. Consult nurserymen's lists. 'Allwood's Yellow', 'Ashington Pink', 'Betty Lou', dark pink; 'Red Pimpernel', scarlet; 'Snowdrift', white and fragrant, and 'Wivelsfield Crimson', are only a few of many good kinds.

Cassia *Leguminosae*

Evergreen shrub from the Argentine, with attractive leaves and yellow flowers. MWT 7° C. (45° F.), but it flowers most of the year in a warm greenhouse.

CULTIVATION. Pot in a large pot in J.I.P. 2, or in rich loam with one-third peat. It can be grown against a wall. Give plenty of water in summer and keep rather dry in winter. Prune in February. Increase by cuttings in heat in spring or summer or by seed. It flowers when small.

Species to grow. *C. corymbosa* (syn. *C. floribunda*), yellow, late summer and autumn. Soon grows tall and needs replacement. Other cassias are available as seed. Most have yellow flowers and are of tropical origin.

Celosia (Cockscomb) *Amaranthaceae*
Half-hardy annuals with garishly coloured, artificial-looking flowers. MWT 10° C. (50° F.)

Cultivation. Sow in March in 18° C. (65° F.). They need light and moist warmth. Pot singly in 3-inch pots in J.I.P. 2 or any rich potting compost, and move on to flower in 6-inch pots.

Species to grow. *C. argentea cristata*, chiefly red and yellow, 1 foot, and the more attractive feathered forms known as *C. plumosa* in similar colours, 1–3 feet.

Celsia *Scrophulariaceae*
Slightly shrubby perennial from Crete and Turkey with handsome spikes of yellow flowers with purple anthers.

Cultivation. Seed sown in a propagating frame in March will flower in the autumn. A sowing in July or August for flowering the following summer produces larger plants. It may also be grown from cuttings taken in spring. Grow in J. I. composts and flower in 6–8-inch pots.

Species to grow. *A. arcturus*, yellow, July to September, 1½–4 feet; *C. cretica* is a biennial and very similar.

Cereus *Cactaceae*
Tall columnar cacti from South America. They usually only flower when large but their fluted stems provide a contrast to the globular cacti.

CULTIVATION. Re-pot in early spring in 3 parts J.I.P. 2 to 1 part crushed brick or other gritty material. Water freely in summer but keep all but dry in winter. Increase by stem cuttings inserted in sand in summer.

SPECIES TO GROW. *C. azureus*; *C. chalybaeus*; *C. flagelliformis*, see APOROCACTUS; *C. jamacaru*, *C. peruvianus* and its variety *monstrosus* which is knobbly all over; *C. strausii* see CLEISTOCACTUS. Other species can be grown equally well. Cristate forms have a distorted appearance which some people find attractive and others repellent.

Cestrum (*Habrothamnus*) *Solanaceae*
Tall evergreen climbing shrubs with clusters of tubular flowers. They can be grown as bushes, standards or climbers where there is plenty of room.

CULTIVATION. They are best planted out and trained up pillars. Otherwise plant them in large pots and re-pot annually in March in J.I.P. 3 or similar compost. Water well while growing, feed when the buds form but keep almost dry in winter. Avoid placing this plant where you brush against it as the bruised leaves smell of boiled milk. Prune mature plants to within two buds of the old wood in February but retain one-third of the new wood on young plants. Increase by cuttings of half-ripened shoots in a propagating frame in late summer.

SPECIES TO GROW. The brightest and best is *C.* × *newellii*, crimson, June and July; *C. aurantiacum*, orange-yellow, summer; *C. purpureum* (syn. *Habrothamnus elegans*), reddish-purple, summer and autumn.

Chamaecereus *Cactaceae*
Prostrate clump-forming cactus from the Argentine with very showy scarlet flowers in spring.

CULTIVATION. See CEREUS for soil and treatment. Increase by detaching small branches and inserting as cuttings in spring and summer.

Species to grow. *C. sylvestrii*, orange-scarlet flowers, and also the hybrid form.

Chamaedorea (*Collinia*) *Palmaceae*
Tropical palms with small elegant fronds that really need more heat, but do survive. MWT 10° C. (50° F.)

Cultivation. All palms need a very high temperature to germinate, 29° C. (85° F.) is desirable, and the seed must be fresh. This miniature palm grows more quickly than a Kentia and is available as a house-plant. In summer it needs plenty of water, shade, warmth and a moist atmosphere. In winter it can be kept damp in the warm but desiccating conditions indoors, and rather drier in the greenhouse; in both cases it should be in full light. Two parts peat to 1 of loam and a little sand is a suitable compost.

Species to grow. *C. elegans bella* (syn. *Neanthe bella*), known as the Parlour Palm, is the one usually available.

Chamaerops (Chusan Palm, *Trachycarpus*) *Palmaceae*
Half-hardy palms with fan-shaped leaves needing frost protection only. They are slow-growing and long-suffering.

Cultivation. Pot very firmly in March or April in J.I.P. 3 with good drainage. Re-pot only every four or five years, but top-dress with fresh soil yearly in spring. Water freely in summer and keep just moist in winter.

Species to grow. *C. fortunei* (syn. *Trachycarpus fortunei*), ultimately tall, *C. humilis*, blue-green leaves, ultimately 6 feet.

Charieis *Compositae*
Small hardy annual from South Africa with bright blue daisy flowers.

Cultivation. Sow in March to flower in June. Use J.I.P. 1 or similar compost.

Species to grow. *C. heterophylla* (syn. *Kaulfussia heterophylla*), blue, 12 inches.

Cherry Pie *see* HELIOTROPIUM

Chilean Crocus *see* TECOPHILAEA

Chilean Jasmine *see* MANDEVILLA

Chincherinchee *see* ORNITHOGALUM

Chinese Jasmine *see* TRACHELOSPERMUM

Chlidanthus *Amaryllidaceae*
Bulbous plant from the Andes. The fragrant yellow flowers appear before the leaves in spring.

CULTIVATION. Pot in April three to a 5-inch pot in J.I.P. 2 or plant 3½ inches deep in the greenhouse border. Water freely in summer and rest, almost dry, in winter. Increase by removing offsets in April. This is difficult to flower.

SPECIES TO GROW. *C. fragrans*, yellow, May or June, 9 inches.

Chlorophytum *Liliaceae*
Popular house-plant with variegated grassy foliage.
MWT 10° C. (50° F.)

CULTIVATION. Easily grown in any compost if kept moist and shaded from strong sunshine. It produces new plantlets at the ends of old flowering stems. These will root if pegged down into a pot of soil. If grown in a basket the young plantlets are ornamental when left hanging round parent plant.

SPECIES TO GROW. *C. comosum variegatum* (sold as *C. capense*).

Chorizema *Leguminosae*
Attractive small evergreen shrub from Australia that can be grown as a bushy pot plant or dwarf climber. MWT 7° C. (45° F.)

CULTIVATION. Pot firmly in a sandy peaty compost or lime-free J.I.P. 2 with a little extra peat. Re-pot in spring every other year when growth starts. Pinch tips of shoots several times when young and prune if necessary immediately after flowering. Do not overwater, particularly in winter. They like plenty of air and a dry atmosphere. They were popular in the past trained over a wire support.

SPECIES TO GROW. *C. cordatum*, quantities of small orange and purple flowers, March to May, 2–4 feet.

Christmas Cactus *see* SCHLUMBERGERA

Chrysanthemum *Compositae*
Whole books are devoted to this favourite flower and whole chapters merely to the terminology used to describe all the possible actions that can be taken to train and control it. Here I give only the bare bones of cultivation for those who wish to try a few plants.

CULTIVATION. For a start rooted cuttings may be bought in spring; subsequently fresh cuttings are rooted each year. These are taken only from the best and healthiest plants that have had perfectly formed flowers. The old plants are cut down to 6 inches high immediately after flowering and the old soil is washed off. They are then planted close together in a box of damp J.I.P. 3 or similar soil and labelled. They need a resting period and a cold frame is suitable if they are protected from frost. They can be induced to grow from December onwards by being brought into warmth. As late rooting reduces the height of the plants and chrysanthemums are apt to be awkwardly tall I think late March is early enough to take cuttings. For show specimen plants, however, the longest possible season of growth is wanted.

To make cuttings sever shoots that spring from the base of old plants just below soil level. The cutting should be about 3 inches long. Trim just below a joint with a razor blade, remove lower leaves and dip cuttings into hormone rooting powder. Insert $\frac{1}{2}-\frac{3}{4}$ inch deep singly in 3-inch pots of J.I.P. 1, or put several round the edge of larger pots. If some dry coarse sand is scattered over the soil, a little will trickle into each hole as the cutting is inserted.

Insert firmly and so that the cutting reaches the bottom of the hole. Warmth at the roots speeds rooting but is not necessary. Water thoroughly and shade lightly. One hopes they will not need watering again until rooted. When they are about 6 inches high pot in 5- or 6-inch pots of J.I.P. 2.

The programme of stopping and disbudding for the particular variety or date of flowering will often be found in the specialist's catalogue. In general the growing point is pinched out when the plants are about 7 inches high and the tips of the resultant side-shoots are often removed four to six weeks later. Do not stop at the same time as potting. Stopping the main stem of a plant induces side-shoots to develop. These are known as the first breaks, and the buds that will develop at their tips are known as 1st crown buds. If these first break shoots are all stopped, a further set of new side-shoots will appear, and the buds that eventually develop at their tips are known as 2nd crown buds. When it has been decided which crown buds are to be allowed to develop the unwanted buds and side-shoots are carefully removed. Those that are close round the chosen terminal bud are allowed to grow for a bit to help draw up the sap, but are gradually removed when they are about half an inch long. Lower unwanted shoots can be removed as soon as seen. When the pots are full of roots the plants can be re-potted into their flowering pots. Use J.I.P. 3 and 8- to 10-inch pots or put two plants in a 9- or 10-inch pot. Pot very firmly indeed and stake with 4-foot canes. Harden off and stand outdoors in a sunny position until the end of September in the South and mid-September in the North. The stakes will need tying to wires to prevent the plants blowing over. Water freely, feed with chrysanthemum fertiliser and keep the shoots tied to the cane. Very late struck cuttings (May) can be put two to a 5-inch pot and stopped once.

The dwarf chrysanthemums that are always in the florists' shops are produced by a régime of day-length and hormone control that is beyond the scope of the ordinary amateur. If kept these plants will become tall and revert to their normal season. For small pot plants that fit the average greenhouse dwarf Poitevine cultivars are suitable and available as rooted cuttings in late spring. They can be stopped once to flower in 6-inch pots or twice to make larger plants in 7- or 8-inch pots.

For cut flowers chrysanthemums are grown in beds and fresh cuttings are best bought each year for this. If chrysanthemums are grown to flower in November and December it is highly desirable to be able to raise the temperature to 10° C. (50° F.). Charm chrysanthemums can be raised from seed to flower the same season.

SPECIES TO GROW. Consult tradesmen's lists for the infinite variety of possible types of flower and plant and dates of flowering. If you are serious join a chrysanthemum society.

Chusan Palm *see* CHAMAEROPS

Cigar Flower *see* CUPHEA

Cineraria *(Senecio)*   *Compositae*
Showy herbaceous perennials grown as biennials. Big heads of daisy flowers in winter or early spring.   MWT 7° C. (45° F.)

CULTIVATION. Sow seeds from April to June for flowering the following winter and early spring. Pot singly in J.I.P. 2 or other compost and keep shaded. Never allow them to get dry, and watch closely for greenfly which are very partial to them. They are happiest in a cold frame until the end of September. Water carefully in winter.

SPECIES TO GROW. Hybrids with large or small flowers in many vivid colours. There are dwarf, intermediate and tall types.

Cissus   *Vitaceae*
Tough climbing house-plant hardy enough for the cool conservatory.   MWT 10° C. (45° F.)

CULTIVATION. This plant is likely to arrive in a greenhouse because it has grown too large in the home. It needs shade and will stand any amount of cutting back. Grow in J.I.P. 2 or similar compost and water sparingly in winter.

SPECIES TO GROW. *C. antarctica* (Kangeroo Vine) evergreen, tendril climber.

Citrus *Rutaceae*
Evergreen trees that include oranges and lemons as well as dwarf ornamental forms suitable for growing in small pots.

MWT 10° C. (50° F.)

CULTIVATION. The Calamondin (*Citrus mitis*) is now the most often grown and is available as a house-plant. Pot very firmly in J.I.P. 3 and do not allow them to get dry at the roots. Syringing and a moist atmosphere helps the flowers to set fruit. It is wise to plunge citrus outdoors in sun from mid-June until late September to ripen the wood. Only water in very dry weather but watch out for insect pests. Increase by cuttings in a warm propagating frame or under mist. Prune to keep in shape. Citrus pips can also be grown.

SPECIES TO GROW. *C. mitis*, white scented flowers and miniature orange fruit. The lemon is *C. limonia*, the citron *C. medica*, the grapefruit *C. paradisi* and the sweet orange *C. sinensis*.

Clarkia *Onagraceae*
Hardy annuals from North America with spikes of showy flowers.

MWT 7° C. (45° F.)

CULTIVATION. Sow in September or October for flowering in May or June. Pinch out tips when about 3 inches high. Best sown in small pots and reduced to one per pot. In early spring put three plants into 6-inch pots or keep singly. Support with sticks and feed when buds form. Use J.I.P. 2 or other compost.

SPECIES TO GROW. Cultivars of *C. elegans* with double flowers in brilliant warm colours and white, 2 feet and upwards.

Cleistocactus *Cactaceae*
Columnar cacti with red tubular flowers.

CULTIVATION. Treat as CEREUS. Keep in full sun and water often when in flower. They branch from the base in time.

SPECIES TO GROW. *C. baumannii*, yellowish spines, orange-scarlet flowers; *C. strausii*, covered with white silky spines, red flowers.

Clematis *Ranunculaceae*
Vigorous evergreen climber from New Zealand with a profusion of showy white flowers in winter and early spring.

CULTIVATION. Plant out in a well-drained greenhouse border in March. Train the shoots up to the roof where they can hang down or cover a wall. This clematis is only suitable for a large conservatory but needs minimal heat. Water freely in summer but little in winter. Increase by layering vigorous young shoots in autumn or spring.

SPECIES TO GROW. *C. indivisa lobata*, white flowers with conspicuous yellow stamens, spring.

Cleome (Spider Flower) *Capparidaceae*
An easily grown annual from tropical America with rather strange flowers over a long season.

CULTIVATION. Sow in March and pot singly in 3-inch pots. In a conservatory they can be useful when flowered three to a 9-inch pot. They grow very quickly and must not be allowed to get pot-bound in the early stages.

SPECIES TO GROW. *C. spinosa* (syn. *C. pungens*) 'Pink Queen', pale pink; and 'Helen Campbell', white, July to September, 3–4 feet.

Cleyera *Theaceae*
Slightly tender Japanese evergreen shrub with handsome variegated foliage for greenhouse decoration in winter.

CULTIVATION. Pot in sandy peat and loam or J.I.P. 2 and water freely in summer when it can be plunged outdoors in light shade. Water moderately in winter. Increase by half-ripe cuttings in summer.

SPECIES TO GROW. *C. fortunei* (syn. *Eurya japonica variegata*) cream and green variegated leaves.

Clianthus *Leguminosae*
Exciting shrubby plants from Australia and New Zealand that can be grown as annuals. MWT 10° C. (50° F.)

CULTIVATION. *C. formosus* (syn. *C. dampieri*) is also known as the Sturt Desert Pea or Glory Pea. It is difficult to grow as the roots often die before it flowers. Sow as early as possible in warmth in small pots and avoid disturbing the roots when re-potting. It trails and can be grown in a basket. Use J.I.P. 2 or try other composts. Keep in full sun and syringe in hot weather. Professionals graft seedlings on to seedling stocks of *Colutea arborescens* sown 10 days earlier. This is a skilled job and should be done before the first true leaves of *C. formosus* develop.

Clianthus puniceus (Lobster's Claw) is easier and hardier and needs a large pot or to be planted in greenhouse border. Water freely in summer and little in winter. Cuttings can be rooted in sand with bottom heat.

SPECIES TO GROW. *C. formosus* (syn. *C. dampieri*), clusters of brilliant scarlet pea flowers with black blotches, and pale green leaves, 1 foot; *C. puniceus*, semi-evergreen and may survive on a sunny wall in mild localities, scarlet, summer. Eventually tall under glass.

Clivia (*Imantophyllum*) *Amaryllidaceae*
South African bulbous plant with evergreen foliage and striking umbels of flowers in early spring. MWT 7° C. (45° F.)

CULTIVATION. Re-pot only occasionally in February in 5- to 12-inch pots, according to size of plant. Use J.I.P. 3 or other rich compost. They bloom more freely when pot-bound but need feeding. Water freely in summer but little in winter. Increase by detaching suckers when re-potting. I grow them for cutting in the ground under the bench in a glass-to-ground greenhouse. Very disease-free.

SPECIES TO GROW. *C. miniata* and its improved cultivars.

Cobaea *Polemoniaceae*
A vigorous tendril climber from Mexico usually grown as a half-hardy annual.

CULTIVATION. Sow in March or early April in a temperature of 21° C. (70° F.). Sow three or four seeds in a 5-inch pot placing the long edge downwards and leaving the upper edge of the seeds uncovered. Keep dark until they germinate and later reduce to one per pot. They like a moist atmosphere and heat. Plant out in the greenhouse border or flower in large pots. Feed frequently and water freely when established.

SPECIES TO GROW. *C. scandens*, purple cup and saucer bells, and a white variety, summer, 10–20 feet.

Cockscomb *see* CELOSIA

Coleus (Flame Nettle) *Labiatae*
Foliage plants with nettle-like leaves in a rich variety of mixed colourings. MWT 10° C. (50° F.)

CULTIVATION. Sow a good strain of seed in warmth early in the year and select the best-coloured seedlings, which tend to be the smallest. Any rich well-drained compost, including all-peat compost, is suitable. Warmth is essential for growth and shade as soon as the sun is strong. Cuttings of particularly well-marked and coloured cultivars which cannot be raised from seed are available commercially in spring. Coleus may survive the winter but it is not really happy under 13° C. (55° F.).

SPECIES TO GROW. *C. blumei* and its cultivars.

Collinia *see* CHAMAEDOREA

Convolvulus *Convolvulaceae*
A varied family, the choice members of which are welcome in the cool greenhouse.

CULTIVATION. *C. cneorum* is a nearly hardy dwarf shrub with white flowers faintly tinged with pink and silver foliage. It is increased by cuttings rooted in sand. *C. mauritanicus* is a tender perennial trailer that will flower in the first season if sown early. It is suitable for hanging baskets. Sow in pots, retaining two per pot and grow in any fibrous compost. It is ever blooming in warm conditions. *C. tricolor* is a half-hardy annual, but may be grown in the same way.

SPECIES TO GROW. *C. cneorum*, white or pink, summer; *C. mauritanicus*, prostrate, hairy leaves, violet-blue flowers; *C. tricolor*, bright blue, white-throated flowers, 1 foot.

Coral Tree *see* ERYTHRINA

Coronilla *Leguminosae*
Easily grown evergreen shrubs from southern Europe with grey-green pinnate leaves and clusters of yellow pea flowers over a long period. It can be grown outdoors in warm districts.

CULTIVATION. Pot in March in J.I.P. 2 or other compost and re-pot each year. Prune to keep in shape. Water freely in summer and moderately in winter. Keep in a sunny airy position. It can stand outdoors in summer. Increase by cuttings of firm young shoots in late summer. These will flower the following spring; or raise from seed.

SPECIES TO GROW. *C. glauca*, yellow, fragrant, and *C. glauca* 'Variegata' with cream variegated leaves, 2–3 feet in pots; *C. valentina*, darker yellow and more tender. They have a long and variable flowering season, through most of the growing period.

Correa (Australian Fuchsia) *Rutaceae*
Small evergreen Australian shrub with scarlet tubular flowers in winter.

CULTIVATION. Re-pot every other year in April or May using J.I.P. 3 or sandy loam and peat. Keep constantly moist but water carefully as they use little water. Trim after flowering. Increase by cuttings of tips of half-ripe shoots in July. Young plants need pinching to make them bushy.

Species to grow. *C.* × *harrisii*, rose-scarlet, late winter, 2–3 feet; *C. speciosa pulchella*, pale almond, winter.

Coryphantha *Cactaceae*
Small cacti, much like *Mammillaria* but with large flowers for their size.

Cultivation. Treat as Mammillaria but grow in full sun.
Species to grow. *C. clava*, red flowers, and *C. erecta*, yellow flowers, are two popular species with cylindrical stems.

Cotyledon *Crassulaceae*
Easily grown South African succulent plants with attractive pale grey foliage. See also Echeveria.   MWT 7° C. (45° F.)

Cultivation. Use a rich sandy compost and treat like Echeveria. Increase by cuttings in spring or late summer or by seed. Do not use leaf cuttings as with so many related plants.

Species to grow. *C. orbiculata* is a somewhat variable succulent shrubby plant with thick leaves that are usually almost white with a fine red edge; *C. undulata*, a single-stemmed plant has grey-green leaves with waved edges. It has orange-red bell flowers, but usually dies after flowering.

Crassula *Crassulaceae*
South African succulent shrubs and herbs, some winter-flowering, and of pleasing form contrasting with other greenhouse plants. See also Rochea.   MWT 7° C. (45° F.) desirable

Cultivation. Grow in rich loamy soil and use pots related to the size of the plants for the large kinds. Three parts J.I.P. 2 to 1 part of coarse grit or sand is suitable. Water freely April to August and then reduce watering. Keep nearly dry from November to March. Increase by stem or leaf cuttings inserted in sandy peat with some crushed charcoal. Allow the surface of cuttings to dry before inserting.

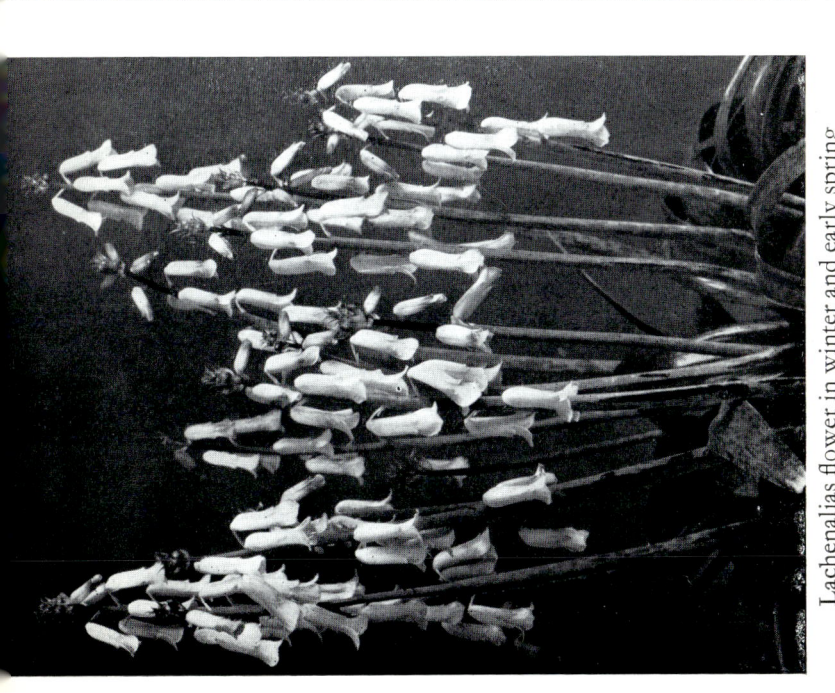

Lachenalias flower in winter and early spring

Cyclamen persicum is the elegant species from which the large florist's cyclamen have been bred

You can see the face of the tiger in *Tigridia pavonia*

Pleione formosana is a small terrestrial orchid that is quite simple to grow

SPECIES TO GROW. *C. coccinea* see ROCHEA; *C. cotyledon* (syn. *Cotyledon arborescens*), slow-growing shrub, ultimately 3–6 feet, rarely flowering but tough house-plant grown for form and foliage; *C. falcata*, to 2 feet, grey leaves, flat heads of scarlet flowers, summer; *C. lactea*, prostrate, heads of white star-shaped flowers at Christmas; *C. portulacea* (syn. *C. argentea*), pink, spring, ultimately a shrub; *C. schmidtii* (syn. *C. impressa*), heads of tiny, but very long-lasting carmine flowers, autumn and winter, 3–4 inches.

Crape Myrtle *see* LAGERSTROEMIA

Crinum (Cape Lily) *Amaryllidaceae*
Very large South African bulbous plants with handsome trumpet flowers. They need space. Frost protection only.

CULTIVATION. Pot singly in March in 9-inch pots of J.I.P. 3, or grouped in a tub and re-pot only every three years or so. Water freely March to October but keep only just moist in winter. Feed in summer after the first year. They can stand outside after flowering until the end of September. Increase by offsets detached in March. They can also be planted out against a south wall in the warmer parts of England.

SPECIES TO GROW. *C. bulbispermum* (syn. *C. capense* and *C. longifolium*), pink or white; *C. moorei*, pink and white; *C.* × *powellii*, rose, and the variety *album*, white; all are summer flowering and 2–3 feet tall.

Crown of Thorns *see* EUPHORBIA

Cryptanthus (Earth Stars) *Bromeliaceae*
Small starfish-like rosette plants from Brazil grown as houseplants and in bottle gardens. MWT 10° C. (50° F.)

CULTIVATION. Treat as BILLBERGIA to which they are related. As they do not hold water in the leaves keep the compost moist in summer and nearly dry in winter. They like a peaty compost containing rotted pine needles, and shade in summer. The flowers are not conspicuous.

SPECIES TO GROW. *C. acaulis rubra,* bronze-red leaves, and *C. bivittatus,* wavy leaves striped with darker green or in a stronger light, buff with reddish stripes, are two species that are often grown, and others can be tried.

Cuphea (Mexican Cigar Flower) *Lythraceae*
Mexican plants with vivid and attractive flowers over a long season. MWT 7° C. (45° F.)

CULTIVATION. Sow in March in warmth. Pot singly in J.I.P. 2 or soil-less compost. Flower in 5- or 6-inch pots. Pinch once or twice to induce bushiness. They like a moist atmosphere and light shade. They begin flowering in July. *C. lanceolata* and *C. miniata* are annuals. The perennials can be increased by cuttings.

SPECIES TO GROW. *C. cyanea,* yellow and red flowers; *C. ignea* (syn. *C. platycentra*), scarlet; *C. lanceolata,* reddish-purple; *C. micropetala,* scarlet with yellow tips; *C. miniata,* pale vermilion, and the variety 'Firefly', scarlet. All 1–2 feet.

Cyclamen *Primulaceae*
Tuberous-rooted plants of great value for their long-flowering season in winter and early spring.
MWT 7° C. (45° F.) but 10° C. (50° F.) preferred

CULTIVATION. Seed sown in August will flower in approximately 16 months. Sow seeds in shallow trays in John Innes or all-peat seed compost. Space the seeds 1 inch apart and cover with ¼ inch of compost. Seed takes five or six weeks to germinate. Pot in 3-inch pots the following March without burying the tiny corms. Seedlings need care and shade from hot sun. In summer they do well plunged in a cold frame but I grow mine on a capillary bench in a shaded greenhouse. John Innes composts suit them. They should be in their 5- or 6-inch flowering pots by July. When established feed until flowering starts. If outside bring into the greenhouse in September.

Alternatively, dry corms can be bought for potting up in August to flower in the winter immediately following. Young plants purchased in spring will flower at the end of the same year. It is also possible to sow seed in warmth very early in the year to flower in 3½-inch pots at the end of the same year. For this you need good growing conditions throughout the year. Cyclamen need a moist atmosphere. They can be watered by any method so long as water is not splashed on the top of the corm. After flowering keep the plants watered until the leaves begin to turn yellow, then gradually reduce watering until they die down. The pots can be put outdoors on their sides in the shade until the tubers are re-potted in August just as new growth is starting to show. They are at their best in the first two years. Always pluck off dead leaves and flowers from the base.

SPECIES TO GROW. *C. persicum* (the original species), white or rose with carmine tips, smaller than hybrids but graceful; hybrids of many colours, some good ones are: 'Afterglow', scarlet; 'Bath Pink', deep pink; 'Giant White'; 'Grandiflora', white with crimson base; 'Mauve Queen', and 'Shell Pink'. The 'Rex' strain have neat silver margined leaves and 'Baroque' cyclamen have frilled flowers. There is a miniature kind called 'Puppet' cyclamen.

Cymbidium *Orchidaceae*
This is a reasonably adaptable orchid for growing in a mixed collection of plants in cool conditions. Apart from the miniature kinds they take a lot of room. The flowers will last for up to three months but it is better for the plant if they are removed after three or four weeks, when they should last another few weeks in water.
MWT 7° C. (45° F.)

CULTIVATION. Flowering plants are six or seven years old and young plants that need growing on for one or two years can be bought more cheaply. A suitable compost consists of 2 parts fibrous loam, 1 part osmunda fibre and 1 part sphagnum moss with a little crushed brick. Add a sprinkling of hoof and horn meal. One can usually buy mixed compost from the nurseryman who supplies the plant. Re-pot only every two years or so in

March or after flowering. Cut away dead roots and also old leafless back bulbs and compost at rear, but leave the front untouched. After re-potting spray the foliage but do not water for a few days. Then soak and allow to get rather dry before watering again. Shade from early March to the end of September and spray the leaves in warm weather. Give less water for a few weeks after flowering and always allow the compost to dry out partially before watering. The pots will need to be large and well crocked for mature plants. Increase by division. Old pseudo-bulbs will make new plants if put in sphagnum moss in a warm propagator. A moist atmosphere is essential for orchids.

SPECIES TO GROW. There are many fine hybrids flowering at various times in the year. Consult grower's lists and join an orchid society.

Cyperus (Umbrella Plant) *Cyperaceae*
Perennial grass foliage plants from the tropics that are available as house-plants. MWT 10° C. (50° F.)

CULTIVATION. Pot in spring in J.I.P. 2 or other compost and keep wet all the year. Shade from strong sun. Seed can be sown in spring.

SPECIES TO GROW. *C. alternifolius gracilis*, about 18 inches; *C. diffusus*, up to 3 feet. Both have stalked tufts of leaves like the ribs of an umbrella.

Cyrtomium *see* FERNS

Cytisus *Leguminosae*
Evergreen shrub from the Canary Islands. This is the 'Genista' of florists, and is often forced into bloom in winter in warm greenhouses. The time of blooming will depend on the temperature.
MWT 7° C. (45° F.)

CULTIVATION. Pot firmly in autumn in J.I.P. 2 in 5–7-inch pots and water freely when growing strongly but less in late summer and autumn. Feed when buds form. Cut shoots hard back after

flowering to within 2 inches of their base. Re-pot occasionally when new growth shows but as it resents root disturbance and tends to grow too large it is better to keep it in the same pot and feed more. Stand outdoors July to September. Increase by cuttings in spring or summer and pinch back.
SPECIES TO GROW. *C. canariensis* (often called *Genista fragrans*), spikes of yellow pea flowers in spring, also its variety *racemosus*, similar.

Daffodil *see* NARCISSUS

Datura (*Brugmansia*) *Solanaceae*
Magnificent plants for the large conservatory that can be grown as half-hardy annuals or planted out permanently in the greenhouse border. MWT 7° C. (45° F.)

CULTIVATION. The shrubby species of datura can bear pruning and so be kept within bounds but they need 12-inch pots. Use J.I.P. 3 or similar rich compost and buy new plants in spring. Water freely in summer and feed regularly when the buds have formed until the flowers are over. Then stand outdoors until the end of September. They can be pruned immediately after flowering, later in the autumn or in March and can be grown as a standard or a bush. Keep almost dry in winter and treat as deciduous in cool conditions. If raised from seed sow in heat in late March or early April. Cuttings of young shoots may be rooted in a propagating frame in spring.

SPECIES TO GROW. *D. chlorantha*, 'Golden Queen', double yellow trumpet flowers, August to October, shrubby; *D. meteloides* (syn. *D. wrightii*), white, violet tinted, 3 feet; *D. suaveolens* (Angel's Trumpet), white, tall shrub. All are late summer flowering with large leaves and huge trumpet flowers.

Davallia *see* FERNS

Dianella *Liliaceae*
Half-hardy perennial from New Zealand with grassy leaves and sprays of whitish flowers followed by decorative blue berries.

CULTIVATION. Plant in conservatory border or in pots of very peaty soil such as 1 part J.I.P. 3 to 2 parts peat. Increase by seed or by division of the roots in spring.

SPECIES TO GROW. *D. intermedia* (Turutu), about 18 inches. *D. caerulea* and *D. laevis* are other species that can be grown.

Dianthus *see* CARNATION

Diascia *Scrophulariaceae*
A pretty little half-hardy annual from South Africa.

CULTIVATION. Sow in spring using J.I.P. 1 or soil-less compost and either pinch twice to make bushy plants or sow in a 5-inch pot and thin to four or five plants, pinching once when 2 inches high. If cut back after flowering they will throw up more flowers. Cuttings root easily.

SPECIES TO GROW. *D. barberae*, rose-pink with yellow throat, late summer, 1 foot.

Dicentra (*Dielytra*) *Fumariaceae*
Hardy tuberous-rooted perennial with elegant leaves and charming flowers in spring under glass.

CULTIVATION. Lift roots from the garden in early autumn and pot in J.I.P. 3 or other compost. Plunge outdoors or in a cold frame until February keeping the pots covered with peat. Bring into the greenhouse and water moderately until growing strongly. Feed when the buds show. The time of flowering will depend on the warmth of the greenhouse. After flowering plunge outdoors but keep watered. Discard after second season.

SPECIES TO GROW. *D. spectabilis* (Bleeding Heart), rosy-crimson, spring, 2 feet.

Didiscus (*Trachymene*, Blue Lace Flower) *Umbelliferae*
Half-hardy annual from Western Australia with lacy clusters of light blue flowers in late summer and autumn.

CULTIVATION. Sow in March in a temperature of 13° C. (55° F.), or later and pot singly. Flower in 5- or 6-inch pots of J.I.P. 2 or other compost. Water freely and shade from hot sun. They will need support and feeding when flowering starts.

SPECIES TO GROW. *D. caeruleus* (syn. *Trachymene caerulea*), pale blue, summer, 15 inches to 2 feet.

Dielytra *see* DICENTRA

Dimorphotheca *Compositae*
South African annuals and perennials with daisy flowers in summer. I am fond of *D. ecklonis* with its elegant white flowers with blue centres and delicate pencilling on the backs of the petals.

CULTIVATION. Sow in February or March as they are useful for early flowering. Use J.I.P. 2 or other compost and sow thinly in 5-inch pots. Thin to three plants per pot. *D. ecklonis* is usually raised from cuttings which root easily in summer. The time of flowering depends on when seed is sown or cuttings taken.

SPECIES TO GROW. *D. aurantiaca*, *D. calendulacea*, *D. sinuata* and their hybrids are all annuals with orange, yellow, salmon, buff or white flowers, 12–18 inches; *D. ecklonis* (syn. *Osteospermum ecklonis*) is perennial, white, 1½–2 feet.

Diplacus *see* MIMULUS

Drosanthemum *see* MESEMBRYANTHEMUM

Earth Stars *see* CRYPTANTHUS

Eccremocarpus *Bignoniaceae*
Quick-growing Chilean evergreen climber, with attractive foliage and racemes of tubular flowers. It flowers the first year from seed if sown in heat early in the year.

CULTIVATION. Sow seed in February in propagating frame or grow from cuttings taken in autumn. Pot singly in 8-inch pots in

May for flowering in the greenhouse using J.I.P. 2 or soil-less compost. Alternatively seed can be sown in late summer and the plants overwintered in small pots.

SPECIES TO GROW. *E. scaber*, orange-red, and variety *aureus*, yellow, late summer, 10–15 feet.

Echeveria *Crassulaceae*

Easily grown succulent plants from the southern parts of North America. They often have attractive rosettes of glaucous leaves and some are winter flowering.   MWT 7° C. (45° F.)

CULTIVATION. Pot in J.I.P. 2 with added grit or in other freely drained compost. They are best in wide shallow pans or pots. The tops of the plants can be cut off and re-rooted when they get leggy. Water freely in summer and much less in winter unless in a warm room. They are also easily raised from seed. Oddly enough both seed and cuttings can be started under mist. See also COTYLEDON.

SPECIES TO GROW. *E.* × *derenosa* 'Worfield Wonder', compact plant, orange-yellow flowers, spring, 6 inches; *E. gibbiflora* (shrubby), leaves flushed with red, flower light red and yellow in winter, and variety *metallica*, with more rounded and bronzed leaves; *E. harmsii* (syn. *Cotyledon elegans*, *Oliveranthus elegans*), large, red, yellow-tipped flowers in July, 12–18 inches; *E. glauca* has attractive grey-green, thick-leaved rosettes that flush with pink when kept rather dry; *E.* × 'Retusa Hybrida', scarlet flowers on 2-foot stems, winter and spring; *E. secunda*, red and yellow, spring, and variety *glauca*, the well-known bedding plant; *E. setosa*, reddish-yellow, early summer, furry leaves; *E. zahnii* 'Hoveyi', narrow grey-green leaves striped with white and pink.

Echinocactus *Cactaceae*

Handsome globular cacti from Mexico that eventually grow enormous and make fine specimens.

CULTIVATION. Treat as CEREUS. Under glass they sometimes scorch in strong sunshine and this should be watched for.

SPECIES TO GROW. *E. grusonii*, prominent ribs and long powerful cream spines, red and yellow flowers only when mature after many years; *E. ingens*, brown spines, yellow flowers when mature.

Echinocereus *Cactaceae*
Fairly small, very spiny cacti with beautiful and showy flowers in summer.

CULTIVATION. Treat as CEREUS to which they are closely related. They mostly form clumps.

SPECIES TO GROW. *E. delaetii*, erect with long white hairs and bright pink flowers; *E. fendleri*, purplish-violet; *E. pectinatus*, roundish stems, free-flowering, pink; *E. pentalophus*, clustered plant with violet-red flowers.

Echinopsis *Cactaceae*
Easily grown barrel-shaped cactus from South America with large pink or white flowers in summer.

CULTIVATION. Treat as CEREUS. Some plants have quantities of offsets and never flower, others have few offsets but flower every year. An offset from a plant that is known to have flowered is a good idea.

SPECIES TO GROW. *E. eyriesii* and hybrids. Other species available are also desirable plants.

Elephant Bush *see* PORTULACARIA

Elephant's Trunk *see* MARTYNIA

Epidendrum *Orchidaceae*
An orchid from the mountains of Mexico where the air is cool and moist. MWT 7° C. (45° F.)

CULTIVATION. Treat as ODONTOGLOSSUM. I have not grown this orchid but I believe it is worth trying in the cool conservatory where the atmosphere is fairly moist. No two people agree as to which orchids are the most adaptable.

Species to grow. *E. vitellinum*, orange-scarlet, late summer, about 1 foot.

Epiphyllum (*Phyllocactus*) *Cactaceae*
These are tall, spineless cacti that have long flat or three-cornered stems and very large and showy flowers. See also Schlumbergera. MWT 7° C. (45° F.)

Cultivation. These plants need to be grown in a moist atmosphere and filtered light. They are not desert plants. They can be grown in pots and hanging baskets. They do not have a lot of root and need support. A well-known grower uses a compost made of 2 parts leafmould (beech), 1 part medium-grade sedge peat and 1 part washed grit or sharp sand. A quart measure of charcoal chippings and the same of well-decomposed cow manure or bonemeal is added to each bushel. The roots need to be kept moist but not wet and the compost needs to be spongy and well drained. Cuttings of mature stems root easily in spring at 16° C. (60° F.). Do not re-pot plants that are in bud, and rest slightly by keeping drier after flowering. Watch for greenfly on the flower buds.

Species to grow. Specialist growers have hundreds of beautiful hybrids with huge flowers in all shades from scarlet to pink and purple as well as white. Most form plants 2–3 feet tall. *E. ackermannii*, crimson, summer; *E.* 'Cooperi', an early hybrid, large, white, scented flowers; *E. oxypetalum* (syn. *E. latifrons*), white, fragrant, night blooming, climbing plant.

Erica (Heath) *Ericaceae*
Small evergreen shrubby plants. Those listed here are known as 'Cape Heaths' and are of South African origin. They need care but little heat and flower in winter and early spring.

Cultivation. These plants need close attention to the simple details of cultivation if they are to be kept for any length of time. Pot very firmly in lime-free J. I. composts or two-thirds peat and one-third silver sand with some pieces of broken pot in the soil and very good drainage. Water very carefully so that soil is constantly moist but never sodden. They use very little water but must not dry out. Cut hard back immediately after flowering and re-pot when necessary, disturbing the roots as little as possible. Plunge outdoors in sun during the summer. Increase by cuttings of side shoots taken in June or July and rooted in sand in a propagating frame or under a bell glass. Alternatively buy in bloom, enjoy and throw away!

SPECIES TO GROW. *E. gracilis*, pink, and its white variety, September to December, 12–18 inches, and *E. hyemalis*, long tubular flowers, pink-tipped white, December and January, are the most popular. *E. canaliculata*, white, January and February, ultimately large and hardy in mild places; *E. pageana*, yellow, March and April. Others may be available from specialist growers.

Eriobotrya (Loquat) *Rosaceae*
Evergreen tree with large handsome leaves that is quickly raised from seed of fruit eaten on Mediterranean holiday.

CULTIVATION. Sow in any potting compost in spring or summer. It can be planted out against a south wall when it becomes too large. It will not fruit in Britain. It is sometimes sold as a houseplant but the leaves tend to brown at the tip when grown indoors.

SPECIES TO GROW. *E. japonica*, handsome corrugated leaves and woolly young growth.

Erythrina *Leguminosae*
Shrub-like plant from the cooler parts of Brazil producing tall shoots topped by spikes of scarlet pea flowers in late summer. They die down to a rootstock like a dahlia in winter. Beware of thorns on the backs of the leaves.

CULTIVATION. Pot and re-pot each year in March or April and soak to start into growth. Give plenty of water while growing but dry off after flowering. Cut back in late October, when the shoots have died down, to within a few inches of the base. Keep dry until the spring. It can be grown in a tub and stood outside in the summer. It seems very free from insect pests. Increase by cuttings removed with a heel in spring and rooted with artificial heat.

SPECIES TO GROW. *E. crista-galli* (Coral Tree), brilliant scarlet, late summer, 5–6 feet.

Eucalyptus (Gum Tree) *Myrtaceae*
Australian evergreen trees with attractive glaucous juvenile foliage. MWT 7° C. (45° F.)

CULTIVATION. Pot up plants in March in J.I.P. 2 or other compost. Seed can be sown either in August or early spring and cuttings taken in June. Water freely in summer. *E. globulus* is used for tropical bedding as it can grow several feet in the first year. Foliage can also be cut.

SPECIES TO GROW. *E. citriodora* (scented leaves), ultimately tall shrub; *E. globulus* (Blue Gum), ultimately tall tree.

Eucnide *Loasaceae*
Half-hardy annual from the western United States with attractive golden-tasselled flowers in summer.

CULTIVATION. Sow in March or April and pot singly in 3-inch pots or directly into 5-inch pots of J.I.P. 2 or other compost, in which they will flower. Keep in full sun and water only moderately. The leaves are slightly irritant to the skin if handled.

SPECIES TO GROW. *E. bartonioides* (syn. *Mentzelia bartonioides* and *Microsperma bartonioides*), buttercup yellow, summer, about 1 foot.

Euphorbia (Spurge) *Euphorbiaceae*
This extremely diverse family includes annuals, perennials, shrubs and trees as well as succulent species that may look like anything from a tangle of barbed wire to a sea anemone.

CULTIVATION. The hardy annual *E. heterophylla*, sometimes known as the annual poinsettia, makes an effective pot plant if sown in March. *E. pulcherrima* (Poinsettia) is a very showy plant that really needs MWT 13° C. (55° F.) but will survive MWT 10° C.

(50° F.). The plants sold at Christmas are dwarfed by chemical means and if you strike cuttings from them in heat in summer they will be taller and flower later. Dry off gradually after flowering and then keep quite dry until the end of April. Then soak the pot and cut back the plant to 4 inches. The shoots which develop are used as cuttings when about 3 inches long. Dip them in powdered charcoal to stop bleeding and root in equal quantities of peat and sand. For potting, loam with a little sand and leafmould is suitable. *E. splendens* (Crown of Thorns) is a prickly succulent shrub. Keep in full sun in small pots of free-draining soil such as 2 parts J.I.P. 2 and 1 part gritty material. Cut back young plants to make them bushy. Euphorbia sap is poisonous. *E. splendens* likes plenty of water when growing but keep dry in winter if leafless, and temperature low. As a room plant it can flower all the year.

SPECIES TO GROW. *E. heterophylla*, annual, 2 feet, in pots; *E. pulcherrima* 'Mikkelsen' strain is hardiest, showy scarlet or pink bracts in winter; *E. milii*, small scarlet bracts most of year, ultimately a shrub but flowers when small, and particularly its variety *splendens*, similar.

Eurya *see* CLEYERA

Eustoma (*Lisianthus* Prairie Gentian) *Gentianaceae*
A beautiful half-hardy Texan plant best grown as a biennial.
MWT 10° C. (50° F.)

CULTIVATION. Sow in June for flowering the following spring. They are very liable to damp off and not easy to grow. Use J.I.P. 2 and overwinter in 3-inch pots and flower in 5- or 6-inch pots. Shade from hot sun. It can be flowered the same year from an early sowing in a warm greenhouse.

SPECIES TO GROW. *E. russellianum*, pale purple bell flowers with white centres and grey-green leaves, 2 feet.

Exacum *Gentianaceae*
Pretty scented biennial with bluish-lilac flowers over a long period.
MWT 10° C. (50° F.)

CULTIVATION. Sow in heat in March to flower in late summer and autumn. They can be sown in late summer and overwintered in a warmer greenhouse. They like equal quantities of loam and peat and need shading in summer and a moist atmosphere.
SPECIES TO GROW. *E. affine*, 1 foot.

Fatshedera *Araliaceae*
Evergreen foliage plant for shade. It is a cross between *Fatsia japonica* and ivy. It is lighter in build than fatsia and needs some support. Frost protection only.

CULTIVATION. Similar to FATSIA. Easily increased by cuttings. Shade in summer.

SPECIES TO GROW. *F.* × *lizei* and variety *variegata* with cream edges to the leaves, ultimately 8 feet.

Fatsia *Araliaceae*
Nearly hardy evergreen shrub from China and Japan with big shiny fig-like leaves. This plant is no trouble. Hardy against a wall outdoors.

CULTIVATION. Pot in J.I.P. 3 or other compost in March and re-pot only when essential or it will soon be too large. Water freely May to September and keep just moist in winter. It can be stood outdoors from May to September if not wanted in the conservatory. It prefers half shade. Increase by seed or 2-inch cuttings of firm young growth, in heat in spring. Small plants are sold as house-plants.

SPECIES TO GROW. *F. japonica* (syn. *Aralia japonica* and *A. sieboldii*), creamy-white flowers in autumn only when mature. It grows slowly to about 8 feet; also variety *variegata*, with white markings on the leaves.

Felicia (Blue Marguerite) *Compositae*
Shrubby perennial from South Africa that can be grown as an annual. Flowering time depends on when seed is sown or cuttings taken.

CULTIVATION. Sow in March for winter flowering and pot singly to flower in 5- or 6-inch pots, or plant out. Pinch once when small to induce bushiness. Increase by cuttings of half-ripened wood in autumn.

SPECIES TO GROW. *F. amelloides* (syn. *Agathaea coelestis*), blue, daisy flowers, 1–2 feet.

Ferns

There are many tender ferns and whole houses can be devoted to their cultivation. Ferns need a moist atmosphere, fresh air and shade from sunshine. They can be very attractive in a greenhouse that has become overshadowed by trees or buildings and in shady positions in any greenhouse with a moist atmosphere.

MWT 7° C. (45° F.)

CULTIVATION. A suitable compost for most ferns consists of equal parts by bulk of loam, granulated moss peat, leafmould and silver sand, with a little charcoal to keep the mixture sweet. The compost needs to be spongy in texture and fibrous loam pulled apart in the fingers is better than sieved loam, except for small plants. Do not ram soil hard or add lime to the compost. EFF soil-less compost seems to suit them. Use rain-water in districts with alkaline water. A little weak feeding may be given to well-established plants. Frequent damping of the surroundings of ferns is beneficial but not syringing of the fronds. Keep everything much drier in cold weather.

SPECIES TO GROW. *Adiantum* (Maidenhair fern) see under ADIANTUM; Asparagus fern see under ASPARAGUS; *Asplenium bulbiferum*, pale green fronds up to 2 feet. It bears bulbils on the fronds; *A. nidus* (Bird's-nest Fern), tropical epiphytic ferns with undivided shiny fronds, MWT 10° C. (50° F.); *Cyrtomium falcatum* (Holly Fern) 'Rochfordii', leathery, glossy fronds, 1–2 feet; *Davallia bullata* (Squirrel's-foot Fern) and *D. canariensis* (Hare's-foot Fern), elegant creeping ferns, MWT 10° C. (50° F.); *Nephrolepis exaltata* and its cultivars; *Platycerium* see under PLATYCERIUM;

Pteris cretica and its crested and variegated forms. This is just a selection from the many possibilities.

Ferocactus *Cactaceae*
Spherical North American cacti, often cylindrical with age. They have prominent ribs with fierce spines and ultimately grow to great size.

CULTIVATION. Treat as CEREUS. Mortar rubble or limestone chips can be added to the compost. Very little water in winter.

SPECIES TO GROW. *F. acanthodes*, reddish spines, orange flowers only when mature; *F. wislizenii* (Barrel Cactus of Arizona), orange, August, when mature.

Ficus (Fig) *Moraceae*
Tropical trees grown as house-plants. When large and sickly they are relegated to the greenhouse. MWT 10° C. (50° F.)

CULTIVATION. All except *F. pumila* prefer a higher temperature but they are tough. Re-pot in late spring and do not over-pot. Use J.I.P. 3 or other fairly rich compost. Water well in summer but very little in winter. Yellow leaves usually mean too much water. They appreciate shade and a moist atmosphere in summer. Sponge leaves when dusty. Brisk heat is desirable to root cuttings of the top 6 inches of the plant. It is possible to ring the bark and cover with damp moss in polythene to root *in situ* indoors. *F. pumila* is a small self-clinging climber sometimes used in baskets in shade or to cling to the north wall of a conservatory.

SPECIES TO GROW. *F. benjamina*, graceful weeping habit, small green leaves; *F. elastica decora* (the best Rubber Plant), large shiny green leaves; *F. e.* 'Doescheri', cream variegated leaves tinged with pink; *F. lyrata* (syn. *F. pandurata*, Fiddle-leaf Fig), huge pale green ribbed leaves; *F. pumila*, creeping plant with small leaves. There is a variegated form.

Flame Nettle *see* COLEUS

Few flowers are more gaudily handsome than the tuberous Begonia

Vallota purpurea, the Scarborough Lily, has scarlet flowers in late summer

Fuchsia 'Mrs. Marshall' is a well-tried favourite

Pimelea ferruginea used to be trained to provide hundreds of heads of bloom in Victorian conservatories

Francoa (Bridal Wreath) *Saxifragaceae*
Perennial herbaceous plant from Chile with graceful spikes of white or pinkish-red flowers rising from a rosette of rather coarse leaves. Useful for cutting. MWT 7° C. (45° F.)

CULTIVATION. Sow seed in March in warmth. They like a compost containing leafmould. Grow in cool airy conditions through the summer and pot on into fairly large pots to flower. They are best renewed from seed but can be kept for another year or divided.

SPECIES TO GROW. *F. ramosa*, 2–3 feet.

Freesia *Iridaceae*
South African bulbous plant with extremely fragrant flowers in early spring. They are rather floppy for pots but may be grown for cutting. MWT 7° C. (45° F.)

CULTIVATION. The modern hybrids raised from seed flower in seven months. Sow April to June for winter flowering. Otherwise pot corms in August 1 inch deep and six to a 5-inch pot or in boxes of J.I.P. 3 or similar rich compost. Plunge outdoors for six weeks until growth starts. Bring into greenhouse but give little water until growing strongly. Keep near the glass and support with sticks. If the corms are to be used another year keep watered and fed until the leaves die down. Then keep dry and in full sun to ripen corms before re-potting in August.

SPECIES TO GROW. *F.* × *hybrida* in many colours including 'Van Staaveren Super Strain', in named colours, 1–2 feet. Consult tradesman's lists for seeds and bulbs.

Fuchsia *Onagraceae*
Quick-growing deciduous shrubs of great charm with a very long flowering season in summer and autumn. They like partial shade and a moist atmosphere.

CULTIVATION. The plants are dormant in winter and should be kept all but dry and free from frost. Cut hard back in February and re-pot in March every year in J.I.P. 3. Start into growth and give plenty of water when they are growing freely. Feed regularly and often, shade lightly and give plenty of fresh air. Buy new plants in April or May and re-pot carefully when received. Pot firmly and pinch several times to make shapely plants. They are easily increased by cuttings of young shoots in spring or half-ripe shoots in August. Young plants can be kept growing through the winter in a minimum of 7° C. (45° F.). *F. fulgens*, *F. procumbens* and *F. triphylla* hybrids should have MWT 10° C. (50° F.).

SPECIES TO GROW. Consult specialist's catalogues for the many greenhouse varieties. Some good ones are: 'Citation', 'Dainty Lady', 'Duke of York', 'Lena', 'Lustre', 'Marinka', 'Mrs. Marshall' and 'Pink Ballet Girl'. *F. fulgens* (Mexico), scarlet tubular flowers until late autumn, 3–6 feet; *F. procumbens* (New Zealand), curious trailing plant, small yellow and purple flowers followed by red fruits; *F. triphylla* cultivars 'Mary', long scarlet flowers born in clusters, 'Thalia', orange-scarlet, similar, and 'Traudchen Bonstedt', pale salmon, all on upright bushes.

Genista *see* CYTISUS

Geranium *see* PELARGONIUM

Gerbera (Barberton or Transvaal Daisy) *Compositae*
Perennial herbaceous plant from South Africa liking sun and a dry atmosphere. Long-lasting flowers for cutting. MWT 7° C. (45° F.)

CULTIVATION. Sow seed in March or buy seedlings of a good strain in spring from a specialist grower. The seed must be new. Shade seedlings until pricked out and established. Pot individually in J.I.P. 2 and keep in light airy conditions. A frame is best for the summer if it is not forgotten. They will begin flowering early the following year and need 6-inch pots or they can be grown in a greenhouse bed. They are unsuitable for automatic watering and resent root disturbance. Keep rather dry in winter unless the greenhouse is warm enough for them to be growing actively. Old plants can be divided. Do not bury the crown of the plant. A temperature above 10° C. (50° F.) is needed for reliable winter flowering. Re-pot in March or April. J.I.P. 2 with a little extra sand is suitable. Avoid overwatering at all times.

SPECIES TO GROW. *G. jamesonii* and single and double cultivars, orange-scarlet through all warm shades to pink and white, summer, 10–18 inches.

Gesneria *see* RECHSTEINERIA and SMITHIANTHA

Gilia *Polemoniaceae*
Very striking half-hardy biennial from the warmer parts of North America with spikes of beautiful scarlet flowers. MWT 7° C. (45° F.)

CULTIVATION. Sow as early as possible for late summer and autumn flowering or in July to overwinter and flower the following year. They need freely drained soil and careful winter watering. Grow three to a 6-inch pot. J.I.P. 2 is a suitable compost. They will need supporting.

SPECIES TO GROW. *G. rubra* (syn. *G. coronopifolia*), crimson-scarlet, up to 3 or 4 feet.

Gladiolus *Iridaceae*
The smaller early flowering gladioli may be grown in pots and the enthusiast can raise scented winter-flowering species from seed.

CULTIVATION. Pot in autumn 1 inch deep and four or five to a 6-inch pot of J.I.P. 3 or other well-drained compost. Plunge outdoors until the beginning of December. Then bring into the greenhouse. If dried off gradually after flowering and then kept quite dry until re-potting they can be grown another year, but new corms are more reliable.

SPECIES TO GROW. The early flowering Nanus Hybrids (sometimes called *G.* × *colvillei* hybrids) such as 'The Bride', white with red markings, April or May, 2–2½ feet; *G. tristis*, scented, pale yellow with purple or reddish markings, which is available as seed.

Globe Amaranth *see* GOMPHRENA

Gloriosa *Liliaceae*
Tuberous-rooted tropical plants that climb by means of tendrils. They have red and yellow lily flowers in summer.
MWT 10° C. (50° F.)

CULTIVATION. Pot the roots singly in March in 6-inch pots of J.I.P. 2 or equal quantities of loam and peat with a little sharp sand. Start into growth with bottom heat and keep as warm as possible. Put in a cane to support them. They resent root disturbance even when resting. Water freely in summer when they appreciate a humid atmosphere. Gradually dry off after flowering and keep quite dry and in a temperature of 10° C. (50° F.) in winter, preferably in the dry warmth of the home.

SPECIES TO GROW. *G. rothschildiana*, crimson and yellow, summer; *G. superba*, orange-yellow and red, summer. Both up to 6 feet.

Glory of the Sun *see* LEUCOCORYNE

Glory Pea *see* CLIANTHUS

Gloxinia *see* SINNINGIA

Golden Spider Lily *see* LYCORIS

Gomphrena (Globe Amaranth) *Amaranthaceae*
Half-hardy annual from India with 'everlasting' flowers.

CULTIVATION. Sow in March, April or May in a temperature of at least 16° C. (60° F.). Pot singly in small pots and flower in 5-inch pots of J.I.P. 2 or soil-less compost. Feed when buds form. To preserve everlasting flowers cut just before they are fully open and hang in bunches upside down in a dry airy place.

SPECIES TO GROW. *G. globosa* with orange-yellow, purple, rose or white flowers, July onwards, 12–18 inches. *G. g.* 'Buddy' with hot purple flowers 1 foot is the most often seen.

Grasses, Ornamental *see* CYPERUS and SCIRPUS

Grevillea *Proteaceae*
Evergreen Australian trees and shrubs useful in a cool conservatory. MWT 7° C. (45° F.)

CULTIVATION. *G. alpina* makes a small compact bush with charming and long-lasting, but not very showy, flowers from Christmas onwards. It is hardy in the south-west. *G. robusta* has silky fernlike leaves and is grown as a foliage and house-plant, usually from seed. Sow in March in a propagating frame inserting the seeds edgeways and ½ inch deep. It may also be increased by half-ripe cuttings in summer. It makes an attractive plant in its second year from seed. *G. alpina* needs pinching when young, but *G. robusta* is grown to a single stem. Water freely April to September, moderately otherwise.

SPECIES TO GROW. *G. alpina* (syn. *G. alpestris*), red and yellow, December to March, 2–4 feet; *G. robusta*, ultimately a tree.

Guernsey Lily *see* NERINE

Gum Tree *see* EUCALYPTUS

Habranthus *see* ZEPHYRANTHES

Habrothamnus *see* CESTRUM

Haemanthus (Blood Lily) *Amaryllidaceae*
Interesting and unusual bulbous plants from South Africa.
MWT 7° C. (45° F.)

CULTIVATION. The large bulbs of *H. coccineus* are likely to be available in July, also *H. albiflos*. *H. katherinae* is never completely dormant but foliage dies off in winter. Pot singly in J.I.P. 2 with the nose of the bulb just showing. Re-pot only occasionally when dormant. The foliage of *H. albiflos* and *H. coccineus* dies down in spring and they should be kept quite dry until growth starts again.

H. katherinae is nearly evergreen and less hardy, MWT 10° C. (50° F.). It is much the most spectacular. Keep them all in sun.

SPECIES TO GROW. *H. albiflos*, white flowers with pompon of stamens, autumn, 1 foot; *H. coccineus*, similar but flowering entirely without leaves, August, 1 foot; *H. katherinae*, orange-red, early summer, 1–2 feet.

Hardenbergia *Leguminosae*

Australian evergreen shrubby climbers with racemes of purple or violet pea flowers even on small plants.

CULTIVATION. They can be raised from seed or cuttings of young shoots and are suitable for growing in a conservatory border or large pots and training up to the roof. Thin out and prune in spring. A peaty sandy soil suits them. Give plenty of water when they are growing actively but little in winter.

SPECIES TO GROW. *H. comptoniana* (syn. *Kennedya comptoniana*), violet-blue, early spring; *H. violacea* (syn. *H. monophylla*), purple to rosy-violet, early spring.

Heath *see* ERICA

Hedera (Ivy) *Araliaceae*

The more ornamental ivies with small leaves are often grown as house-plants and can trail from the edge of the staging in greenhouses.

CULTIVATION. Pot in J.I.P. 1 or soil-less compost and always keep just moist. They need very little water in winter. Increase by layering and also by cuttings. Full light enhances the colouring of the variegated kinds but shade in summer. Pinch in spring to keep them branching.

SPECIES TO GROW. The many varieties of the common ivy *H. helix* with variously shaped and coloured leaves. My favourite is *H. h.* 'Glacier', with silvery-grey mottled leaves. It is hardy. *H. canariensis* varieties are less hardy and particularly resent overwatering in winter.

Hedychium *Zingiberaceae*
Large canna-like plants from Asia with handsome leaves and fragrant spikes of flowers. Suitable for large conservatories.
MWT 7° C. (45° F.)

CULTIVATION. *H. gardnerianum* is the hardiest and very impressive when in flower in a border. They can be grown in large pots or tubs and need plenty of water from April to October. It is best to cut them down after flowering and keep nearly dry through the winter. If it is warm and wet they grow continuously. Re-pot when needed in March and increase by dividing the roots.

SPECIES TO GROW. *H. coccineum*, orange-red, 4–6 feet; *H. coronarium*, white, summer, 3–4 feet; *H. gardnerianum*, yellow with red filaments, late summer, 3–6 feet.

Heeria *see* SCHIZOCENTRON

Heliotropium *Boraginaceae*
Soft-wooded shrubs from Peru with very sweetly scented flowers. They can be grown as half-hardy annuals. MWT 10° C. (50° F.)

CULTIVATION. They can be grown from cuttings in either spring or preferably late summer but are now usually raised from seed. The kinds readily available are dwarf hybrids which flower all the summer. Re-pot annually in March and keep moist in summer and nearly dry in winter. Sow seeds in heat in March or earlier if you can keep them warm or buy young plants in May. J.I.P. 2 is suitable. Pinch to make bushy and prune old plants hard back in early spring.

SPECIES TO GROW. Hybrids of *H. peruvianum* (Cherry Pie) in shades of violet and purple, also white, 1–3 feet.

Helxine (Mind your own business) *Urticaceae*
Very small creeping plant from Corsica sometimes used to carpet the ground under greenhouse staging.

Cultivation. Let it mind its own business elsewhere. It can spread alarmingly indoors and out. The golden-leaved form *Helxine soleirolii* 'Aurea' is less rampant.

Heterocentron *see* Schizocentron

Hippeastrum *Amaryllidaceae*
Very handsome South American bulbous plants, often wrongly called Amaryllis (which see), but needing a higher temperature. They are warm greenhouse plants but included here because they are so often grown and do survive lower temperatures.

mwt 10° C. (50° F.)

Cultivation. The time of flowering of the hybrids depends on the amount of heat. Prepared bulbs for Christmas flowering are grown indoors and all will flower earlier indoors. When kept cool flowering is unlikely before April. They can be urged to flower by starting them plunged in a warmed bed. They are more or less evergreen but dried off and sold as dry bulbs from December to March. Pot up when received in 6-inch pots of j.i.p. 2 with a little crushed charcoal. Treat any roots with care and only half bury the bulb. Keep just moist but do not water freely until the leaves start growing. The flower bud appears first. After flowering keep well watered and feed occasionally until no more leaves develop. Then reduce watering (August) and dry off for two or three months before encouraging growth again. Re-pot every other year. Increase by offsets which can be kept growing all the year in as much warmth as possible.

Species to grow. Hybrids amongst which scarlet and white predominate. They have big trumpet flowers 6 or more inches across on stout stems. An old hybrid, *H.* × *johnsonii*, red with white stripes, is rare but graceful; *H.* × *ackermannii*, deep crimson-red, late summer; *H. aulicum*, scarlet with widely separated petals, winter, 1½ feet; *H. vittatum*, white with scarlet stripes, up to 3 feet. These and other species are sometimes available commercially.

Holly Fern *see* Ferns

Honey Flower *see* MELIANTHUS

Howea *see* PALMS

Hoya (Wax Flower) *Asclepiadaceae*
Evergreen shrubby plants with sparse fleshy leaves and exquisite clusters of waxy flowers in late summer. MWT 7° C. (45° F.)

CULTIVATION. *H. carnosa* from south China and Australia can sometimes be persuaded to cling like ivy. It is a slender climber with enchanting hanging umbels of flowers. Hoyas do best in rough peaty soil with charcoal and some sand. Water freely in summer but very sparingly in winter. The variegated form is slow-growing. *H. bella* is more tender (MWT 10° C. (50° F.)) and a smaller plant with drooping branches. It is sometimes grafted on *H. carnosa* to give it more vigour. Both need supporting on a framework in pots. *H. bella* is often allowed to hang in a basket. Re-pot only occasionally in March. Increase by layering or by cuttings in warmed propagating frame. Do not remove flower stalks as there will be more flowers at the foot of these stalks the following year.

SPECIES TO GROW. *H. bella* (syn. *H. paxtonii*), pure white flowers with violet centres, up to 2 feet; *H. carnosa*, blush-white with reddish centre, ultimately 10–12 feet; *H. c. variegata* has cream edges to the leaves.

Hyacinthus (Hyacinth) *Liliaceae*
Hardy and showy spring flowering bulbous plants for winter colour where there is little heat.

CULTIVATION. Pot singly in 5-inch pots of J.I.P. 2 or other compost in September with nose of bulb just showing. Do not compact soil beneath the bulb or the bulb will rise up and the roots will come out of the soil. Plunge outdoors until bud is through the neck of the bulb (six to eight weeks), before bringing into the greenhouse. Accustom them to the light gradually and do not let them dry out. They can also be grouped almost touching in bowls of fibre and kept in a cool dark place under cover. Specially prepared bulbs flower at Christmas.

SPECIES TO GROW. Florist's hyacinths are derived from *H. orientalis* of the Mediterranean region. There are named cultivars in many shades from pale pink to scarlet, pale blue to purple, yellow and white. 'Cynthella' hyacinths are smaller and more graceful examples of the same type and suitable for bowls. The Roman Hyacinth is derived from *H. orientalis albulus* and is smaller and flowers before Christmas.

Hydrangea *Saxifragaceae*
Deciduous flowering shrubs of most value in the shady conservatory.

CULTIVATION. The earliness of flowering depends on the warmth available but they can be grown in pots with only frost protection. For blue flowers the compost must be lime-free, and a blueing compound can be used. J.I.P. 2 without chalk is suitable. Water freely from May to October but only sparingly in winter. Feed regularly and remove old flower heads and weak shoots but leave strong main shoots as these will bear flowers next year. After flowering stand the plants outdoors until October when the leaves fall. Cuttings of non-flowering shoots about 4 inches long root easily from April onwards through the summer. They will need shade and steady moisture but can be plunged outdoors when well rooted. Pinch out the leading shoots unless you want single-stem plants. The heavy flower heads need staking under glass.

SPECIES TO GROW. *H. macrophylla* 'Hortensia' cultivars.

Hylocereus *Cactaceae*
Epiphytic night-flowering cacti with tall climbing stems from tropical forest regions of central and southern America.
MWT 10° C. (50° F.)

CULTIVATION. These plants need ample room, rich loamy soil and plenty of water in summer. They have aerial roots that cling to trees and triangular jointed stems. They need shade and warmth to develop their flowers and should be fixed to the rafters or a trellis in a large greenhouse.

SPECIES TO GROW. The best known is *H. undatus* (syn. *Cereus undatus* and *C. triangularis*), enormous fragrant white flowers in late summer. See also SELINICEREUS.

Hymenocallis (*Ismene* Spider Lily; Peruvian Daffodil)
Amaryllidaceae
Bulbous plants, mainly from South America, with umbels of sweetly scented white or yellow flowers somewhat like fringed daffodils.

CULTIVATION. Pot singly in winter in lime-free J.I.P. 2 and re-pot only every three years or so. Feed occasionally. Keep all but dry during the winter resting period.

SPECIES TO GROW. *H. narcissiflora* 'Advance' (syn. *H. calathina* and *Pancratium calathinum*), white, summer, 1½–2 feet, almost hardy; *H.* × *festalis*, similar; *H. harrisiana*, white, about 1 foot, MWT 10° C. (50° F.); *H.* × *spofforthiae* 'Sulphur Queen', yellow, 2 feet, MWT 10° C. (50° F.). All are summer flowering.

Iberis (Candytuft) *Cruciferae*
This easily grown, free-flowering but rather despised hardy annual is willing to flower in winter and spring under glass.

CULTIVATION. Sow a pot or two at a time in any compost and thin to three plants per pot, or even one per 5-inch pot. For winter flowering June, July and August are the months to sow.

SPECIES TO GROW. There are two main types in catalogues, the white hyacinth-flowered kinds about 15 inches high, *I. amara hyacinthiflora*, and the *I. umbellata* varieties, rose-pink to carmine and purple, 6–12 inches.

Imantophyllum *see* CLIVIA

Impatiens *Balsaminaceae*
Tender annuals, and perennials grown as annuals, from India and tropical Africa. They have succulent stems and showy flowers most of the year. MWT 10° C. (50° F.)

CULTIVATION. The annual *I. balsamina* is a quick growing, rather coarse plant that needs a lot of water. The *I. holstii* and *I. sultanii* varieties, often called 'Busy Lizzies', are much more attractive and easily increased by cuttings in warm conditions. A glass of water in a warm room is a simple method. The newly rooted cuttings need to be kept on the dry side until established in soil. The plants become leggy in time and are best replaced but can be cut back. They can also be raised from seed in warmth (at least 16° C. (60° F.)) early in the year. They like peat and leafmould and any rich compost. Feed regularly when established. Shade from sun but keep in strong light or flowering will stop.

SPECIES TO GROW. *I. balsamina* (Balsam), camellia-flowered hybrids, double, in many colours, 1½–2 feet, and dwarf form, 1 foot; *I. holstii*, brilliant scarlet flowers and reddish stems, and various coloured hybrids; *I. olivieri*, tall bushy plant with lilac flowers suitable for large conservatory; *I. petersiana*, deep red flowers and dark red leaves and stems, about 2 feet; *I. sultanii*, scarlet, 1–2 feet, and various coloured hybrids, also dwarf F_1 hybrids, 9 inches.

Ipomoea (Morning Glory) *Convolvulaceae*
Annual twining climber from tropical America with sensational brilliant blue trumpet flowers. See also PHARBITIS and QUAMOCLIT.

CULTIVATION. Soak seeds for a day and sow in small pots at the beginning of April, preferably in a propagator. They stop growing and the leaves go white if the temperature falls in the early stages. Sow more than you need and try to keep the plants above 10° C. (50° F.). Later transfer to larger pots without disturbing the roots. Two or even three on a trellis in a 5-inch pot can produce a magnificent display for several weeks. Remove faded flowers and feed occasionally. The flowers fade each afternoon but I have often had thirty out at a time in a 5-inch pot. Larger plants will grow in the greenhouse border or large pots. Grow in sun. They flower three months from sowing.

SPECIES TO GROW. *I. learii* see PHARBITIS. *I. rubro-caerulea* (syn. *I. tricolor* and *Pharbitis tricolor*), brilliant blue and variety *praecox*; *I. versicolor* see *Quamoclit lobata*.

Iris *Iridaceae*

The bulbous irises, although hardy, can be grown under glass for early flowering as cut flowers and the early miniature kinds are very welcome.

CULTIVATION. *I. danfordiae*, *I. histrioides* and *I. reticulata* are all neat miniature plants best grown in alpine pans or shallow pots. Pot in September or October and keep only just moist until growth starts. They do not require heat and are best in a cold frame until near flowering. After flowering either plant out the whole potful in the garden, or water until leaves fade. Then keep quite dry in the sun until autumn when they are planted out. *I. reticulata* is very sweetly scented and often does well in the same pot a second year. *I. susiana* is a rhizomatous iris with large mournful but distinguished flowers. Pot singly in a 5- or 6-inch pot in J.I.P. 2 when received in autumn. Water moderately until July and then keep absolutely dry on a shelf in the sun until October.

SPECIES TO GROW. *I. danfordiae*, golden-yellow, January, 5 inches; *I. histrioides major* (plunge outdoors until in bud), ultramarine, January, 4 inches; *I. reticulata*, purple-blue and variety 'Cantab', paler, both fragrant, February, 6 inches; *I. susiana* (Mourning Iris), single huge flower netted dark purple on lighter ground, March or April, about 2 feet; *I. xiphium × tingitana* (Dutch iris) hybrids of which 'Imperator', dark blue, and 'Wedgwood', lighter blue, are good in pots, April, 18–24 inches.

Ismene *see* HYMENOCALLIS

Isolepis *see* SCIRPUS

Ivy *see* HEDERA

Ixia (African Corn Lily) *Iridaceae*
Bulbous plant with brilliant flowers on wiry stems in May.

CULTIVATION. Pot in September or October about six to eight to a 5-inch pot, 1 inch deep in J.I.P. 2. Plunge in peat in a cold frame or leave under the greenhouse staging until growth shows. Then keep in full sun from January and water moderately, until the leaves die down. Then keep quite dry until re-potting in the autumn. Increase by offsets removed when re-potting. They should flower in their second year. Seed takes three or four years to flower.

SPECIES TO GROW. Usually available mixed but sometimes as named hybrids, early summer, 18 inches; *I. viridiflora* with electric greeny-blue flowers is interesting, early summer, 1 foot.

Jacaranda *Bignoniaceae*
Blue flowered tree from Brazil with charming ferny foliage when young. MWT 10° C. (50° F.)

CULTIVATION. Sow in at least 16° C. (60° F.) as early in the year as they can be kept warm. They start slowly and need well-drained sandy soil. They are attractive for several years in pots. They survive lower temperatures but lose their leaves in winter. They will stand cutting back and will flower when large. Cuttings of side shoots can be rooted in warmth in summer.

SPECIES TO GROW. *J. mimosifolia* (syn. *J. ovalifolia*), lavender-blue, ultimately tall.

Jacobinia (*Justicia*) *Acanthaceae*
Herbaceous and shrubby plants from the hotter parts of central and south America that can be grown with MWT 10° C. (50° F.). CULTIVATION. Jacobinias were favourite greenhouse plants but

are rare today. They are best frequently renewed from cuttings like fuchsias but need heat to root. Old plants, given warmth and water in spring, will produce cuttings. Stop young plants often as they are inclined to legginess. They will flower in 5-inch pots and should be pruned severely and rested after flowering. They need plenty of water in spring and summer and must not dry out in winter. Re-pot annually in J.I.P. 3 or similar compost.

SPECIES TO GROW. *J. carnea* (syn. *Justicia carnea*) is the hardiest and easiest, pink, late summer, up to 6 feet; *J. chrysostephana*, yellow, winter; *J. ghiesbreghtiana*, scarlet, winter, 1–1½ feet; *J. pauciflora* (syn. *Libonia floribunda*), scarlet tubular flowers with yellow tips, autumn and early winter, 2 feet; *J.* × *penrhosiensis*, crimson, winter; *J. suberecta*, herbaceous creeping plant, orange-red.

Japanese Hyacinth *see* OPHIOPOGON

Jasminum (Jasmine) *Oleaceae*
Evergreen twining and scandent shrubs to train up walls and pillars where there is space.

CULTIVATION. *J. polyanthum* is a very fast-growing easy climber with extremely fragrant clusters of pink-backed white flowers in late winter. It roots at every joint that trails on the ground and needs controlling, although young plants can be grown in pots trained on a wire hoop. *J. primulinum* has no scent. Increase by cuttings in spring. J.I.P. 3 is a suitable compost.

SPECIES TO GROW. *J. azoricum*, white, summer and winter; *J. polyanthum*, white, late winter; *J. primulinum* (syn. *J. mesnyi*), yellow, early spring.

Jovellana *Scrophulariaceae*
Summer flowering slightly shrubby plant closely related to calceolaria.

CULTIVATION. The seed is slow to germinate and the plant likes shade and moisture. It is a New Zealand plant rarely seen in Britain.

Species to grow. *J. sinclairii*, syn. (*calceolaria violaceae*), panicles of small lilac flowers with reddish spots, 1½ feet.

Jubaea *see* Palms

Justicia *see* Jacobinia

Kalanchoe *Crassulaceae*
Interesting succulent plants from tropical Africa. *K. blossfeldiana* is sold as a flowering pot plant for most of the year.

mwt 10° C. (50° F.)

Cultivation. When bought in flower plants need to be kept in bright light and well watered. When the flowers are over cut back to a good pair of leaves and keep nearly dry in winter. Commercial growers sometimes restrict daylight to between 8½ and 10 hours in June and July to induce flowers in autumn. Naturally, *K. blossfeldiana* flowers in spring and summer. Increase by cuttings in July or by seed sown in heat in March. Young plants need warmth and water. The other species mentioned are grown for their attractive leaves. They can be grown in j.i.p. 2 with added grit or a sandy loam with some leafmould and coarse grit. The drainage must be good. This is a big family of interesting plants for those specialising in succulents.

Species to grow. *K. blossfeldiana* hybrids with scarlet or yellow flowers; 'Vulcan' is a compact red one, up to 1 foot. *K. beharensis*, huge velvety leaves, ultimately tall; *K. marmorata*, blue-green leaves mottled with brown; *K. tomentosa*, small silver plushy leaves with ginger edges; *K. uniflora* (syn. *Bryophyllum uniflorum*) is a small creeping plant with pink bell flowers.

Kalosanthes *see* Rochea

Kangeroo Paws *see* Anigozanthus

Kangeroo Vine *see* Cissus

Plumbago capensis is a popular climber with pale blue flowers

Tibouchina urvilleana, better known as *T. semidecandra*, has both leaves and flowers of rich texture and elegance

The scarlet flowers of *Clianthus puniceus*, the Lobster's Claw, have a predatory look

Tolmeia menziesii is better known as the Pig-a-back plant

Kaulfussia *see* CHARIEIS

Kennedya *see* HARDENBERGIA

Kentia *see* PALMS

Kleinia (Candle Plant) *Compositae*
If you are fascinated by how odd plants can be, try this one! It is a succulent from Cape Province having glaucous blue jointed stems like strings of sausages with small ivy leaves sprouting out of them. MWT 7° C. (45° F.)

CULTIVATION. The plant is easily increased by cuttings of the detachable joints. Several plants growing in a pan of soil as for ASTROPHYTUM are quite decorative. Keep nearly dry in winter and always in strong light.

SPECIES TO GROW. *K. articulata* (syn. *Senecio articulatus*), the yellowish-white flowers are said to be evil-smelling but the point of the plant is its form.

Lachenalia (Cape Cowslip) *Liliaceae*
Interesting South African bulbous plants with spikes of long-lasting flowers in winter. MWT 7° C. (45° F.)

CULTIVATION. Pot in August or early September half an inch deep and six to a 5-inch pot in J.I.P. 2 or similar fairly rich compost. Plunge the pots in a cold frame or otherwise keep cool and shaded for two months. Then keep near the glass in the greenhouse and water moderately. Keep watered until June or when the foliage dies down. Then keep pots dry and in the sun until re-potting in August.

SPECIES TO GROW. Hybrids and varieties of *L. aloides* (syn. *L. tricolor*), particularly 'Nelsonii', golden-yellow tinged green, and *L. a. luteola*, lemon yellow tipped green and red, early spring, 9 inches; *L. bulbifera* (better known as *L. pendula*), coral red, tipped green and purple, December, 9 inches.

Lagerstroemia *Lythraceae*
Evergreen flowering shrub from Asia to plant against a greenhouse wall. MWT 7° C. (45° F.)

CULTIVATION. Plant in a sunny position in freely drained soil with extra peat. Trim back in February. Increase by cuttings of young shoots in warmth.

SPECIES TO GROW. *L. indica* (Crape Myrtle), clusters of frilly pink flowers in summer, ultimately large.

Lampranthus *see* MESEMBRYANTHEMUM

Lantana *Verbenaceae*
Evergreen shrubs with showy flowers the first year from seed.
MWT 7° C. (45° F.)

CULTIVATION. Plants raised from seed sown in heat in March will flower in the autumn. Cuttings root easily in August. Some of the old hybrids increased only by cuttings are the best if you can get them.

SPECIES TO GROW. Hybrids of *L. camara* in various colours (mostly orange and yellow), July to October, 1½–3 feet.

Lapageria *Liliaceae*
A very beautiful evergreen twining shrub from Chile for the frost-free greenhouse with a moist atmosphere and shade in summer.

CULTIVATION. Plant out in the greenhouse border. Well-drained lime-free soil is essential. If grown in a tub 3 parts by bulk of fibrous peat, 1 part loam, ½ part sharp sand and some charcoal is a suitable compost. Water freely from April to September. Keep only just moist in winter. Increase by layering in spring or autumn.

SPECIES TO GROW. *L. rosea*, rose-crimson, late summer and autumn.

Lasiandra *see* TIBOUCHINA

Lemaireocereus (Organ-pipe Cactus) *Cactaceae*
Handsome and fast-growing columnar cactus from Mexico where it is used for hedges. MWT 7° C. (45° F.)

CULTIVATION. Treat as *Cereus*. Grow in full sun.

SPECIES TO GROW. *L. marginatus* (syn. *Pachycereus marginatus*), ultimately up to 20 feet. Other species also attractive when young.

Lemon *see* CITRUS

Lemon-scented Verbena *see* LIPPIA

Leptospermum *Myrtaceae*
Half-hardy evergreen shrubs with tiny leaves and a mass of attractive flowers in early summer.

CULTIVATION. *L. scoparium* grows quickly from seed, but the hybrids do not come true and should be increased by cuttings in May. This plant loves capillary watering but soon becomes large. Any light acid or neutral soil suits it and it is hardy in the south-west. Pot in spring. It can be plunged outdoors after flowering until late September.

SPECIES TO GROW. *L. scoparium* (Manuka or Tea Tree of New Zealand), white flowers and hybrids in various shades from white to crimson, single and double, 2 feet and upwards.

Leucadendron *Proteaceae*
The Silver Tree of Table Mountain is attractive in pots when young if you can get the seed.

CULTIVATION. Sow seeds in spring and be very careful not to break the roots at any time. Germination is slow. The silky evergreen leaves make a pleasant contrast to other plants. J.I.P. 2 is suitable.

SPECIES TO GROW. *L. argenteum* (Silver Tree), ultimately a tree.

Leuchtenbergia *Cactaceae*
Very odd Mexican cactus, the only species of its genus. It has a root like a parsnip and yellow flowers.

CULTIVATION. Grow in deep pots of very porous soil such as 3 parts of J.I.P. 2 to 1 part gritty material that includes some lime-stone chips. Keep in full sun.

SPECIES TO GROW. *L. principis*, yellow, 9–12 inches.

Leucocoryne *Amaryllidaceae*
Attractive bulbous plant from Chile with fragrant clear blue or light purple flowers with white centres in spring.

CULTIVATION. Pot in autumn and treat as FREESIA.

SPECIES TO GROW. *L. ixioides odorata* (Glory of the Sun), pale blue to light purple, sweetly scented, spring, about 1 foot.

Libonia *see* JACOBINIA

Lilium (Lily) *Liliaceae*
Most hardy lilies can be grown under glass where they do not do well in the garden, and some tender lilies are quite quickly raised from seed.

CULTIVATION. Pot immediately they are received in autumn, with the exception of *L. candidum* and *L. testaceum* which should be planted in August. J.I.P. 2 may be used, or 3 parts by bulk rich fibrous loam, 1 part leafmould or peat and some coarse sharp sand. The soil must be lime-free for *L. auratum*, *L. brownii* and *L. japonicum*. They are usually planted singly in a 6- or 7-inch pot or three in a 10-inch pot. The stem-rooting lilies should be planted deep in the pot and only just covered, leaving room for topdressing in the spring. They are best kept just moist, plunged in a cold frame or in a cool cellar until growth shows but protected from frost. Topdress the stem-rooting kinds when about 2 feet tall, preferably adding a proprietary lily food to a fine rich compost. Water freely only when growing strongly, but never allow them to get dry. Watch out for greenfly that can quickly ruin the plants. After flowering keep moist in a cool place and allow the leaves to die down naturally. Bring in before frost and re-pot when necessary in late autumn, being careful not to injure live roots. Increase by removing offsets in October or by seed. *L. formosanum* and *L. philippinense*, if sown in early autumn, flower the following summer in a MWT 10° C. (50° F.) greenhouse. *L. regale* takes two to three years.

SPECIES TO GROW. *L. auratum* (Golden-rayed Lily of Japan), ivory with yellow and crimson markings, scented, stem-rooting, needs a large pot and has many varieties, July to August, 3–8 feet; *L. brownii*, cream inside, chocolate outside, stem-rooting, July, 3–5 feet; *L. candidum* (Madonna Lily), white, basal rooting, full sun, June, 2–5 feet; *L. formosanum*, white, often rosy-purple outside, September, 4–7 feet, and variety *pricei*, much shorter; *L. hansonii*, orange-yellow, stem-rooting, June to July, 4 feet; *L. japonicum* (syn. *L. krameri*), pink, stem-rooting, August, 4–8 feet; *L. longiflorum*, white, fragrant, stem-rooting and varieties, July, 3–6 feet; *L. regale*, white, rosy-purple outside, fragrant, stem-rooting, July, 3–6 feet; *L. speciosum*, white suffused and spotted with claret-red, July to September, 1–4 feet. There are named forms and variations of colouring. This is one of the best under glass. Flowering times of all lilies will depend on the warmth of the greenhouse. *L. brownii*, *L. formosanum*, *L. longiflorum* and *L. speciosum* can all be forced. There are many fine American and other hybrid lilies: 'Brandywine', apricot, 'Enchantment', nasturtium-red, 'Prosperity', lemon-yellow, and a few others are even available prepared for Christmas flowering in the house.

Lily *see* LILIUM

Limonium (Sea Lavender; Statice)　　　　*Plumbaginaceae*
Half-hardy annuals known for their 'everlasting' flowers and perennial kinds from the Canaries flowering the first year from seed.

CULTIVATION. Sow in March or April and later pot singly in J.I.P. 2 or other compost. *L. suworowii* has arresting pink spires of bloom and needs a lot of water. For drying cut the flowers as soon as they are fully opened and hang in a cool place.

SPECIES TO GROW. *L. perezii*, pale lavender to purple, autumn, 18 inches; *L. puberulum* 'Blue Spray', late summer, shrubby; *L. suworowii*, lavender-rose, 18 inches.

Linaria (Toad Flax) *Scrophulariaceae*
A hardy annual from Morocco with many hybrids that make pretty spring-flowering plants from an autumn sowing.

CULTIVATION. Sow in September or March in 5-inch pots of J.I.P. 1 or soil-less compost and thin to six per pot. Keep near the glass and water very sparingly in winter. Give twiggy support.

SPECIES TO GROW. Hybrids of *L. maroccana* in many colours, 9–12 inches.

Lippia (Lemon-scented Verbena) *Verbenaceae*
Half-hardy deciduous shrub from Chile with insignificant flowers but grown in the greenhouse for the glorious scent of its crushed leaves. Hardy outdoors in warm districts.

CULTIVATION. Re-pot in March in J.I.P. 3. Water freely in summer but keep only just moist in winter. Prune hard back in February to within an inch of the base of last year's growth. Increase by cuttings taken with a heel in early summer under mist or in a propagating frame.

SPECIES TO GROW. *L. citriodora* (syn. *Aloysia citriodora*), lilac, August. It can be kept at 2 feet.

Lisianthus *see* EUSTOMA

Lobelia *Campanulaceae*
Perennial and annual plants from South Africa and Australia grown for bedding but useful under glass for constant flowering and freedom from pests.

CULTIVATION. Sow in spring and transplant a small cluster of seedlings into a 5-inch pot of J.I.P. 2 or any compost and treat as one plant. They grow taller under glass and flower until Christmas. Autumn-sown plants will overwinter if required and they will cover soil under staging. They seem immune to greenfly. *L. tenuior* has larger flowers for a shorter season and needs the usual half-hardy annual treatment.

SPECIES TO GROW. *L. erinus*, compact varieties in light blue, dark blue, mauve, crimson with white eye and white, 4 inches; trailing varieties 'Blue Cascade', light blue, 'Sapphire', deep blue with white eye; *L. tenuior* (syn. *L. ramosa*), upright growth and brilliant purple-blue flowers, about 1 foot.

Lobster's Claw *see* CLIANTHUS

Loquat *see* ERIOBOTRYA

Lotus *Leguminosae*
Silver-leaved trailing perennial from the Canary Islands with clusters of scarlet pea flowers. MWT 10° C. (50° F.)

CULTIVATION. Pot in March in J.I.P. 2 with a little charcoal or an equal mixture of loam and leafmould with a little sand. It looks well hanging from a basket. Water carefully in summer and keep only just moist in autumn and winter. It likes sun. Increase by division in early spring or by cuttings rooted in slight warmth in late spring.

SPECIES TO GROW. *L. bertholetii* (syn. *L. peliorrhynchus*), scarlet, June.

Luculia *Rubiaceae*
Evergreen shrubs from temperate parts of East Asia with large heads of fragrant pink and white flowers. These large and long-lived plants are sometimes found in old conservatories, but are neglected today. MWT 7° C. (45° F.)

CULTIVATION. Plant in spring against the back wall and restrict the root run to about 3 feet square as for a fig. The soil should be sandy loam and peat. They like moisture and very good drainage. Prune well back after flowering. Young plants can be grown in pots. Increase by cuttings taken with a heel and rooted in silver sand in the autumn. Keep under mist or in an enclosed propagator until rooted. This may take two months. Seed takes about three years to reach the flowering stage.

SPECIES TO GROW. *L. gratissima*, pink, late autumn, ultimately tall; *L. pinceana*, similar, white tinged with pink, a smaller plant.

Lychnis (Viscaria) *Caryophyllaceae*
Easily grown hardy annual from the Mediterranean region with masses of flowers over a fairly long period.

CULTIVATION. Seed can be sown in spring for summer flowering or in autumn for spring flowering. Pot singly in 3-inch pots and later in 5-inch pots of J.I.P. 2 or soil-less compost. Water with care and keep near the glass in winter. Give twiggy support.

SPECIES TO GROW. *L. coeli-rosa* (syn. *Agrostemma coeli-rosa* and *Silene coeli-rosa* but normally sold as Viscaria), rosy-purple, 1 foot; and varieties *oculata* and *nana* with hybrids in shades of scarlet, crimson, pink, blue and white.

Lycoris *Amaryllidaceae*
Bulbous plants from China and Japan flowering in late summer after the leaves have died down. MWT 7° C. (45° F.)

CULTIVATION. Treat as NERINE.

SPECIES TO GROW. *L. aurea* (Golden Spider Lily), late summer, about 1 foot; *L. incarnata*, very pale pink, 12–18 inches; *L. radiata*, deep pink, 15–18 inches; *L. sanguinea*, crimson.

Maidenhair Fern *see* ADIANTUM

Mammillaria *Cactaceae*
A vast family of small globular and sometimes cylindrical cacti

that mostly grow in clusters and flower freely. Many have red fruits after the flowers.

CULTIVATION. Pot in spring in any cactus compost such as 3 parts J.I.P. 2 to 1 part coarse sand or grit and a little crushed charcoal. Water regularly in summer and shade from hot summer sun. Keep nearly dry in winter. There are some 200 species to choose from and I leave it to you. *M. bocasana* (Powder-puff Cactus) is very appealing. Increase by removing offsets, and by seed which is interesting and quite quick. Some plants may flower within a year.

Mandevilla (Chilean Jasmine) *Apocynaceae*
Beautiful deciduous climber from the Argentine that is only a success when planted out and is good for training up to the roof of a conservatory. MWT 7° C. (45° F.)

CULTIVATION. Plant at the end of March. A well-drained peaty soil with plenty of sharp sand suits it. Water freely and syringe while growing, but keep rather dry in winter. Cut back weakly sideshoots in winter. Increase by cuttings of firm sideshoots under mist or in a propagating frame in late spring. Keep the young plants in pots for the first two winters.

SPECIES TO GROW. *M. suaveolens*, fragrant creamy-white flowers, summer, up to 20 feet.

Manuka *see* LEPTOSPERMUM

Marigold *see* CALENDULA

Martynia (Elephant's Trunk or Unicorn Plant) *Martyniaceae*
Unusual half-hardy annual from warm parts of North America with gloxinia-like flowers in late summer followed by strange fruits.

CULTIVATION. Sow singly in small pots in March and pot on to 5- or 6-inch pots of J.I.P. 2 or similar compost. They like a moist atmosphere. Water freely and feed when buds show.

Species to grow. *M. louisiana* (syn. *M. annua* and *Proboscidea annua*), cream or yellow and sometimes reddish-purple spotted flowers, late summer, about 2 feet.

Mask Flower *see* Alonsoa

Matthiola (Stock) *Cruciferae*
Hardy annuals and biennials with spikes of scented flowers in summer or winter grown mainly for their fragrance.

Cultivation. All stocks should be sown very thinly and never allowed to become starved or pot-bound. The smaller and paler leaved seedlings usually have double flowers. Ten Week Stocks are sown in March and treated as half-hardy annuals for bedding out but can be flowered in pots. The Mammoth or Beauty kinds are treated similarly or preferably sown in summer for winter flowering. Intermediate or East Lothian stocks flower in autumn from a spring sowing and in spring from late summer sowing. Pot singly in small pots and soon re-pot in 6-inch pots. So-called 100 per cent double strains are available of all but East Lothian stocks. The double seedlings show up by their paler colour if grown at over 10° C. (50° F.).

Species to grow. Hybrids of *M. incana* and *M. sinuata* known as 'Ten Week Stocks', particularly 'Mammoth' or 'Beauty' varieties, 1–2 feet; Intermediate or East Lothian stocks, bushy, about 18 inches. Brompton Stocks (biennial) and Column stocks can also be grown under glass and the hardy annual *M. bicornis* (Night-scented stock) is valued for scent alone and not for show.

Melaleuca *Myrtaceae*
Evergreen shrubs from Australia related to Callistemon and with a similar type of bottle-brush flower but smaller leaves.

Cultivation. Re-pot in March or April, otherwise treat as Callistemon. Prune lightly after flowering. Increase by cuttings in late summer.

SPECIES TO GROW. *M. fulgens*, red, June, ultimately tall; *M. wilsonii*, red to pink, summer, 4–6 feet.

Melianthus (Honey Flower) *Melianthaceae*
Semi-woody evergreen shrub from South Africa with extremely decorative glaucous pinnate leaves with serrated edges.

CULTIVATION. Easily raised from seed and grown as a pot plant when young in J.I.P. 2 or 3. It can also be planted out in the greenhouse border and trained up a wall or pillar. Do not put it where it will get knocked as the bruised leaves have a disagreeable scent. It is hardy against a wall in mild districts if the roots are protected.

SPECIES TO GROW. *M. major*, reddish-brown flowers in summer but grown for the leaves, ultimately tall under glass if supported.

Mentzelia *see* EUCNIDE

Mesembryanthemum *Aizoaceae*
A large and varied family of succulent plants from South Africa and elsewhere. Some are shrubby plants with brilliant daisy flowers that are useful in the sunny conservatory with a dry atmosphere. The correct naming of these plants has overcome almost everyone.

CULTIVATION. Pot in spring in 3 parts J.I.P. 2 to 1 part coarse sand. Water freely in summer but allow the soil to dry between waterings. Keep all but dry in winter. Cuttings root easily and are best taken after flowering and only the young plants kept through the winter.

SPECIES TO GROW. *M. roseum* (syn. *Lampranthus roseum*) is the most often seen shrubby kind, brilliant dark pink flowers.

Metrosideros *see* CALLISTEMON

Mexican Coral Drops *see* BESSERA

Microsperma *see* Eucnide

Mignonette *see* Reseda

Milla *Liliaceae*
Unusual Mexican bulbous plant with a number of pure white scented flowers on a 2-foot stem in late summer.
MWT 7° C. (45° F.)

Cultivation. These bulbs can be planted out of doors in late spring and stored indoors in the winter in dry sand but they are better suited to the cool greenhouse. Plant three to a 6-inch pot in J.I.P. 2. Dry off gradually after flowering and store quite dry through the winter either in their pots or in dry sand, preferably in a temperature around 13° C. (55° F.). They are good for cutting.

Species to grow. *M. biflora*, white, late summer, 2 feet.

Mimosa *see* Acacia

Mimulus (*Diplacus* and Musk) *Scrophulariaceae*
Evergreen shrubby plant from California with an endless succession of trumpet flowers. There are also small herbaceous hybrids with attractive spotted flowers.

Cultivation. Pot *M. glutinosus* in spring in J.I.P. 2 or soil-less compost and re-pot annually. Keep in full sun and water well in summer. Train up a cane or other support. Prune to keep it in shape in February or March. It can be kept bushy by hard pruning if preferred. Increase by cuttings of firm young shoots in spring or summer in a propagating frame or under mist. Various hybrid musks grown as half-hardy annuals are easy and attractive plants in small pots at the edge of a capillary bench. Otherwise put charcoal in the soil and stand the pots in saucers of water in warm weather.

Species to grow. *M. glutinosus* (syn. *Diplacus glutinosus*), apricot and variety *puniceus*, orange-red, summer and autumn, up to 5 feet.

Dwarf hybrid mimulus with large spotted flowers in various colours, 6-9 inches.

Mina *see* QUAMOCLIT

Mind your own business *see* HELXINE

Mitraria *Gesneriaceae*
Nearly hardy evergreen climbing shrub from Chile with pendant orange-scarlet tubular flowers that can be grown in a cool, partially shady greenhouse with a humid atmosphere in summer.

CULTIVATION. Pot in March in 2 parts turfy peat to 1 of sand. Water freely in spring and summer but give much less water in winter. Feed regularly in summer. Increase by cuttings of young shoots in summer.

SPECIES TO GROW. *M. coccinea*, orange-scarlet, summer.

Monstera *Araceae*
Mexican climbing plants with slit and holed leaves that are grown as house-plants but become too large for the home.

MWT 10° C. (50° F.)

CULTIVATION. I have grown *Monstera deliciosa* well below this temperature although it is not advisable, particularly after life indoors. It only makes new growth in warm conditions. Increase by seed (which is slow) or by a cutting made of the top of an old plant. Both require as much heat as you can muster.

SPECIES TO GROW. *M. deliciosa* (syn. *Philodendron pertusum*) is the hardiest and can produce edible fruit; *M. pertusa* 'Borsigiana' is a smaller plant and the one now commonly sold as a house-plant.

Moon Cacti *see* SELENICEREUS

Morning Glory *see* IPOMOEA

Musk *see* MIMULUS

Naegelia *see* SMITHIANTHA

Nandina *Berberidaceae*
A decorative bamboo-like plant that is hardy in many districts but can be useful in the very cool conservatory.

CULTIVATION. Plant in rich, moist soil in the greenhouse border in spring. Increase by cuttings of ripened shoots in sand in a propagating frame in early autumn.

SPECIES TO GROW. *N. domestica* 'Purpurea', pinnate leaves tinged red in spring and autumn, panicles of white flowers, 2–6 feet.

Narcissus (Daffodil) *Amaryllidaceae*
Easily grown hardy plants that are nevertheless welcome under glass in early spring. They flower some three weeks earlier than outdoors even without heat and are best grown with only a minimum of artificial heat.

CULTIVATION. Pot in August or September in J.I.P. 2. Virtually any compost can be used. They do not like forcing and can be kept in a cold frame and only brought into the greenhouse after Christmas. My own plan is to grow new or expensive kinds indoors the first year giving them good soil and plenty of room in large pots and then to plant out the whole potful as it stands in May. The usual method is to water until the leaves die down and then keep dry until planting time in the autumn. For maximum show indoors two staggered layers of bulbs may be potted one above the other.

SPECIES TO GROW. One can get bulbs that have been raised in Great Britain, Holland or Ireland and consulting bulb catalogues is a recurring joy. Those listed below are good garden varieties that are particularly suitable for growing in pots, but there are hundreds to choose from. They are of all types and listed under their official classification numbers where you will find them in catalogues.

  1a. 'Dawson City', 'Golden Harvest', 'Winter Gold'
  1b. 'Bonython', 'Queen of the Bicolours'

1c. 'Beersheba', 'Mrs. E. H. Krelage', 'Scapa'
2a. 'Carbineer', 'Carlton', 'Havelock', 'Scarlet Elegance'
2b. 'John Evelyn', 'Daisy Schäffer', 'Signal Light'
2c. 'White Nile'
5b. 'Silver Chimes'
6a. 'February Gold', 'Peeping Tom'
7b. 'Cherie', 'Trevithian'
8. 'Bridal Crown' (double), 'Geranium', 'Scarlet Gem'
9. 'Actaea'

Nasturtium *see* TROPAEOLUM

Neanthe *see* CHAMAEDOREA

Nemesia *Scrophulariaceae*
Beautiful South African half-hardy annuals grown for bedding but decorative under glass.

CULTIVATION. Sow in March for summer bedding and from April to June for late summer and autumn flowering in pots. If sown in September they can be overwintered to flower in spring in MWT 7° C. (45° F.).

SPECIES TO GROW. Hybrids of *N. strumosa*, in many colours including 'Blue Gem', brilliant clear blue; 'Fire King', scarlet; also 'Carnival' mixture with large flowers on compact plants, and 'Suttonii' in separate colours or mixed. All 8 inches to 1 foot.

Nemophila (Californian Bluebell) *Hydrophyllaceae*
Quick-growing North American hardy annual trailing plant.

CULTIVATION. Sow thinly in 5-inch pots of J.I.P. 1 or soil-less compost in September in a cold frame and bring into the greenhouse in October. Water sparingly through the winter. They will flower in early spring or in June from a spring sowing.

SPECIES TO GROW. *N. menziesii* (syn. *N. insignis*), bright blue, trailing.

Neoregelia *Bromeliaceae*
Epiphytic plants from Brazil grown as house-plants. They usually have rosettes of shiny leaves that go scarlet in the centre at flowering time although the flowers themselves are not conspicuous.
MWT 10° C. (50° F.)

CULTIVATION. Keep the central cup full of water (rain water is best). These strange plants mostly grow on trees in nature and can be grown fixed to pieces of wood or branches with copper wire as well as in pots. The roots must be in a suitable compost encased in sphagnum moss if on wood. Compost as for AECHMEA, which see. Increase by detaching offsets and rooting them in as high a temperature as possible. Keep the roots nearly dry in winter but the cup filled. Hanging plants will need frequent dipping or syringing in hot weather. Shade from the end of March to the end of September.

SPECIES TO GROW. *N. carolinae tricolor*, showy ivory-striped leaves, rose-tinted in strong light and centre turning carmine; *N. marechatii*, green leaves, flushed wine red and centre turning crimson; *N. meyendorfii*, pale green leaves and pink centre; *N. spectabilis*, crimson tipped and sometimes flecked leaves and purple centre. With all these plants the centre of the rosette changes colour as flowering time approaches. The flowers are not showy and appear in the water in the central vase. The main rosette is apt to die after flowering, leaving sideshoots. Many other species are becoming available as bromeliads increase in popularity.

Nephrolepis *see* FERNS

Nerine *Amaryllidaceae*
Handsome and easy South African bulbous plants flowering in the autumn. MWT 7° C. (45° F.)

CULTIVATION. Pot during resting period in July or August and re-pot only every four years or so. Leave the neck and shoulder of the bulb exposed, and pot firmly in 4-inch pots using J.I.P. 2. Give

The trumpet flowers of a shrubby Datura are often 7 or 8 inches long

Passiflora × *allardii* is a handsome Passion Flower

Collecting cacti can become an absorbing hobby

The sculptured leaves of *Cotyledon undulata* are its greatest attraction

no water until growth shows. The flower stem should appear first in September or even late August. Water freely when growth is active until the leaves turn yellow in May, when the plants should be dried off gradually and kept completely dry until growth shows again. At the first sign of growth stand the pots in water and soak to moisten soil thoroughly. Then treat as before. Summer dryness in full sunshine is essential to success. If the roots are not disturbed, the bulbs can be put into a larger pot after flowering. They do best when crowded but must be fed when in active growth. Add a little bonemeal to the compost when re-potting, which is normally done in the resting period.

SPECIES TO GROW. *N. flexuosa alba*, white flowers on a tall stem; *N. sarniensis* (Guernsey Lily), scarlet, and its many beautiful hybrids in a variety of colours. The 'Borde Hill Hybrids' are outstanding.

Nerium (Oleander; Rose Bay) *Apocynaceae*
Attractive and easily grown evergreen shrubs from the Mediterranean region with fragrant flowers in summer. Every part of the plant is very poisonous.

CULTIVATION. They grow quickly from seed but the best kinds are increased by cuttings of well-ripened shoots. These can be rooted in water in summer and then potted up. Pot or plant in spring in J.I.P. 3 or other rich compost. Water copiously from May to September but very little from November to March. Unless the ventilation is very good they need slight shade in summer under glass. They start flowering at a height of 2 feet but ultimately become tree-like. They can stand outside in tubs in summer. To ensure flowering it is necessary to remove small sideshoots if they appear just below the flower buds before these have expanded. Feed during summer and prune lightly immediately after flowering. Flowers develop from the previous year's shoots.

SPECIES TO GROW. Hybrids of *N. oleander*, with single or double flowers, crimson, rose, white or yellow, June to October, 6–12 feet.

Nicotiana (Tobacco Plant) *Solanaceae*
Perennials from Brazil grown as annuals for their very sweetly scented flowers.

CULTIVATION. Sow in March or April, prick out into 3-inch pots and soon re-pot in fairly large pots as they grow fast and need a lot of water. Feed when flowers are developing and shade from hot sun.

SPECIES TO GROW. *N. affinis* (syn. *N. alata*), white, very fragrant, 3 feet, and hybrids that are shorter and sometimes less fragrant, from white to dark crimson and purple. The 'Sensation' hybrids do not close in daylight. All flower from July onwards, 15 inches to 2½ feet.

Nidularium *Bromeliaceae*
Almost indistinguishable from NEOREGELIA, which see.
MWT 10° C. (50° F.)

SPECIES TO GROW. *N. innocentii*, large rosette of dark green leaves flecked purple and with purple reverse. Centre turns crimson and small flowers barely emerge from the water in central cup.

Nierembergia *Solanaceae*
A perennial from the Argentine grown as a half-hardy annual. It has a profusion of violet-blue cup-shaped flowers.

CULTIVATION. They can be grown in an alpine pan in J.I.P. 2 or in soil-less or other compost in 4-inch pots on a capillary bench when they will be considerably taller. Sow thinly in March or April and reduce seedlings to three per 4-inch pot or thereabouts. If sown later they will probably begin flowering the following March. Shade when in flower. They can be cut back in autumn and kept fairly dry in winter to bloom a second year. Cuttings can be rooted in August.

SPECIES TO GROW. *N. caerulea* (syn. *N. hippomanica*), violet-blue, summer, 8–15 inches.

Norfolk Island Pine *see* ARAUCARIA

Notocactus *Cactaceae*
Attractive cacti from Brazil and Uruguay.

CULTIVATION. Pot in spring using 3 parts J.I.P. 1 to 1 part gritty material. Best grown in half shade in summer. Water sparingly at all times.

SPECIES TO GROW. *N. apricus*, yellow; *N. leninghausii*, pretty ginger spines, yellow flowers when mature, ultimately tall; *N. ottonis*, free-flowering, yellow; *N. tabularis*, free-flowering, yellow and red flowers.

Ochna *Ochnaceae*
Deciduous flowering shrub from South Africa grown for its ornamental fruit. MWT 10° C. (50° F.)

CULTIVATION. A peaty compost with sand and free drainage suits these plants. Increase by cuttings of half-ripe shoots in summer.

SPECIES TO GROW. *O. serrulata* (syn. *O. multiflora*), racemes of yellow flowers in spring followed by black fruits surrounded by a red calyx.

Odontoglossum *Orchidaceae*
A fairly tough epiphytic orchid from Guatemala with very large flowers in autumn and winter. It would like a higher temperature but is possible with MWT 7° C. (45° F.).

CULTIVATION. Grow in 2 parts osmunda fibre and 1 part sphagnum moss and re-pot every two or three years in spring when growth has started. Shade from the end of February to the end of September. Reduce watering after flowering and keep quite dry in December and January. Start watering again the moment new growth shows but allow to get nearly dry between waterings.

SPECIES TO GROW. *O. grande*, yellow marked with chestnut-brown, autumn and winter, 6–9 inches.

Oleander *see* NERIUM

Oliveranthus *see* ECHEVERIA

Ophiopogon (Japanese Hyacinth) *Liliaceae*
Dwarf perennial foliage plant with variegated strap-shaped leaves. Useful ground-cover in greenhouse bed.

CULTIVATION. Grow in any ordinary compost and increase by division of the roots. It is difficult to be sure which variety one has, but the only one I have seen offered commercially is *O. jaburan* 'Variegatus'. There seem to be forms with yellow striped, and with white striped, leaves, the former having purple, and the latter white, flowers. They like moisture in the summer and can be used outdoors then, but keep rather drier in the winter and re-pot in March only when the roots are crowded.

SPECIES TO GROW. *O. jaburan*, of which there are various forms with white to lilac flowers like small hyacinths in summer and leaves striped with white or yellow.

Opuntia (Prickly Pear) *Cactaceae*
Cacti, some of which grow large and make handsome specimens.

CULTIVATION. Pot in March in a porous compost such as J.I.P. 1 or 2 with added gritty material. Use pots of reasonable size unless you wish to keep the plants small, and re-pot at least every other year in spring. From the end of October until the middle of March keep dry if the temperature is below 7° C. (45° F.) and otherwise only water enough to prevent the plants shrivelling. Grow in full sun. Increase by using one or two pads as cuttings in spring. Root them in sand. Only mature plants flower. Water freely in summer but allow the compost to dry between waterings.

SPECIES TO GROW. *O. basilaris*, no spines, large deep purple flowers; *O. leucotricha*, long white hairy spines, yellow flowers, *O. microdasys* (Rabbit's ears), pretty small pads dotted with yellow or white tufts of bristles; *O. santa-rita*, thin round blue-green pads and yellow flowers.

Orange *see* CITRUS

Organ-pipe Cactus *see* LEMAIREOCEREUS

Ornithogalum *Liliaceae*
Bulbous plants from the Mediterranean region and South Africa, the first with fragrant and the second with very long-lasting flowers.

CULTIVATION. Pot *O. arabicum* August to November 1 inch deep and three to a 6-inch pot of J.I.P. 2 or similar compost. Water moderately and keep in a sunny position. When the leaves turn yellow keep dry until growth starts again. Re-pot annually. Treat *O. thyrsoides* similarly, but plant when available (before April). This is known as the Chincherinchee after the sound made by the flower heads rustling in the wind. The petals are dry and long-lasting.

SPECIES TO GROW. *O. arabicum*, white with black centre on a 2-foot stalk, spring; *O. thyrsoides* (Chincherinchee), raceme of white flowers, and variety *aureum*, yellow, summer, about 18 inches.

Osteospermum *see* DIMORPHOTHECA

Pachycereus *see* LEMAIREOCEREUS

Pachyphytum *Crassulaceae*
Mexican succulent plants with globular leaves covered with white bloom and bell flowers similar to Echeveria. MWT 7° C. (45° F.)

CULTIVATION. Treat like ECHEVERIA to which they are closely related. Indeed, crosses made between them are called Pachyveria.

SPECIES TO GROW. *P. bracteosum*, greyish-white, sugar-plum leaves, bright red flowers on 8–12-inch stalks; *P. oviferum*, mealy leaves like sugar almonds, reddish flowers.

Palms *Palmaceae*
When young, palms are foliage plants that can be kept in small pots. Although slow-growing most are ultimately large and prefer a warm greenhouse. MWT 10° C. (50° F.)

CULTIVATION. Palms need considerable heat for seed to germinate and are delicate in the early stages. In general it is better to buy young plants. Re-pot yearly in late spring without disturbing the ball of soil. A mixture of equal quantities of fibrous loam, either peat or leafmould, and sand is suitable. Feed regularly in summer and also shade. They appreciate spraying in hot weather. There are hundreds of palms from all parts of the world. Those listed below are as suitable as any in cool conditions and likely to be available.

SPECIES TO GROW. *Chamaedorea elegans bella* (syn. *Neanthe bella*) is the Parlour Palm, and tender, see CHAMAEDOREA; *Chamaerops fortunei* and *C. humilis* are almost hardy, see under CHAMAEROPS; *Jubaea spectabilis*, fairly hardy from Chile; *Kentia belmoreana* (syn. *Howea belmoreana*) is the Curly Palm, and *K. forsteriana* (syn. *Howea forsteriana*) is the Thatch leaf Palm—both like as much heat as you can give them; *Phoenix canariensis* (syn. *Phoenix jubae*) is a native of the Canary Islands and similar to *P. dactylifera*, the Date Palm, which is sometimes raised from a stone; *P. roebelenii* is the most graceful dwarf palm and should have suckers removed from its base if they develop; *P. rupicola* is similar but ultimately large.

Pancratium *see* HYMENOCALLIS

Parochetus *Leguminosae*
Almost hardy prostrate perennial plant from Nepal. It has clover leaves and blue pea flowers and can be used for covering soil under the staging.

CULTIVATION. This plant spreads very rapidly and can be increased by removing rooted pieces in the autumn. It can also be raised from seed sown in the spring.

SPECIES TO GROW. *P. communis* (Shamrock Pea), blue, 3 inches.

Parodia *Cactaceae*
Small round free-blooming cacti. MWT 7° C. (45° F.)

CULTIVATION. Treat as NOTOCACTUS.

SPECIES TO GROW. *P. aureispina*, golden spines, yellow flowers; *P. maassii*, orange-red flowers; *P. sanguiniflora*, plant woolly on top, blood-red flowers.

Parrot's Bill *see* CLIANTHUS

Passiflora (Passion Flower) *Passifloraceae*
Vigorous tendril climbers only really suitable where there is a lot of space overhead although they can be grown in tubs for a time.
MWT 7° C. (45° F.) except for *P. caerulea*

CULTIVATION. Plant in March in fibrous loam with plenty of peat and sand. The roots should be restricted to encourage flowering. Water freely in summer and keep fairly dry in winter. Prune to within two buds of the old wood in winter and remove weak shoots in spring. Increase by cuttings of young shoots with a heel in spring in a propagating frame.

SPECIES TO GROW. *P.* × *allardii*, white shaded pink with purple centre; *P. antioquiensis* (syn. *Tacsonia van volxemii*), large rich rose-red flowers; *P. caerulea*, white with blue centre and variety 'Constance Elliot', ivory white; *P. mixta quitensis* (syn. *Tacsonia mixta quitensis*), long-tubed pink to orange-red flowers in late summer; *P. racemosa*, racemes of vivid scarlet flowers.

Pelargonium (Geranium) *Geraniaceae*
The greenhouse zonal pelargoniums (commonly called geraniums) flower almost continuously and are most rewarding plants. There are also miniature and ornamental leaved cultivars. Regal pelargoniums, with large velvety blooms, are very showy for a shorter season and these, too, can be compact plants. The ivy-leaved kinds can climb or trail, while scented-leaved and other species offer infinite variety. MWT 7° C. (45° F.) to 10° C. (50° F.) ideal

CULTIVATION. Preferably buy new plants in April or May and re-pot in 5-inch pots using J.I.P. 2 or 3. Increase by cuttings which root very easily in any sandy mixture, particularly in late summer. Choose the firm-growing tips of healthy plants and cut off with a razor blade just below the third joint. Insert cuttings singly in 2-inch pots or round the edge of larger pots. Many people remove all but the top two developing leaves. Shade them from hot sun but keep on the open staging. They root quite well out of doors in a shaded spot at this time of year. Re-pot individually in small pots when well rooted and pinch out the growing point to make them bushy. Water fairly freely in summer but keep rather dry in winter and never allow to get sodden. Old plants can be pruned back into shape, but young plants are the most satisfactory. With a temperature of 10° C. (50° F.) or more and sufficient light zonal pelargoniums will flower all the year. For good winter flowering plants are prevented from flowering in the summer. The colouring is apt to be poor without supplementary lighting.

Regal pelargoniums: these flower mainly between May and July although they will probably start in April if the MWT is above 4° C. (40° F.). Flowering can be adjusted somewhat by removing buds and pinching, or by rooting cuttings at different times from March to September. June and July are the best months for taking cuttings. Treat as described in the previous paragraph and pot on as they grow, to flower in 6- or 7-inch pots. Feed when the flowers are forming. After flowering one can stand or plunge them outdoors in a sunny position to ripen the growths. Then cut them back to within three buds of the old wood and put them in a frame or under the staging. Do not water but syringe occasionally until growth starts again. Then re-pot, carefully removing enough of the old compost to enable them to fit into a size smaller pot. Keep rather dry through the winter and re-pot again into larger pots in the early spring. This saves space and prevents overwatering in the winter. Regal pelargoniums are very attractive to whitefly.

SPECIES TO GROW. There are hundreds of kinds and this is a personal choice.

Hybrid Zonals: single flowers 'Beatrice Clay', orange-salmon;

'Beatrix Little', currant-red, compact plant; 'Caledonia' (syn. 'Mrs. Sears'), pale mauve-pink; 'Caledonian Maiden', dark cherry-red, good winter bloomer; 'Doris Moore', deep cherry-red, neat growth; 'Elizabeth Cartwright', carmine-red; 'Jane Campbell', deep orange; 'John Cross', rose-pink; 'Mauretania', palest pink with darker zone; 'Prince Regent', salmon-pink; 'Staplegrove Fancy', white suffused reddish-pink; 'Target', scarlet. *Double flowers* 'A. M. Mayne', magenta-purple; 'Dagata', pale rosy-mauve; 'Colonel Drabbe', turkey-red with white centre; 'Dodd's super double', deep pink, very vigorous; 'Gustav Emich', guardsman-scarlet; 'Mrs. Lawrence', pale pink; 'Orangesonne', orange; 'Princess Alexandra', shell-pink with a silver leaf with white edge. 'Irene' varieties are very free-blooming and vigorous for indoor or bedding. They are American introductions. 'Irene', crimson (mother of all 'Irenes'); 'La Jolla', medium crimson; 'Party Dress', palest pink; 'Modesty', white (sometimes slightly pink); 'Rose Irene', rose-pink, white eye; 'Toyon', scarlet.

Miniature Zonals: to 8 inches 'Celia', rose-pink with white eye; 'Fleurette', deep salmon; 'Granny Hewitt', crimson; 'Kleine Liebling' (syn. 'Little Darling'), cherry pink, and variegated leaf cultivar also; 'Red Black Vesuvius', scarlet, black leaves; 'Sunstar', orange; 'Virgo', white.

Ivy-leaved Pelargoniums 'Butterflies', cyclamen-purple; 'Galilee', the double rose-pink window-box geranium; 'La France', double imperial purple; 'L'Elegante', leaves variegated cream and purple, single flowers, white with purple feathering; 'Lilac Gem', double pale mauve, dwarf neat plant. Plants with striking white-veined leaves introduced from Australia are sold as 'Crocodile' and 'White Mesh' or sometimes 'Alligator', 'Sussex Lace' and 'Fishnet'.

Hybrid Ivies (between zonal and ivy-leaved in habit) 'Achievement', double, bright cherry; 'Millfield Gem', double, pale pink with darker markings.

Regal Pelargoniums 'Applause', pink and frilly; 'Aztec', white blotched with strawberry and brown; 'Black Magic', nearly black; 'Carisbrooke' (syn. 'Ballerina'), large ruffled flowers, pale pink, blotched carmine; 'Grand Slam', bright cherry veined and blotched purple; 'Grandma Fischer', salmon-orange with dark blotches; 'Lavender Grand Slam', lavender with purple markings; 'Rogue', mahogany-crimson, compact plant; 'White Glory', a good white.

Miniature Regals 'Catford Belle', rosy-purple with darker markings; 'Sancho Panza', dark purple with paler edges.

Species Some wild species are more interesting than decorative, but the following are attractive: *P. echinatum*, variable white, pink or purple flowers with darker blotches and *P.* × *echinatum* 'Miss Stapleton', with more vivid flowers; *P. graveolens* 'Lady Plymouth', which combines prettily cut and silver variegated leaves with delightful scent and small pink flowers, is one of my favourite plants; *P.* × 'Kewense', narrow petalled crimson flowers in summer; *P. violarium* (syn. *P. tricolor*), attractive grey-leaved plant with pansy-like flowers in summer.

There are many scented-leaved species and zonal pelargoniums with brilliantly coloured leaves which should be smelt and seen before choosing.

Pentapterygium *Ericaceae*
Epiphytic shrubs from the Himalayas that can be grown in hanging baskets or pots. MWT 7° C. (45° F.)

CULTIVATION. I have not tried these plants but a lime-free and very peaty compost with some added sand is said to suit them. Increase by cuttings rooted in sand in warm conditions.

SPECIES TO GROW. *P. serpens*, bright red hanging bell flowers; *P. rugosum*, white, marbled purple or red, followed by purple berries; also *P.* 'Ludgvan', intermediate between the two species with pale pink flowers, veined deeper pink, and pale purple berries; all are 1–3 feet with sparse arching branches.

Persea (Avocado Pear) *Lauraceae*
The stones of avocado pears will grow into pleasant small trees with laurel-shaped leaves but grow too large for the greenhouse long before they bear fruit. MWT 10° C. (50° F.)

Peristrophe *see* JUSTICIA

Peruvian Daffodil *see* HYMENOCALLIS

Petunia *Solanaceae*
Effective half-hardy perennials grown as annuals mainly for summer bedding. They flower continuously from June.

CULTIVATION. They are normally sown in March or early April, preferably with the extra warmth of a propagating frame or warmed bench. They are plants that like sunshine but need to be kept constantly moist at the roots. They do very well on capillary benches. For bedding sow in early April and plant outdoors at the end of May or the beginning of June. If kept under glass pot singly and give support or allow to trail.

SPECIES TO GROW. Single and double and F_1 hybrids in many lovely colours, from 9 inches to 2 feet. The single large-flowered fringed types and the small F_1 double hybrids are good with glass protection.

Phacelia *Hydrophyllaceae*
Easily grown hardy annual from California with gentian-blue bell flowers.

CULTIVATION. Sow where they are to flower in September, March or April; I think thin sowing in a 5-inch pot of J.I.P. 2 or similar compost and reducing the seedlings to three is a good idea. Keep them in good light and water very cautiously in winter. They flower in March from an autumn sowing.

SPECIES TO GROW. *P. campanularia*, gentian-blue, spring or summer according to sowing time, 6–9 inches.

Pharbitis (Blue Dawn Flower) *Convolvulaceae*
Beautiful very quick-growing evergreen twining climber that becomes deciduous in a cool greenhouse.   MWT 7° C. (45° F.)

CULTIVATION. Plant in the greenhouse border or grow in a large pot of J.I.P. 2. It is closely related to morning glory but perennial.

Water freely in summer. Increase by cuttings of sideshoots in a propagating frame or by layering. It can also be raised from seed. It grows too strongly for the very small greenhouse.

SPECIES TO GROW. *P. learii* (syn. *Ipomoea learii*), brilliant dark blue flowers turning to magenta, late summer and autumn. *P. tricolor* see IPOMOEA.

Phlox *Polemoniaceae*
Half-hardy annuals that can be grown effectively in pots.

CULTIVATION. Sow seed in late summer and autumn for spring flowering and in spring for summer flowering. Treat as NEMESIA.

SPECIES TO GROW. *P. drummondii*, the compact hybrids are the most convenient for pots, all shades crimson to white, scarlet and mauve, 6–12 inches.

Phoenix *see* PALMS

Phyllocactus *see* EPIPHYLLUM

Pig-a-back Plant *see* TOLMIEA

Pimelea *Thymelaeaceae*
Small and free-flowering evergreen shrub from Australia. These were popular conservatory plants in Victorian times but only one species seems to be available today. MWT 7° C. (45° F.)

CULTIVATION. Grow in pots of sandy peaty soil or lime-free J.I.P. 2. Re-pot after flowering. They do not use much water but the soil must never be really dry even in winter. After flowering remove dead flowers and cut back shoots up to two-thirds of their length to keep the plants shapely. They get leggy very easily and it is difficult to buy a well-shaped plant. They can be plunged outdoors after flowering until late September. Increase by cuttings of new shoots in spring.

SPECIES TO GROW. *P. ferruginea* (syn. *P. decussata*), heads of rose-pink tubular flowers at the tips of the branches, spring and early summer, 1½–2½ feet.

Pittosporum *Pittosporaceae*
A family of evergreen shrubs with attractive foliage that are used by florists and hardy in warm districts.

CULTIVATION. Pot in spring in J.I.P. 2. Water freely in summer and less in winter. Increase by cuttings in propagating frame in summer. They can be put outdoors in a sheltered position from June to October. *P. eugenioides* and *P. tobira* are grown as houseplants when small, but all will ultimately become large bushes or trees.

SPECIES TO GROW. *P. eugenioides*, pale green crinkled leaves, and *P. e.* 'Variegatum', with white markings; *P. tenuifolium* 'Silver Queen', silver variegated wavy leaves; *P. tobira* (syn. *P. chinense*), whorls of glossy leaves, orange-scented cream flowers in summer, and *P. t.* 'Variegatum', with silver markings on the leaves.

Platycerium (Stag's-horn Fern) *Rubiaceae*
Strange epiphytic fern from the temperate parts of Australia.
MWT 10° C. (50° F.)

CULTIVATION. As it grows on trees in nature it can be hung up wired to a piece of wood with a lump of rough peat and sphagnum moss in equal quantities over its roots. It will grow in any orchid compost and can also be grown in a pot or a basket. It must be kept moist but not sodden, and shaded from sunlight.

SPECIES TO GROW. *P. alcicorne* (syn. *P. bifurcatum*), slow-growing to a considerable size.

Pleione *Orchidaceae*
The easiest orchid for cool conditions. Small terrestrial orchids with beautiful flowers on short stalks before the leaves develop in winter and early spring.

CULTIVATION. Pot several together in pans or half-pots. The pseudobulbs should be less than half buried and may need support until rooted. I have grown them without difficulty in a variety of composts that were open and freely drained. A recommended mixture is 2 parts loam, 1 part peat, 1 part sphagnum moss and ½ part sharp sand. Re-pot when they become crowded directly after flowering. Water until leaves die down naturally and keep almost dry in winter until growth starts again. Shade in summer. Oddly enough they do well on capillary benches except when dry in winter.

SPECIES TO GROW. All are very similar and the naming is sometimes confused. *P. formosana* (syn. *P. pricei*), varying shades of rosy-lilac with fringed cream lip spotted with brown. *P. hookeriana* and *P. maculata* are sometimes offered. All 4–6 inches.

Pleroma *see* TIBOUCHINA

Plumbago *Plumbaginaceae*
A favourite climbing shrub from South Africa with pale blue or white phlox-like flowers in summer.   MWT 7° C. (45° F.)

CULTIVATION. This adaptable plant can be trained against a wall or grown in pots and kept shrubby. Pot or plant in March and re-pot annually in 6–9-inch pots of J.I.P. 3. Water freely and syringe in summer but keep pretty dry at the roots from October to March. Young plants should be pinched back but let the climbers grow and only prune after flowering. Climbers can be kept to a single stem like a vine and all plants can be pruned quite hard if necessary. Increase by cuttings of semi-matured shoots with bottom-heat in spring and summer.

SPECIES TO GROW. *P. capensis*, pale blue and *P. c.* 'Alba', white.

Poinsettia *see* EUPHORBIA

Polianthes (Tuberose) *Amaryllidaceae*
Bulbous plant from Mexico with sweet-smelling white flowers.

They can be forced at various seasons but if planted when available in spring will flower in late autumn. Good cut flower. Not a pretty plant. MWT 7° C. (45° F.)

CULTIVATION. Pot singly and deeply in 5-inch pots of J.I.P. 3 and do not water until growth shows. Keep them near the glass. Discard after flowering.

SPECIES TO GROW. *P. tuberosa*, double flowered form, up to 3 feet.

Polygala *Polygalaceae*
Easily grown South African evergreen shrub with pale green leaves and magenta pea flowers intermittently.

CULTIVATION. Re-pot in March in J.I.P. 3 with added peat or a compost of 2 parts peat and 1 part each of fibrous loam and sand. Cut back after flowering. Water freely in summer when it likes a moist atmosphere. Keep just moist in winter. It can be plunged outdoors in half shade from July to the end of September. Increase by cuttings about 3 inches long in propagating frame in spring.

SPECIES TO GROW. *P. myrtifolia grandiflora* 'Dalmaisiana', 2–5 feet.

Pomegranate *see* PUNICA

Poor Man's Orchid *see* SCHIZANTHUS

Portulacaria (Elephant Bush) *Portulaceae*
Succulent shrub from South Africa that loses its leaves in drought or cold. It has nearly black stems and small shiny succulent leaves.
MWT 7° C. (45° F.)

CULTIVATION. This plant is easily grown in any light porous compost. Cuttings of young shoots root readily. It flourishes in a hot dry atmosphere which can be useful. I like its odd artificial look.

SPECIES TO GROW. *P. afra*, ultimately a tall bush; and its variegated form.

Pot Marigold *see* CALENDULA

Prairie Gentian *see* EUSTOMA

Prickly Pear *see* OPUNTIA

Primula *Primulaceae*
Invaluable plants that are raised from seed to flower all through the winter and spring in the cool greenhouse. MWT 7° C. (45° F.) except for *P.* × *kewensis* and *P. malacoides* which can be grown with frost protection only.

CULTIVATION. Sow in pans of J. I. seed compost or similar compost, prick out as soon as possible and pot singly in 3-inch pots of J.I.P. 1 about a month later. Keep as cool as possible in summer. A partially shady place outdoors is suitable if watering is not neglected. In September re-pot into flowering pots of 5 or 6 inches, being very careful to keep the neck of the plant at the same level as before and not to bury it. The pots must be in the greenhouse before the first frost. Water with care avoiding wetting the crown of the plant and remove decayed leaves at once. *P.* × *kewensis* should be sown in March, *P. obconica* and *P. sinensis* in April or May and *P. malacoides* from April to June as it is the quickest to mature. A few people are sensitive to one or more primula species and suffer severe skin reactions after handling the plants.

SPECIES TO GROW. *P.* × *kewensis*, buttercup yellow, winter and spring; *P. malacoides*, lavender, and hybrids from white and pale pink to crimson, winter and spring; *P. obconica*, hybrids, shades of crimson, blue, pink, salmon and white, mainly spring; *P. sinensis*, hybrids in all shades of crimson, rose, blue, white and orange and its 'stellata' varieties with star-shaped flowers, winter and spring. They are all from 9–12 inches tall.

Prostanthera (Australian Mint Bush) *Labiatae*
Evergreen shrubs from Australia with aromatic foliage and lilac or purple flowers in winter and spring.

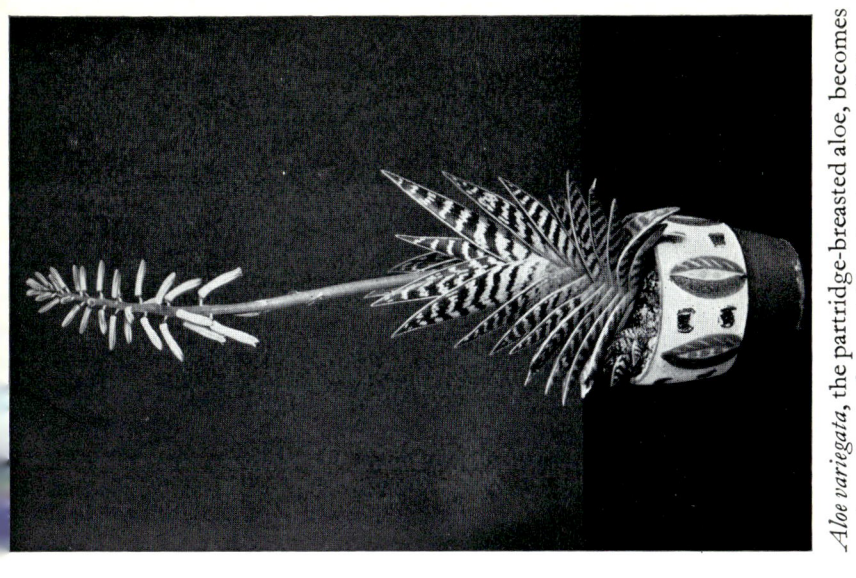

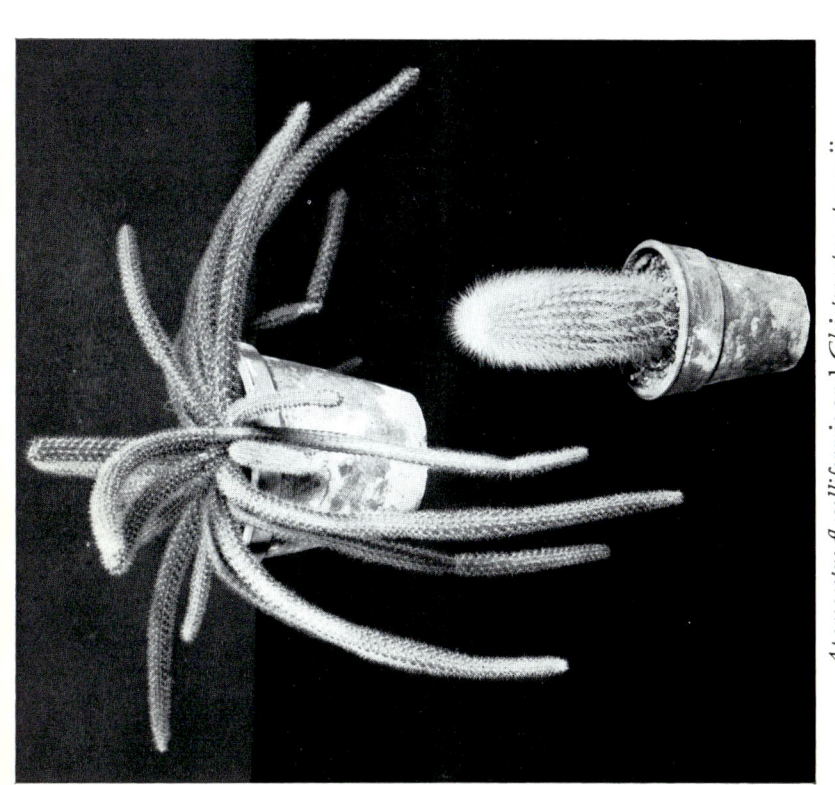

Aporocactus flagelliformis and *Cleistocactus straussii*

Aloe variegata, the partridge-breasted aloe, becomes the colour of a partridge in strong sunlight

A collection of succulents

Aeonium haworthii   *Sedum morganianum*   *Crassula cotyledon*
        Echeveria hybrid   *Agave americana*

CULTIVATION. Grow in peaty soil in the greenhouse border or in pots of lime-free J.I.P. 2 with a little extra peat. Plant in spring and pinch young plants to make them bushy. Increase by cuttings in summer or from seed.

SPECIES TO GROW. *P. melissifolia parvifolia*, bright lilac, early spring; *P. rotundifolia*, purple, April and May, 4 feet and upwards.

Pteris *see* FERNS

Punica (Pomegranate) *Punicaceae*
The dwarf pomegranate is a very small and attractive deciduous shrub with glossy leaves and scarlet flowers in late summer.

CULTIVATION. Pot in late autumn in J.I.P. 3 or similar compost. Water freely in summer and keep in full sun. Keep only barely moist when dormant. Prune lightly after flowering. Increase by cuttings of half-ripened shoots in July, preferably with heat, or by seed in spring.

SPECIES TO GROW. *P. granatum* 'Nana', which flowers freely when only about 3 inches high, is the best in pots.

Quamoclit *Convolvulaceae*
Showy South American twining climber, grown as an annual and closely related to Pharbitis.

CULTIVATION. Sow in March in a temperature of 18° C. (65° F.). Otherwise treat as PHARBITIS, which see.

SPECIES TO GROW. *Q. lobata* (syn. *Ipomoea versicolor* and *Mina lobata*), crimson changing to orange, June to September; *Q. pennata* (Cypress Vine, syn. *Ipomoea quamoclit*), deep scarlet and variously coloured hybrids.

Rat's Tail Cactus *see* APOROCACTUS

Rebutia *Cactaceae*
Easily grown and free-flowering small cacti.

CULTIVATION. Pot in spring in compost as for CEREUS with good drainage. Water regularly from March to August and shade from hot sun. Reduce watering in autumn and give almost none from October to March. Increase by removing offsets.

SPECIES TO GROW. *R. miniscula* is the best known, scarlet flowers in March; *R. marsoneri* has yellow flowers and others are equally attractive. All bloom in spring and early summer.

Rechsteineria *Gesneriaceae*

The plant known as *Gesneria cardinalis* is now included here as well as a fascinating tuberous plant from Brazil with silver furry leaves and pale orange tubular flowers.   MWT 10° C. (50° F.)

CULTIVATION. They can be treated like the ordinary tuberous begonias. *R. leucotricha* likes a drier atmosphere and more light, and can be grown indoors. Pot up tubers singly and only half-buried in spring. Use J.I.P. 2 or a well-drained peaty mixture. Water sparingly until growing strongly and dry off in the autumn. Keep dry in their pots in a warm place until re-potting in spring.

SPECIES TO GROW. *R. cardinalis compacta* (syn. *Gesneria cardinalis compacta*), velvety green leaves and orange-scarlet flowers in summer, about 9 inches; *R. leucotricha* (Brazilian Edelweiss), a white woolly stalk with four silver leaves and a bunch of tubular flowers on top, older plants make several tiers of leaves and flowers, about 1 foot.

Rehmannia *Scrophulariaceae*

Herbacious perennial from China with showy spikes of foxglove-like flowers.

CULTIVATION. Sow seed in May, pot singly and put in flowering pots (6- or 7-inch) using J.I.P. 3 in the following March. If kept a second year they can be divided and re-potted in March. Plants can be bought in the spring. Shade in summer and water freely. Keep fairly dry in winter.

SPECIES TO GROW. *R. angulata*, red and scarlet and its hybrids, summer, 1–3 feet.

Reseda (Mignonette) *Resedaceae*
Old-fashioned annual grown for its fragrance. MWT 7° C. (45° F.)

CULTIVATION. Sow in August or September for spring flowering. Sow thinly in flowering pots of J.I.P. 2. Spring sowings will produce flowers through the summer.

SPECIES TO GROW. Improved cultivars of *R. odorata* such as 'Goliath', 'Machet' and 'Red Monarch' with reddish spikes of flowers, 1–1½ feet.

Rhipsalidopsis *Cactaceae*
Small epiphytic cactus from Brazil with flat pendant joints and pink flowers. MWT 10° C. (50° F.)

CULTIVATION. As for EPIPHYLLUM.

SPECIES TO GROW. *R. rosea*, dwarf plant, pink.

Rhipsalis (Mistletoe Cactus) *Cactaceae*
These plants have curious thin green stems, small flowers and white berries. They are shade-loving epiphytes to grow in the company of bromeliads and epiphytic plants generally.
MWT 10° C. (50° F.)

CULTIVATION. Grow in suspended pots or baskets in similar compost mixtures as for bromeliads or orchids.

SPECIES TO GROW. Choose any that attract you from among the many weird species.

Rhododendron *Ericaceae*
Evergreen winter-flowering shrubs for the large conservatory. The cool greenhouse is not warm enough for Javanese rhododendrons but the tender hybrids of Himalayan species flower in January and need greenhouse protection. For the smaller members of this family see under AZALEA.

CULTIVATION. Although not difficult these are not plants for the careless grower. They must have a humid atmosphere and regular care. They are best planted out in the greenhouse border. A suitable soil is equal parts peat, lime-free loam and coarse sand. The drainage must be very good. Plant and also re-pot when necessary immediately after flowering. If grown in pots they can be stood outdoors from June to September. Water freely from March to September, preferably with rain-water. Syringe daily in hot weather. Water carefully in winter but never allow to dry. No pruning is necessary but faded flowers must be removed.

SPECIES TO GROW. Hybrids of Himalayan rhododendrons, 'Countess of Haddington', white, flushed rose, scented; 'Fragrantissimum', white, tinged pink, scented; 'Lady Alice Fitzwilliam', white, scented. Various hardier species can also be grown, *R. thomsonii*, blood red, March, is an attractive one. A specialist nursery should be consulted.

Rhynchospermum *see* TRACHELOSPERMUM

Richardia *see* ZANTEDESCHIA

Rochea *Crassulaceae*
South African succulent sub-shrub with showy heads of scarlet flowers. It is sometimes sold as a flowering pot plant.

CULTIVATION. Grow in J.I.P. 2 with a little sharp sand added and in pots of reasonable size. Water moderately in summer and keep rather dry in winter. Old flowering stems should be reduced by two-thirds in the hope that sideshoots will flower the following year. Feed after the first year and re-pot if necessary in spring. Cuttings root easily in March but only flower in the second summer. Pinch out tips to make bushy plants. The flower stems need support. MWT 7° C. (45° F.) is ideal.

SPECIES TO GROW. *R. coccinea* (syn. *Crassula coccinea* and *Kalosanthes coccinea*), scarlet, early summer, 1 foot; *R. falcata* see CRASSULA *falcata*.

Rosa (Rose) *Rosaceae*
Although hardy, roses can be grown under glass for perfect and

lasting blooms in early spring. The Fairy Rose flowers in ten weeks from seed.

CULTIVATION. Purchased plants can be potted very firmly in October in J.I.P. 3 or a mixture of 3 parts turfy loam to 1 part well-rotted manure with a little sharp sand. They are best on rugosa stocks in pots, and for finest results rugosa stocks are potted in autumn and budded the following June or July. Plants raised from cuttings on their own roots are also suitable. Leave the potted plants outdoors until early or even late December unless the weather is very severe. In January prune really hard back to outside buds and water very lightly until growth starts. Then spray daily with clear water until buds show colour. Remove side buds if large blooms are wanted.

In June plunge outdoors or remove from pots and plant out without disturbing the roots and re-pot in October. They must be kept watered and occasionally fed. After the first year start feeding when buds show. Re-pot every other year. Plants from the open ground should not be forced much in their first year. Plants in pots can be bought in September. Miniature roses can be grown singly in small pots or grouped together. The Fairy Rose is easily raised from seed sown in March and treated as a half-hardy annual. Allow three plants per 5-inch pot.

SPECIES TO GROW. Consult a catalogue for full descriptions of many hybrid tea roses. The following are good under glass but they are only a selection: 'Ena Harkness', 'Ellinor Le Grice', 'Lady Sylvia', 'McGredy's Ivory', 'McGredy's Yellow', 'Ophelia', 'Picture', 'William Harvey', 'William Moore'. Floribundas are good in pots and also dwarf polyanthas and miniature roses: the Fairy Rose is sometimes called *Rosa polyantha nana*.

Rubber Plant *see* FICUS

Rose Bay *see* NERIUM

Saintpaulia (African Violet) *Gesneriaceae*
Dwarf tropical plants with dark fleshy leaves and vividly violet

flowers. The cool greenhouse is a good nursing home for sick saintpaulias in the warmer months but they really like a temperature that does not fall below 16° C. (60° F.).

CULTIVATION. This plant must have a moist atmosphere and good light but shade from sun. It is successful in centrally heated homes and under artificial lights if the air round the plant is kept moist. A suitable compost is 3 parts peat, 1 part loam and 1 part sharp sand. Keep moist but never sodden. New plants can be raised from leaf cuttings. Choose a medium-sized leaf and cut off with a razor blade. Insert the leaf stalk ½ inch deep in equal mixture of peat and sharp sand. Support the leaf with a label. Tiny plantlets will appear in time which should be grown on singly to flower about a year later. Old plants can be divided. They can also be raised from seed in warm conditions.

SPECIES TO GROW. *S. ionantha* has a multitude of cultivars with both single and double flowers in many shades of purple, mauve, pink and white. They need a temperature of 16° C. (60° F.) to thrive and flower freely for long periods.

Salpiglossis *Solanaceae*
A tall half-hardy annual from Chile with beautifully veined velvety trumpet flowers in rich colours in summer and autumn.

CULTIVATION. Sow in March or April in a temperature of 18° C. (65° F.). Pot singly in 3-inch pots, pinch out growing point and later pot on to 5-inch pots or grow three together in larger pots. They may also be sown in early August for spring flowering and kept in small pots until early in the year. Give support and water very carefully until they are growing strongly. J.I.P. 2 is a suitable compost for the flowering pots.

SPECIES TO GROW. Hybrids of *S. sinuata*, 18 inches to 3 feet.

Saxifraga *Saxifragaceae*
Easily grown plant for shady conditions. Produces innumerable plantlets on pendant stems as well as spikes of pinkish-white flowers. MWT 7° C. (45° F.)

CULTIVATION. It can be grown in hanging baskets with the plantlets hanging round it or in small pots from freshly rooted runners each year. Use any ordinary compost and water very sparingly in winter.

SPECIES TO GROW. *S. stolonifera* (syn. *S. sarmentosa*) (Mother of Thousands), and *S. s. tricolor* which is smaller and has leaves marked with white and red and needs MWT 10° C. (50° F.).

Scarborough Lily *see* VALLOTA

Schizanthus (Butterfly Flower; Poor Man's Orchid) *Solanaceae*
Half-hardy annuals from Chile with a long flowering season and showy orchid-like flowers.

CULTIVATION. Sow seed in August, preferably in a cold frame, and later pot singly. They can be flowered in 6-inch pots of J.I.P. 3 if big plants are not wanted. Keep them near the glass and support with sticks. Pinching produces bushy plants but is not essential. Final potting is done in February. They flower from March to May and will flower in August and September from a spring sowing. There is no more rewarding annual in a cool conservatory in spring.

SPECIES TO GROW. Hybrids of *S. pinnatus* (sometimes called *hybridus grandiflorus*). There are dwarf types of about 18 inches and tall growers to 4 feet. Background colours are white through mauve and pink to red shades with a variety of attractive darker markings.

Schizocentron *Melastomataceae*
Unusual herbaceous creeping plant from Mexico with brilliant magenta flowers. Suitable for hanging baskets or as ground cover for tubs of shrubs. MWT 7° C. (45° F.)

CULTIVATION. Grow in J.I.P. 2 with a little extra peat or in soilless compost. Increase by division of rooted pieces.

SPECIES TO GROW. *H. elegans* (syn. *Heeria elegans* and *Heterocentron elegans*), rosy-purple or magenta, May to June.

Schlumbergera (Christmas Cactus) *Cactaceae*
Epiphytic cacti from Brazil with showy flowers at the tips of the branches in winter. MWT 10° C. (50° F.)

CULTIVATION. These plants have flat drooping branches and are often grafted on to selinicereus. Use soil mixtures as for EPIPHYLLUM and grow in a pot small for the size of the plant, repotting every other year in May. Keep shaded in summer and moderately moist. If you are going to use it for home decoration bring indoors at the end of September. If moved about and subjected to changes of temperature when buds are forming they may drop. Christmas cacti flower from November to January in a warm room and February to April in a cool greenhouse. After flowering keep rather dry for a few weeks. Well-tended plants live for many years. They can be cut back after flowering if necessary. The cut ends should be dusted with powdered charcoal. Increase by taking cuttings two joints long, after flowering and insert three or four together in a small pot of porous compost. Treat as one plant.

SPECIES TO GROW. *S.* × *buckleyi* (syn. *S. bridgesii* but better known as *Zygocactus truncatus*) is the Christmas Cactus with brilliant carmine fuchsia-like flowers in winter and *S. gaetneri* (Easter Cactus) with dark scarlet flowers in early spring are the most often grown.

Scilla *Liliaceae*
Dwarf bulbous plants of interest in pots.

CULTIVATION. *S. sibirica* 'Spring Beauty' is absolutely hardy with brilliant blue flowers that are welcome in a poorly heated greenhouse in spring. Pot from August to November 1 inch deep and close together in J.I.P. 2 or other compost. Plunge outdoors or keep in a cool place for at least eight weeks. They can also be grown in fibre in bowls. If grown in soil and kept watered until the leaves die down they can be re-potted in the autumn or planted in the garden. *S. violacea* is a South African plant grown for its foliage. Allow bulbs to multiply in pot. Keep dry when leaves die down until growth starts in autumn.

SPECIES TO GROW. *S. sibirica* 'Spring Beauty', blue, February, 6 inches; *S. violacea*, leaves purplish blotched with green, green flowers in spring, about 6 inches.

Scirpus (*Isolepis*) *Cyperaceae*
Perennial marsh grass sometimes grown as a foliage plant. A potful looks like a mop of bright green hair.

CULTIVATION. Pot in J.I.P. 2 in March. Water very copiously in summer, moderately in winter. Grow in small pots or hanging baskets. Increase by division in March or raise from seed sown in spring.

SPECIES TO GROW. *S. cernuus* (syn. *S. gracilis* and *Isolepis gracilis*), 6 inches.

Sea Lavender *see* LIMONIUM

Sedum *Crassulaceae*
Foreign relatives of our stonecrops, particularly those from Mexico, provide some very attractive and trouble-free plants for the front of the staging or for mixed bowls. The flowers are of secondary importance.

CULTIVATION. *S. sieboldii* is herbaceous and the others evergreen succulents. Pot in spring in a porous compost such as J.I.P. 1 with a little added coarse sand. Water little from October to April and always sparingly. Increase by cuttings in summer inserted in very sandy compost. The winter temperature should not be above 10° C. (50° F.).

SPECIES TO GROW. *S. morganianum* looks like a glaucous green chain, trailing; *S. pachyphyllum*, grey-green club-shaped leaves with red tips, pale yellow flowers in spring; *S. sieboldii*, glaucous leaves, pink flowers, October, trailing, and *S. s. medio-varigatum* with yellow centres to the leaves; *S. treleasei*, blue-green leaves, pale yellow flowers, up to 1 foot.

Selaginella *Selaginellaceae*
Moss-like plants that can be used to cover ground under the staging or among ferns. They are related to ferns and need similar conditions. MWT 7° C. (45° F.)

CULTIVATION. Grow in light porous soil in shade and keep constantly moist. They can be grown in pots or hanging baskets in J.I.P. 2 with added sand and charcoal. Increase by layering the fronds at any time of year or by cuttings in the warmer months. Insert several cuttings in a pot and grow on together.

SPECIES TO GROW. *S. kraussiana* is the hardiest and comes in a variety of trailing forms. All the others need at least MWT 10° C. (50° F.).

Selenicereus (Moon Cactus) *Cactaceae*
Tall climbing or trailing cacti with narrow stems and huge flowers that open at night. MWT 7° C. (45° F.)

CULTIVATION. Treat as HYLOCEREUS. Slightly less tender. Increase by cuttings bearing aerial roots in summer.

SPECIES TO GROW. *S. grandiflorus*, white, scented, early summer; *S. macdonaldiae*, even larger white flowers, not scented, early summer.

Senecio *see* CINERARIA and KLEINIA

Setcreasea *see* TRADESCANTIA

Shamrock Pea *see* PAROCHETUS

Shrimp Plant *see* BELOPERONE

Silene *see* LYCHNIS

Silver Tree *see* LEUCADENDRON

Sinningia *Gesneriaceae*
This is the correct name of gloxinia, the popular velvety-leaved and trumpet-flowered bulbous plant. It does best in a warm greenhouse until the flowers open.

CULTIVATION. Start the tubers in small pots of light peaty soil in March in a temperature of 18° C. (65° F.). Do not quite bury the tubers and always keep just moist. Move to larger pots in the greenhouse as the weather warms up and keep shaded. They like a growing temperature of 16° C. (60° F.). Feed when buds form. Dry off gradually after flowering and store in their pots where they will not be below 10° C. (50° F.). They can be raised from seed sown early in the year but they need warm moist conditions to reach the flowering stage in the season.

SPECIES TO GROW. Hybrids of *S. speciosa* in a variety of plain, bicolor and speckled colours, up to 1 foot.

Slipper Flower *see* CALCEOLARIA

Smithiantha (*Gesneria, Naegelia*) *Gesneriaceae*
Handsome spikes of bell flowers rise above plush-covered leaves. These warm greenhouse plants can be grown if a moist atmosphere and 10° C. (50° F.) can be maintained.

CULTIVATION. Buy rhizomes in March and pot singly and just barely covered in 5-inch pots. Equal parts of leafmould, peat and loam with some sharp sand is a suitable compost or J.I.P. 2 can be used. Keep them as warm as possible and water very sparingly until the roots are growing well. Water freely when growing strongly and feed weekly when flowering begins. When they start to die down in October or later, stop watering and rest in their pots until re-potting and starting into growth in the spring. Do not store below 10° C. (50° F.).

SPECIES TO GROW. British and American cultivars should be purchased from a specialist grower. These plants are being improved all the time and come in a wide variety of warm colours, late summer and autumn, 18 inches to 2 feet.

Snapdragon *see* ANTIRRHINUM

Solanum *Solanaceae*
The little trees with orange berries sold at Christmas are *Solanum capsicastrum* (winter cherry) from Brazil. The others are climbers grown for their flowers.

CULTIVATION. Raising *S. capsicastrum* from seed is a job for the dedicated with time on their hands. Buy it and be thankful for the skills of the trade. If it becomes sick, water it with a solution of Epsom Salts, ½ ounce to the gallon. *S. jasminoides* is a half-hardy climber from Brazil with white flowers. Add leafmould and sand to the greenhouse border. *S. wendlandii* is the most spectacular member of the family and needs MWT 10° C. (50° F.). It will grow up to the roof but can be in a big pot when young. Restrict the roots or plant in poor soil to keep it in bounds when planted out.

SPECIES TO GROW. *S. capsicastrum*, orange berries, winter, about 1 foot; *S. jasminoides alba*, white flowers with yellow centres, hardy in warm districts; *S. wendlandii*, large lilac-blue flowers in summer.

Sollya (Australian Bluebell Creeper) *Pittosporaceae*
Small Australian evergreen twining shrubs with clusters of pale blue flowers in early summer.

CULTIVATION. Pot in 6-inch pots of lime-free J.I.P. 2 or plant in very peaty soil with a little sand. Water freely while growing but keep only just moist in winter. Grow in full sun and feed occasionally in summer. Train on a pillar or small trellis. Increase by cuttings of young shoots taken with a heel in spring.

SPECIES TO GROW. *S. heterophylla* (syn. *S. fusiformis*) and *S. parviflora* (syn. *S. drummondii*), both blue, 3–6 feet.

Sparaxis *Iridaceae*
South African bulbous plant with brightly coloured bell-flowers in spring.

CULTIVATION. Treat as IXIA.

SPECIES TO GROW. Hybrids of *S. grandiflora* and *S. tricolor* in many colours (usually sold mixed), April and May, 1–2 feet.

Sparmannia *Tiliaceae*
Fast-growing, semi-woody, evergreen flowering shrub from South Africa with very large pale green leaves. MWT 7° C. (45° F.)

CULTIVATION. Pot in March or April in J.I.P. 3 or similar compost. It likes both sun and syringing but is sometimes grown as a house-plant. Cut hard back each February and rest with little water for four to six weeks. Feed in summer. Increase by cuttings in spring in a propagating frame. The plants can stand outdoors from July to September.

SPECIES TO GROW. *S. africana* (African hemp), and variety *flore pleno*, white flowers at unpredictable times, up to 10 feet in time, but flowers at 2 feet.

Spider Flower *see* CLEOME

Spider Lily *see* HYMENOCALLIS

Spiraea *see* ASTILBE

Stag's-horn Fern *see* PLATYCERIUM

Star Cactus *see* ASTROPHYTUM

Statice *see* LIMONIUM

Stock *see* MATTHIOLA

Stenocarpus *Proteaceae*
Australian evergreen tree with large shiny oak-like leaves.

CULTIVATION. This is an easily grown house-plant that ultimately grows large. Pot on fairly frequently. Treat like GREVILLEA to which it is related. It can be raised from seed.

Species to grow. *S. sinuatus*, mature specimens have scarlet flowers.

Strelitzia (Bird of Paradise Flower) *Musaceae*
Mature plants have very striking purple and orange flowers like the heads of exotic birds. MWT 10° C. (50° F.)

Cultivation. Pot in J.I.P. 2 with a little extra grit. It needs good drainage and plenty of water in summer but very little in winter. Flowering plants will need very large pots or to be planted in a border. It can be increased by detaching suckers in spring. Seed takes something like seven years to flower and germination is erratic.

Species to grow. *S. reginae*, ultimately a large plant, purple and orange flowers, April.

Streptanthera *Iridaceae*
Small South African bulbous plant with neat attractive foliage and bright flowers in late spring.

Cultivation. As for Ixia.

Species to grow. *S. cuprea coccinea*, glowing orange-scarlet with black centre, early June, 9 inches.

Streptocarpus (Cape Primrose) *Gesneriaceae*
Favourite warm greenhouse plant from tropical Africa with flowers reminiscent of a sinningia. I include it here as young plants can be bought and grown on even if seed is troublesome without more heat. MWT 10° C. (50° F.)

Cultivation. Buy young plants in May. They flower in 5-inch pots of J.I.P. 2 and must be shaded from hot sun. They appreciate a moist atmosphere and occasional feeding when buds form. The plants need to be kept rather dry in winter and re-potted in March. Large plants can be divided into separate crowns.

Species to grow. *S.* × *hybridus*. There are cultivars with purple, mauve, pink, crimson or white flowers often beautifully marked with contrasting colours, about 1 foot. *S.* 'Constant Nymph', violet-blue and constantly flowering, is a very good plant.

Streptosolen *Solanaceae*
Evergreen climber from Colombia with effective orange flowers from June until late autumn.   MWT 7° C. (45° F.)

CULTIVATION. Small plants can be grown in pots of J.I.P. 2 or other compost but it is best in sandy soil in a sunny greenhouse border. Pot or plant in March. Water freely April to September but keep fairly dry in winter. Prune flowered shoots hard back immediately after flowering. Increase by cuttings of young side growths in spring or summer in propagating frame.

SPECIES TO GROW. *S. jamesonii*, orange-scarlet, summer, 6–8 feet.

Sturt Desert Pea *see* CLIANTHUS

Swan River Daisy *see* BRACHYCOME

Tacsonia *see* PASSIFLORA

Tea Tree *see* LEPTOSPERMUM

Tecophilaea (Chilean Crocus)   *Amaryllidaceae*
Rare and very expensive small bulbous plant from Chile with gentian-blue white-throated lily flowers in early spring.

CULTIVATION. Pot in August rather deeply at the rate of four to a 5-inch pot using J.I.P. 2 or rich sandy loam. The pots can be plunged to the rim in a sunny frame until December. They like sun and fresh air and are more or less hardy. Increase by means of offsets removed in August or by seed.

SPECIES TO GROW. *T. cyanocrocus*, blue, early spring, 4–6 inches; also variety *leichtlinii* with a white throat.

Throatwort *see* TRACHELIUM

Thunbergia (Black-eyed Susan) *Acanthaceae*
Annual climber from tropical Africa suitable for pots.
MWT 10° C. (50° F.)

CULTIVATION. Sow in propagating frame in March. Pot singly in small pots of J.I.P. 1 or other compost and flower in 5- or 6-inch pots of a richer mixture. They must be supported with canes or allowed to hang from a basket. Water freely and shade from sun. They like a moist atmosphere.

SPECIES TO GROW. *T. alata*, colours vary from cream to orange with dark purple throat, summer and autumn, up to 7 feet.

Tibouchina *Melastomataceae*
My favourite greenhouse shrub. Evergreen shrub from Brazil with showy purple flowers for long periods and attractive hairy leaves. MWT 7° C. (45° F.)

CULTIVATION. Pot or plant in spring in fibrous loam or J.I.P. 2. It is best in the border or a tub after the first year. It must be pinched when young and trained against a wall as it quickly becomes leggy. It can be grown as a bush or wall shrub. Prune in February or March. Increase by cuttings of firm young shoots in spring or summer in a propagating frame.

SPECIES TO GROW. *T. urvilleana* is said to be the correct name of the plant that is best known as *T. semidecandra*, formerly *Lasiandra macrantha* and *Pleroma macranthum*. Royal purple flowers through summer and autumn, ultimately large.

Tigridia *Iridaceae*
Mexican bulbous plant with a succession of fleeting but glorious flowers in summer.

CULTIVATION. Pot and re-pot in April, deeply, six to a 6- or 7-inch pot using J.I.P. 3. They are best plunged in damp peat until growth shows. Water carefully until growing strongly. Feed when flowers start. After flowering dry off gradually and keep quite dry and

Streptocarpus 'Constant Nymph' lives up to its name

Celsia cretica, the Cretan Mullein, is a biennial sometimes grown in pots

Cestrum purpureum can be grown as a shrub or a climber

Hedychium gardnerianum is a handsome plant in autumn

Rehmannia angulata is an unusual perennial from China

frost-free from November to April. They can be grown in a warm border outdoors and treated like gladioli.

SPECIES TO GROW. *T. pavonia*, usually only sold in a mixture of colours, mainly orange-scarlet with crimson spots, also yellow, pinkish-crimson, mauve and white with various markings suggestive of the face of a tiger. Flowers in June and July, about 2 feet.

Toad Flax *see* LINARIA

Tobacco Plant *see* NICOTIANA

Tolmiea (Pig-a-back Plant) *Saxifragaceae*
Hardy herbaceous perennial plant grown as a pot plant for its attractive foliage and charming habit of developing little plantlets on its leaves.

CULTIVATION. Grow in cool shady conditions in any ordinary compost. J.I.P. 2 is suitable. Water freely in summer but carefully in winter. Increase by layering and then detaching the small plantlets that form at the top of the leaf stalks of the older leaves.

SPECIES TO GROW. *T. menziesii*, green flowers in summer, best renewed frequently from plantlets, up to 2 feet.

Torenia *Scrophulariaceae*
Half-hardy annual from Vietnam with a mass of attractive flowers in late summer.

CULTIVATION. This is a plant that needs warmth and a moist atmosphere. Sow in March or April in 16° C. (60° F.). Pot singly and pinch several times to make the plants bushy. J.I.P. 2 is suitable for the flowering pots of 5 or 6 inches. They will need support unless allowed to hang from baskets. They need full light when young but shade from hot summer sun.

SPECIES TO GROW. *T. fournieri*, lavender-blue with yellow throat, about 9 inches and its variety *grandiflora*, similar but larger, and *alba*, with white flowers, about 1 foot.

Trachelium (Throatwort) *Campanulaceae*
Sub-shrubby perennial from south Europe grown for its dense heads of tiny blue flowers. It is responsive to skilled cultivation.
MWT 7° C. (45° F.)

CULTIVATION. This plant will grow and flower in one season in 5-inch pots if treated as a half-hardy annual but better plants are produced by growing it slowly as a biennial. Pot firmly and pinch several times to make a shapely plant with a number of flowering heads. A good plant takes space and a big pot. A poor plant is easy but not very ornamental. Feed when pots are full of roots. J.I.P. 2 is suitable. It can be sown from February to June and will flower when you allow its tall flowering stems to develop.

SPECIES TO GROW. *T. caeruleum*, mauvy-blue, 18 inches to 3 feet.

Trachelospermum (*Rhynchospermum*) *Apocynaceae*
Easily grown evergreen twining shrub with sweetly scented white flowers. Sometimes known as Chinese Jasmine and grown outside in sheltered places.

CULTIVATION. Small plants can be grown in pots of J.I.P. 3 and trained on stakes or wires, otherwise plant in the greenhouse border. Pot or plant in March. Prune to keep in shape immediately after flowering. Water freely in summer and syringe. Increase by cuttings in a propagating frame in summer.

SPECIES TO GROW. *T. jasminoides* (syn. *Rhynchospermum jasminoides*), white, summer, 15 feet.

Trachycarpus *see* CHAMAEROPS

Trachymene *see* DIDISCUS

Tradescantia (Wandering Jew) *Commelinaceae*
Perennial trailing foliage plants for shady positions. They come from tropical America and are barely warm enough in winter in the cool greenhouse but are universally grown.
MWT 10° C. (50° F.)

CULTIVATION. Cuttings root readily in a glass of water in a warm room and equally so in damp soil. Several can be put together in the pot in which they will grow in any ordinary compost. The correct names of the species you may come across is a matter for the experts. The plants sold as house-plants may be *Dichorisandra*, *Setcreasea* or *Zebrina* as well as *Tradescantia*, and will be chosen by appearance rather than name.

SPECIES TO GROW. These are attractive. *T. albiflora*, green leaves striped and bordered with white and sometimes flushed pink; *T. fluminensis* (syn. *T. fluviatilis*), variegated forms similar to the foregoing; *T.* 'Quicksilver' is a recent introduction with larger pale green leaves finely striped with white; *T. sillamontana*, silvery woolly leaves and bright mauve-pink flowers; *Setcreasea purpurea*, purple striped foliage; *S. striata*, dark green, silver-striped leaves; *Zebrina pendula*, deep green to purple leaves with silver bands and *Z. p. quadricolor* with even more vivid markings that include white and pink.

Transvaal Daisy *see* GERBERA

Tritonia *Iridaceae*
Small bulbous plants from South Africa related to *Montbretia*.

CULTIVATION. Pot in October or November in J.I.P. 3 or other rich compost, putting about six bulbs in a 5-inch pot. Do not water until growth shows. Re-pot only every two or three years. Dry off gradually after flowering and keep dry until November. Increase by offsets.

SPECIES TO GROW. *T. crocata*, vivid orange to scarlet is the most readily available, but any can be grown; *T. hyalina* has pale orange flowers and is good for cutting; all about 1 foot.

Tropaeolum (Nasturtium) *Tropaeolaceae*
Easily grown hardy annual from South America. Quite effective for hanging baskets in spring.

CULTIVATION. There are double forms that have to be increased by cuttings, best taken in July. Otherwise sow singly in small pots of seed compost in late summer and later put in baskets or 5-inch pots and train upwards or allow to hang. Water sparingly in winter and do not use rich soil.

SPECIES TO GROW. Hybrids of *T. majus* such as 'Golden Gleam', climbing or trailing, yellow to scarlet. Also 'Hermione Grasshoff', scarlet and constantly flowering, from cuttings.

Tuberose *see* POLIANTHES

Tulipa (Tulip) *Liliaceae*
Hardy bulbous plants that can be flowered early in the cool greenhouse.

CULTIVATION. All kinds of tulips except a few rare species can be grown under glass and the choice is large. Pot from September to November in J.I.P. 2 or 3, just burying the bulbs and putting them very close together. Plunge in a cold frame or out of doors buried in peat or sand for 8–10 weeks. Then bring into the greenhouse and water freely when growing strongly.

SPECIES TO GROW. Consult tradesmen's lists and choose those recommended for forcing. 'Duc van Thol' tulips are very early and short stemmed and can be grown in pans or bowls but are now rarely offered. Early single tulips such as 'Bellona', golden-yellow; 'Brilliant Star', scarlet; 'Couleur Cardinal', darker scarlet; 'General de Wet', orange, and 'Prince of Austria', orange-scarlet, are good. Early double tulips with peony-like flowers can also be grown in bowls. These can be followed by the Mendel, Triumph, Cottage and Darwin tulips if a succession is wanted until May. *T. praestans* 'Fusilier' with several small orange-scarlet flowers on each stem and attractive leaves is a good pot plant but do not force, 1 foot.

Turutu *see* DIANELLA

Umbrella Plant *see* CYPERUS

Unicorn Plant *see* MARTYNIA

Vallota (Scarborough Lily) *Amaryllidaceae*
Handsome South African bulbous plant with scarlet trumpet flowers in autumn. It is best bought in a pot and not as a dry bulb.

CULTIVATION. Pot firmly in J.I.P. 2. Water very sparingly until established. Re-potting is best done in June or July and only every two or three years. Keep in full sun with plenty of water in summer but only just moist when not in active growth. It does not lose its leaves in winter. Increase by removing offsets when re-potting.

SPECIES TO GROW. *V. speciosa* (syn. *V. purpurea*), bright scarlet, late summer or autumn, up to 18 inches.

Veltheimia *Liliaceae*
South African bulbous plant with handsome leaves and flowers like small red-hot pokers in early spring.

CULTIVATION. Pot in August or September, singly in 6-inch pots. Use J.I.P. 3 or similar compost and leave the nose of the bulb showing. Water moderately while growing and feed when flowers are forming. Dry off gradually after flowering. Re-pot every other year. Other varieties are similar but rarely available.

SPECIES TO GROW. *V. viridifolia* (syn. *V. capensis*), pink and green flowers, March or April, about 1 foot.

Viscaria *see* LYCHNIS

Wandering Jew *see* TRADESCANTIA

Wattle *see* ACACIA

Wax Flower *see* HOYA

Winter Cherry *see* SOLANUM

Zantedeschia (Richardia; Calla; Arum Lily) *Araceae*
Large fleshy rooted South African marsh plants often called Arum Lilies. *Z. aethiopica* is hardy in some parts of the country. Under glass they flower in spring according to the temperature, probably March or April. The others do better with MWT 10° C. (50° F.).

CULTIVATION. Pot and re-pot *Z. aethiopica* yearly in August or early September in J.I.P. 3, putting a single root in a 7-inch pot or two or three in a 10- or 12-inch pot. Water moderately at first and then freely. When in full growth they can stand in a saucer of water. At the end of May they can be planted out in the garden until the autumn but they must be kept well watered and in rich soil. The other species are tender. Keep only just moist when dormant in winter and do not plant out.

SPECIES TO GROW. *Z. aethiopica* (syn. *Richardia africana*), white, spring, 1½–2½ feet; *Z. elliottiana*, yellow flowers and white spotted leaves, summer; *Z. rehmannii*, a dwarf plant with small pink flowers in summer, about 1 foot.

Zebrina *see* TRADESCANTIA

Zephyranthes (Zephyr Flower) *Amaryllidaceae*
Small bulbous plants from South America and the Caribbean with lily flowers in summer. MWT 7° C. (45° F.)

CULTIVATION. Pot in early spring before growth starts. Use J.I.P. 2 and bury the bulbs rather deeply putting four or five in a 6-inch pot. Water freely when growing and keep only just moist through the winter. Re-pot only occasionally as they flower more freely when crowded. Increase by removing offsets when re-potting.

SPECIES TO GROW. *Z. grandiflora* (syn. *Z. carinata*), rosy-pink, summer, 6–12 inches; *Z. robustus* (syn. *Habranthus robustus*), a similar, slightly larger plant, early autumn; *Z. rosea*, rose-pink, late summer, 5–10 inches.

Zinnia *Compositae*
Half-hardy annuals from Mexico with brilliantly coloured flowers that are good for cutting but often fail in the British summer.

CULTIVATION. Sow in April or May for late summer and autumn flowering. Pot singly in 5- or 6-inch pots of J.I.P. 3 and remove all sideshoots, thereby producing one really large flower. Alternatively pinch out the growing point for a bushy plant with smaller flowers. The miniature cultivars make good pot plants.

SPECIES TO GROW. Hybrids of *Z. elegans* of every conceivable shape and size, warm bright colours and green, double flowers, 9 inches to 2½ feet.

Zygocactus *see* SCHLUMBERGERA

Index

Abutilon, 126; from cuttings, 84
Acacia, 127; from cuttings, 84
Achimenes, 123, 127; flowering and resting time, 103
Adiantum, 127, 175
Aechmea, 123, 128
Aeonium, 129
African corn lily, 129, 190
African hemp, 129, 237
African violet, 122, 129, 229; from leaf cuttings, 83
Agapanthus, 129; flowering and resting time, 103
Agathaea, 130, 174–5
Ageratum, 130; from seed, 98
Aggregate: in composts, 64; on staging, 52
Agrostemma, 131, 200
Aichryson, 129, 131
Air circulation and ventilation, 21; air-circulating fans, 50–1
Alignment and aspect of greenhouse, 19, 20
All-peat composts, 61; and fast growth in early stages, 97
Aloe, 131
Alonsoa, 131
Aloysia, 131, 198
Aluminium: greenhouses, 22; paint on greenhouses, 22
Amaryllis, 132, 184; flowering and resting time, 103
Ampelopsis, 132
Anigozanthus, 132
Annuals: autumn-sown hardy, 93; climbing, 94; half-hardy, 93–4
Antirrhinum, 132; from seed, 94, 98
Ants as pests, 113
Aphelandra, 133
Aphides, 113
Aporocactus, 123, 133; as free-flowering, 110

Aralia, 134
Araucaria, 134
Ardisia, 134
Artifical Light in Horticulture, 74
Arum lily, 134, 246
Asbestos sheeting for staging, 26
Asclepias, 134
Asparagus fern, 135, 175
Aspidistra, 135
Aspirated thermostats, 39
Asplenium, 175
Astilbe, 135
Astrophytum, 136
Australian blue bell creeper, 136, 236
Australian fuchsia, 136, 159
Australian mint bush, 136, 224
Automatic watering, *see* Capillary, Watering
Automation, electrically-controlled, 28–32; *see also* Electricity
Avocado pear, 218
Azalea, 136

Babiana (baboon-root), 137; flowering and resting time, 103
Balsam, 188
Barberton daisy, 137, 178
Barrel cactus, 176
Bauera, 138; from cuttings, 84
Bedding plants, 124; bedding pelargoniums, 122
Begonia, 120, 138; from leaf cuttings, 83; flowering and resting time, 103; hybrid, 139
Belladonna lily, 132
Beloperone, 139
Beneficial Insects (Min. of Ag.), 118
Bessera, 139; flowering and resting time, 103
Biennials, 94
Bilbergia, 123, 140
Billardiera, 140

248

INDEX

Bird of Paradise flower, 238
Bird's-nest fern, 175
Bituminous paint, a danger of using, 22
Black-eyed Susan, 140, 240
Blackleg affecting pelargoniums, 117
Bleeding heart, 140, 166
Blinds for greenhouse shading, 51
Blood flower, 134–5, 140
Blood lily, 140, 181
Blue dawn flower, 140, 219
Blue gum, 140, 172
Blue lace flower, 141, 166
Blue marguerite, 141, 174
Boiler conversion, 35–6; boiler heats, 34–5
Bonemeal, uses of, 25, 63, 107
Border in greenhouse, soil for, 25, 26, 63
Boronia, 141; from cuttings, 84
Botrytis, 50, 117
Bottle-brush flowers, 141, 144, 202
Bottom heat, 82
Bougainvillea, 141; from cuttings, 84
Box (panel) ventilation under staging, 21
Brachycome, 141; from seed, 94, 98
Bridal wreath, 142, 177
Browallia, 142; from seed, 98
Brugmansia, 142, 143, 165
Brunfelsia, 142
Bryophyllum, 143, 192
Bud drop, cause of, 111–12
Bulbous (and related) plants, 100–3; advantage of, 100; purchase of, 79; flowering and resting times, 103–4; evergreen, 101
Busy Lizzie, 143, 188
Butterfly flower, 143, 231

Cacti and succulents, 105–10; cause of non-flowering, 109; purchase of, 79, 106; repotting of, 106, 109; soil for, 107; space requirement of, 121; to re-root, 109; plastic pots for, 56; some epiphytic, 108, 109; root-rot of, 109; stem and leaf cuttings, and raising from seed, 84, 109–10; list of free-flowering, 110; using composts for, 107; *see also* Capillary benches
Calamondin, 143, 155
Calceolaria, 143; from cuttings, 84; from seed, 94, 98
Calendula, 143; from seed, 98
Californian bluebell, 144, 207
Calla lily, 144, 246
Callistemon, 144; from cuttings, 85
Camellia, 144; from cuttings, 85
Campanula, 145; from cuttings, 85; from seed, 94, 98

Candle plant, 146, 193
Candytuft, 146, 187
Canham, A. E., *Artificial Light in Horticulture*, 74
Cantua, 146; from cuttings, 85
Cape cowslip, 146, 193
Cape heaths, 146, 170
Cape lily, 146, 161
Cape primrose, 146, 238
Capillary benches for watering, 26, 31, 66–72, 119; construction of, 70; as unsuitable for cacti, 105; capillary trays of glass fibre, 70
Capsid bugs, 113–14
Carnations, 80, 121–2, 146–7; feeding of, 65; leaf rust of, 118; perpetual flowering, 121; red spider affecting, 115; taking cuttings of, 85; tortrix moth affecting, 114; wilt of, 117
Cassia, 147; from cuttings, 85
Celosia, 148
Celsia, 148; from cuttings, 85; from seed, 98
Centrally heated homes, and greenhouse temperatures, 16
Cereus, 148
Cestrum, 149; from cuttings, 85
Chamaecereus, 149; *C. silvestrii* as free-flowering cactus, 110
Chamaedorea, 150
Chamaerops, 150
Charcoal, uses of, 64
Charieis, 150
Cherry pie, 151, 183
Cheshunt compound, 117
Chilean crocus, 151, 239
Chilean jasmine, 201
Chimney bellflower, 145
Chincherinchee, 151, 213
Chlidanthus, 151; flowering and resting time, 103
Chlorophytum, 151
Chlorosis, treatment of, 62
Chorizema, 151
Christmas cactus, 151, 232
Chrysanthemum, 80, 120, 121–2, 152–4; capsid bugs, earwigs and eelworm affecting, 113, 114; leaf rust of, 118; leaf miners of, 115; raised from cuttings, 85; recommended compost for, 59
Chusan palm, 150, 154
Cigar flower, 154, 162
Cineraria, 94, 98, 154; from seed, 94, 98; leaf, rust of, 118
Cissus 154
Citrus, 155; from cuttings, 85
Clarkia, 155; from seed, 93, 98
Cleanliness, 60, 111

249

INDEX

Cleistocactus, 155
Clematis, 156
Cleome, 156
Cleyera, 156
Clianthus, 157; from cuttings, 85
Climate variations in one structure, as ideal, 18
Clivia, 101, 102, 157
Cobaea, 158; from seed, 94, 98
Cockscomb, 148, 158
Coleus, 158
Colloidal copper, against Grey mould, 117
Composts, 54, 55, 57–62; all-peat, 61; for cacti and succulents, 107; for cuttings, 83; for lime-haters, 61, 62, 96; for orchids, 63; for potting, 57–63; Croxden soil-less, 60, 61, 62; Eclipse peat, 60; Eff soil-less, 60; formulae, 58–9; Garford soil-less, 60; J. Arthur Bowers', 60; John Innes, 13, 57–60, 61, 64, 125 seqq.; J. I. Base fertiliser, 58–9; J.I. for fine seeds, seeds generally, 58, 96; J.I. for cuttings, 83; J.I. for desert plants, 107; J.I. used with chemical feed, 65; Levington, 61; Powlings, 60
Concrete greenhouse, 22
Condensation problems, 18, 23, 24, 50
Convection heaters, 37
Convolvulus, 158
Coral tree, 159, 171, 172
Coronilla, 159; from cuttings, 85
Correa, 159
Coryphantha, 160
Cotyledon, 160
Crape myrtle, 161, 194
Crassula, 160; from cuttings, 85
Cresylic acid as soil steriliser, 26
Crinum, 161
Crocks in pots, 56–7
Crown of thorns, 161, 173
Croxden soil-less compost, 60
Crushed brick, in potting, 64
Cryptanthus, 161
Cuphea, 162; from cuttings, 85; from seeds, 94, 98
Curly palm, 214
Cuttings, 81–6; and mist propagation, 82, 88–92; soft and half-ripe, 82–3
Cyclamen, 162; suggested treatments, 101–2, 162–3; from seed, 94, 98; flowering and resting time, 103
Cymbidium, 163
'Cynthella' hyacinths, 186
Cyperus, 164
Cypress vine, 225
Cyrtomium, 164, 175
Cytisus, 164; from cuttings, 85

Daffodil, 165, 206
Damping down of floor, 52–3
Damping off, to prevent, 117
Date palm, 214
Datura, 165; from cuttings, 85
Daylight, manipulation of, 74
Dazomet for soil sterilisation, 26
DDT, 114
Derris preparations, 112, 113, 116
Desiccation, affecting seedlings and cuttings, 81, 96
Dianella, 165
Dianthus (*see also* Carnation), 146–7, 166
Diascia, 166; from seed, 98
Didiscus, 166; from seed, 98
Dieltrya, 166, 167
Dimorphotheca, 167; from seed, 98
Diplacus, 167, 204
Double glazing of greenhouse, 24
Drosanthemum, 167, 203
'Dry period', *see* Bulbous plants, resting times
Dutch iris, 189
Dutch lights as greenhouse structure, 20

Earth stars, 161, 167
Earwigs, 114
East Lothian stocks, 202
East-west siting of greenhouse, 20
Eccremocarpus, 167; from seed, 94, 98
Echeveria, 168; from cuttings, 83, 85
Echinocactus, 168
Echinocereus, 169; species, as free-flowering cacti, 110
Echinopsis, 169; *E. eyriesii* as free-flowering cactus, 110
Eclipse peat compost, 60
Eelworms, 114
Eff soil-less compost, 60
Electricity for greenhouse, use, 28–32, 36–46; measuring house for, 41–3; to calculate load, 39–45; electric extractor fans, 21, 49; electric soil-warming cable, 43–4; use of electric seed propagators, 95–6
Electricity in your Garden, 43
Elephant bush, 169, 223
Elephant's trunk, 169, 201
Encyclopaedia of greenhouse plants (cool greenhouse), 125–247
Epidendrum, 169
Epiphyllum, 123, 170
Epiphytic plants, 123
Erica, 170; from cuttings, 85
Eriobotryia, 171
Erythrina, 171; from cuttings, 85
Eucalyptus, 172; from cuttings, 85; from seed, 98
Eucnide, 172; from seed, 94, 98

250

INDEX

Euphorbia, 172; from cuttings, 85; poisonous sap of, 173
Eurya, 156, 173
Eustoma, 173
Everlasting flowers, 180, 197
Exacum, 173
Extractor fan ventilation, 21, 49

Fairy rose, 229
Fan and pad ventilation, 52
Fan heaters, 21
Fan ventilation, 21, 49–50; air-circulating fans, 50–1
Fatshedera, 174; from cuttings, 85
Fatsia, 174; from cuttings, 85
Feeding, 64–5; of carnations and tomatoes, 65; foliar, 65
Felicia, 174; from cuttings, 85; from seed, 98
Ferns, 121
Ferocactus, 176
Ficus, 176
Fiddle-leaf fig, 176
Fig, 176
Fir bark, prepared for potting, 64
Fish meal, uses of, 25, 63
Flame nettle, 158, 176
Florists' hyacinths, 186
Flowers of sulphur, in compost mixtures, 62
Fluorescence, *see* 'Warm White' tubes; in home plant display, 75
Foliage plants from seed, 94
Foliar feeding, 65
Formaldehyde, for soil sterilising, 26, 63
Frames: frost-free; heated, for overwintering, 45; propagating, 45–6, 95–6; with soil-warming cable, 44; *see also* Heated bench, 45
Francoa, 177
Free-standing greenhouse, 19
Freesia, 177; from seed, 98, 102; flowering and resting time, 103; need of replacing, 102
Fuchsia, 177; from cuttings, 85; winter flowering of, 74; affected by white fly, 116
Fumigating smokes, 115, 116, 117

Garden Centres, buying plants from, 77–8
Gardening Chemicals (RHS), 112
Garford soil-less compost, 60
Genista, 164–5, 178
Geraniums: buying, 79; *see* Pelargonium, 215–18
Gerbera, 178; from seed, 98
Germination temperature, 95

Gesneria, 179, 226, 235; *G. cardinalis*, 226; value of Gesneriads, 123
Gilia, 179
Gladiolus, 179; *nanus* hybrids, 102; flowering and resting time, 103
Glass, choice and care of, 23–4; shading, 51–2
Globe amaranth, 179, 180
Gloriosa, 179; flowering and resting time, 104
Glory of the Sun, 180, 196
Glory pea, 157, 180
Gloxinia, 103, 180, 235; from leaf cuttings, 85
Glug-bottles in watering, 67, 70
Golden-rayed lily of Japan, 196, 197
Golden spider lily, 180, 200
Gomphrena, 180
Grapefruit, 155
Grasses, ornamental, 164, 181, 233
Greenfly, 197; aphides generally, 113
Greenhouse: all metal, 20, 21, 22, 23; aspect of, 19; automation in, 28–32; bench in, 26–7; *see also* Capillary benches; blinds for, 51; bulbous plants for, 100–4; buying plants for, 76–9; cacti and succulents for, 105–10; cleanliness in, 60, 111; frames supplementing, *see* Frames; damping down floor of, 52–3; double glazing of, 24; Dutch lights as basis of, 20; encyclopaedia of plants for, 125 seqq.; flowers from cuttings for, 81–6; flowers from seed for, 93–9; galvanised steel, 22; general-purpose, best form for, 20; general-purpose floor, 25; hardwood, 22; heating of, 33–46; insulating, 73–4; manure in, 63; minimum temperatures, 16, 41; overcrowding, 76; path inside, 25; pests and diseases in, 111–18; propagating frames inside, 44–5; reinforced concrete structures, 22; replacing glass in, 23; shading, 51–2; shrubs and climbers in, 81, 94; softwood, 21–7; specialising in, 119–24; staging in, 23, 26; structural considerations, 18–27; as tenant's fixture, 23; ventilating, 47–53; waterproofing, 22
Grevillea, 181; from cuttings, 85; from seed, 94, 98
Grey mould, 117
'Grow-Lux' fluorescent tubes, 75
Growth cabinets, 74
Growth rooms, artificial illumination of, 73
Guernsey lily, 181, 209
Gum tree, 172, 181

INDEX

Habranthus, 181, 246
Habrothamnus, 149, 181
Haemanthus, 181; flowering and resting time, 104
Half-hardy annuals, 93-4
Half-ripe cuttings, 82
Hardenbergia, 182
Hard-wood cuttings, 83
Hardwood greenhouses, 22
Hare's-foot fern, 175
Heated bench, 45
Heath, 170-1, 182
Heating of cool greenhouse, 33-46; by electricity, 38-46; fan-type, 36-9; by oil-fired boiler, 34-6; gas or oil-fired ducted air system, 36; paraffin stove or boiler for, 33-5; portable heater, 33; soil-warming cables, 43-5; solid-fuel boiler, 35; space heating by mineral insulated cables, 38; tubular, 37; tubular compared with convector, 37
Hedera, 182
Hedychium, 183; flowering and resting time, 104
Heeria, 183, 231
Heliotropium, 183; from cuttings, 85; from seed, 94, 98
Helxine, 183
Henry Doubleday Research Association, 112-13
Heterocentron, 184
Himalayan rhododendrons, species and hybrids, 227, 228
Hippeastrum, 184; flowering and resting times, 104
Holly fern, 175, 184
Honey flower, 185, 203
Horticultural Trades Association, 125
Howea, 185
Hoya, 185; from cuttings, 85
Humidity factors, 18, 19, 47-53; *see* Condensation; and paraffin heating, 34; coping with in automation, 30-1; orchids and, 52, 123
Hyacinthus, 102, 185-6
Hydrangea, 186; from cuttings, 85
Hygrometers, 31, 53
Hylocereus, 186
Hymenocallis, 187; flowering and resting times, 104

Iberis, 187; from seed, 93
Imantophyllum, 157, 187
Impatiens, 188; from cuttings, 85; from seed, 98
Indian azaleas, 137
Indoor plant-growing rooms, 19; indoor rock gardens, 106

Insecticides, systemic, 113
Insulation by plastic sheeting, 24
Intermediate stocks, 202
Ipomoea, 188; from seed, 94, 98
Iris, 189; bulbous, 102; flowering and resting times, 104
Irradiation in seed-raising, 74
Ismene, 187, 189
Isolepis, 190, 233
Ivy, 182, 190
Ivy-leaved pelargoniums, 217
Ixia, 103, 190; flowering and resting times, 104

Jacaranda, 190; from seed, 94
Jacobinia, 190; from cuttings, 85
Japanese azaleas, 136, 137
Japanese hyacinths, 191, 212
Jardin Exotique at Monte Carlo, 106
J. Arthur Bowers' compost, 60
Jasminum, 191; from cuttings, 86
Javanese rhododendrons, 227
John Innes composts, *see* Composts
Jovellana, 191
Jubaea, 192, 214
Justicia, 190, 192

Kalanchoe, 192; from cuttings, 86; from seed, 98
Kalosanthes, 192, 228
Kangaroo paws, 132, 192
Kangaroo vine, 155, 192
Kaulfussia, 150, 193
Kennedya, 182, 193
Kentia, 193, 214
Kleinia, 193, 234
Kurume azaleas, 137

Lachenalia, 102, 103, 193; flowering and resting times, 104
Lagerstroemia, 194
Lampranthus, 194
Lantana, 194
Lapageria, 194
Lasiandra, 194, 240
Latin names, 16
Leaf cuttings, 83
Leaf miners, 115
Leafmould, 64
Leaf rust, 118
Lean-to and span roofs, 19-20
Lemaireocereus, 195
Lemon, 155
Lemon-scented verbena, 195, 198
Leptospermum, 195; from cuttings, 86
Leucadendron, 195
Leuchtenbergia, 196
Leucocoryne, 196; flowering and resting times, 104

INDEX

Levington compost, 61
Libonia, 190, 196
Light factor, 19–20, 73–5; four principal uses of light in horticulture, 75
Lilium, 196, 197; buying lilies, 79; from seed, 99
Lime-hating plants, compost for, 61, 62
Limonium, 197; from seed, 94, 99
Linaria, 198; from seed, 93, 99
Lippia, 198
Liquid feeds, 65
Lisianthus, 173, 198
Loam: for compost, 59; to sterilise, 26, 59, 60, 63
Lobelia, 198; from seed, 99
Lobster's claw, 157, 199
Loquat, 171, 199
Lotus, 199
Lucalia, 199; from cuttings, 86
Lychnis, 200; from seed, 93, 99
Lycoris, 200; flowering and resting times, 104

Macpenney system of automatic watering, 69
Madonna lily, 196, 197
Maidenhair fern, 127, 200
Malathion, 115, 116
Malmaison carnations, 147
Mammillaria, 200; *M. boscana* as free-flowering cactus, 110
Mandevilla, 201; from cuttings, 86
Manuka, 201
Manure, green and animal, 25, 64, 65
Marigold, 143–4, 201, 224
Martynia, 201; from seed, 99
Mask flower, 131, 202
Matthiola, 202; from seed, 99
Maximum and minimum thermometer, 30, 47
Mealy bugs, 115
Melaleuca, 202
Melianthus, 203
Mentzelia, 172, 203
Mesembryanthemum, 203; from cuttings, 86
Metrosideros, 203
Mexican cigar flower, 162
Mexican coral drops, 139, 203
Microsperma, 172, 204
Mignonette, 204, 227
Mildew, 117
Milla, 204; flowering and resting times, 104
Mimosa, 127, 204
Mimulus, 204; from cuttings, 86
Mina, 205, 225
Mind your own business, 183, 205

Miniature: cyclamen, 163; cymbidium, 163; rose, 229; royal pelargonium, 218; zonal pelargonium, 217
Mist propagation, 31, 48, 87–92; for leafy cuttings, 81–2; seed-raising under, 97; unit for, in greenhouse, 87–92
Mistletoe cactus, 227
Mitraria, 205; from cuttings, 86
Mollis azaleas, 137
Monstera, 205
Moon cactus, 205, 234
Morning glory, 188, 205; from seed, 94, 98
Moulds, 117
Mourning iris, 189
Musk, 204, 205

Naegelia, 123, 206, 235
Nandina, 206; from cuttings, 86
Narcissus, 102, 165, 206
Nasturtium, 243
Neanthe, 150, 207
Nemesia, 207; from seed, 94, 99
Nemophila, 207; from seed, 93, 99
Neoregelia, 123, 208
Nephrolepsis, 175–6, 208
Nerine, 102, 208; flowering and resting times, 104
Nerium, 208
Nettles, attracting whitefly, 116
Nicotiana, 210
Nidularium, 123, 208, 210
Nierembergia, 210; from cuttings, 86; from seed, 94, 99
Night-storage heaters, 38
Nomenclature, 16–17
Norfolk Island pine, 134, 211
Notocactus, 211; *N. apricus*, *N. ottonis* and *N. tabularis* as free-flowering cacti, 110

Ochna, 211
Odontoglossum, 211
Oil heating, 33–5, 36
Oleander, 209, 212
Oliveranthus, 168, 212
Ophiopogon, 212
Opuntia, 212, 224
Orange, 155
Orchids, 52, 123, 211; potting, 63; Orchid Society of Great Britain, 123
Organ-pipe cactus, 195, 213
Ornithogalum, 213; flowering and resting times, 104
Osmunda fibre for potting, 63
Osteospermum, 167, 213
Overcrowding of greenhouse, 76
Overwatering, *see* Watering

INDEX

Pachycereus, 213
Pachyphytum, 213
Pachyveria, crosses between Echeveria and Pachyphytum, 213
Painting of greenhouse, 22
Palms, 214
Pancratium, 187, 214
Parlour palm, 214
Parochetus, 214
Parodia, 214; *P. aureispina* as free-flowering cactus, 110
Parrot's bill, 157, 215
Partridge-breasted aloe, 131
Passiflora, 214; from cuttings, 86
Passion flower, 215
Peat, *see* Compost; some uses of, 25, 61, 90, 97; buying, 64
Pelargonium, 84, 86, 122; buying, 79; hybrid ivies, 217; made to flower in winter, 74; choice and growing methods, 214–18
Pentapterygium, 218
Perennials grown as annuals, 94
Peristrophe, 218
Perpetual-flowering carnations, 80, 121
Persea, 218
Peruvian daffodil, 187, 219
Pests, 111–18; biological control of, 112–13; *Pest control without poisons* (HDRA), 112
Petunia, 219; from seed, 94, 99
Phacelia, 219; from seed, 93, 99
Pharbitis, 219
Phlox, 220
Phyllocactus, 170, 220
Pig-a-back plant, 220, 241
Pimelia, 220; from cuttings, 86
Pittosporum, 221
Plants from: cuttings, 80–6; seed, 93–9; plant-buying, 76–9
Plastic bags, domes, used for cuttings, 84, 92
Plastic film, for greenhouse lining, 24; for capillary benches, 70
Platycerium, 123, 175, 221
Pleione, 221
Pleroma, 222
Plumbago, 222; from cuttings, 86
Poinsettia, 172–3, 222
Polianthes, 102, 222
Polygala, 223; from cuttings, 86
Pomegranate, 225
Poor man's orchid, 223, 231
Portulacaria, 223
Potash (and other plant requirements), 65
Pot marigold, 143–4, 224
Pots, clay and plastic, 55–6; for cacti, 108; for capillary watering, 55, 68, 71; plastic, for seeds, 96; useful sizes, 56

Potting, 56–64; composts for, 59–65
Powder-puff cactus, 201
Prairie gentian, 173, 224
Pricking out, 96, 97
Prickly pear, 212, 224
Primula, 224; from seed, 94, 99; winter-flowering, 94
Propagating frames, 45–6
Propagation by: cuttings, 81–6; mist methods, 87–92; seed-raising, 81, 93–9
Prostanthera, 224; from cuttings, 86
Pteris, 176, 225
Punica, 225; from cuttings, 86
Pyrethrum, 112, 113, 116

Quamoclit, 225; from seed, 94, 99
'Quarantine' for new plants, 111

Rabbit's ears, 212
Rat's tail cactus, 133, 225
Rebutia, 225; *R. minuscula* as free-flowering cactus, 110
Rechsteineria, 103, 226
Red spider mite, 113, 115
Regal pelargoniums, 215, 216, 217, 218; whitefly of, 116
Rehmannia, 226; from seed, 99
Reseda, 227
Rest period for bulbous (and similar) plants, 101–4
Rex begonias, 138; from leaf-cuttings, 83
Rhipsalidopsis, 123, 227
Rhipsalis, 227
Rhododendron, 227
Rhynchospermum, 228
Richardia, 228, 246
Rochea, 160, 228; from cuttings, 86
Roman hyacinth, 186
Roof angle, 18–20
Roof ventilators, 49
Rooting of cuttings, 83–4
Rosa, 228, 229; from seed, 99; miniatures, 229
Rose bay, 209, 229
Rotting of cuttings, 82
Rubber plant, 176, 229

Saintpaulia, 122–3, 129, 229; from leaf cuttings, 83
Salpiglossis, 230; from seed, 94, 99
Sand: in cuttings mixtures, 84; in propagating, 64, 84; as potting medium, 62; on capillary benches, 68, 71
Saxifraga, 230
Scale (pest), 116
Scarborough lily, 245
Scented-leaved pelargoniums, 218
Schizanthus, 231; from seed, 93, 99

INDEX

Schizocentron, 231
Schlumbergera, 123, 232; from cuttings, 86; *S.* × *buckleyi* as free-flowering cactus, 110
Scilla, 102, 232
Scirpus, 233
Sea lavender, 197, 233
Seaweed as fertiliser, 25, 65
Sedum, 233; from cuttings, 86
Seed: boxes, pans, trays, 56, 96; composts for sowing, 58, 96; growing from, 93–9; small electric propagators for, 96; in vermiculite and peat, 97; sowing under mist, 97; pricking out, 96, 97; purpose of irradiation of, 74
Selaginella, 234
Selenicereus, 234
Senecio, 154, 234
Sequestrene, against iron deficiency, 63, 112
Setcreasea, 234
Shading of greenhouse, 51–2
Shamrock pea, 214, 234
Shrimp plant, 139, 234
Side-wall ventilation, 21
Silene, 234
Silver tree, 195, 234
Sinningia, 123, 235; from leaf cuttings, 83; temperature for, 103
Slipper flower, 143, 235
Smithiantha, 103, 123, 235
Snapdragon, 133, 236
Soil, 57–65; soil thermometer, 46; soil-warming cables, 43–5; soil-less composts, 55, 60, 61, 62; sterilising of, 26, 63
Sollya, 236; from cuttings, 86
Span-roof and lean-to greenhouses, 19, 21
Sparaxis, 236; flowering and resting times, 104
Sparmannia, 237; from cuttings, 86
Specialisation, 119–24
Sphagnum moss for potting, 63, 211
Spider flower, 156, 237
Spider lily, 187, 237
Spiraea, 135, 237
Spurge, 172–3
Squirrel's foot fern, 175
Staging in greenhouse, 52
Stag's horn fern, 221, 237
Star cactus, 136, 237
Statice, 197, 237
Sturt desert pea, 157, 239
Stem-rooting lilies, 196
Stenocarpus, 237
Sterilisation, 26, 63
Stocks, 202, 237

Strelitzia, 238
Streptanthera, 238; flowering and resting time, 104
Streptocarpus, 238; from leaf-cuttings, 83; from seed, 99
Streptosolen, 239; from cuttings, 86
Sulphur: spraying, against botrytis, 117; use of flowers of sulphur in compost, 62
Swan River daisy, 141, 239
Syringeing: against red spider, 115; against thrips, 116

Tacsonia, 239
Tea tree, 195, 239
Tecophilaea, 239; flowering and resting times, 104
Temperatures: minimum, 16; role of ventilation in, 20; weapons against excessive, 51
Ten week stock, 202
Thatch leaf palm, 214
Thermal factors of structural materials, 41
Thermostatic control, 35, 36, 38–46, 48, 49, 88, 91, 95, 96; of fan heaters, 37–8; of heated bench, 45; best type of thermostat, 38; placing of thermostat, 39
Thiram fungicides, 118
Three-quarter span, advantage of, 19
Thrips, 116
Throatwort, 242
Thunbergia, 240; from seed, 99
Tibouchina, 240; from cuttings, 86
Tigridia, 102, 240; flowering and resting times, 104
Toad, as woodlice eater, 116
Toadflax, 198, 241
Tobacco plant, 210, 241
Tolmiea, 241
Torenia, 241; from seed, 94, 99
Trace elements, 65
Trachelium, 242; from seed, 94, 99
Trachelospermum, 242; from cuttings, 86
Trachycarpus, 242
Trachymene, 242
Tradescantia, 242; from cuttings, 86
Transvaal daisy, 178, 243
Trays, clay and plastic, for seeds, 56
Trickle-line watering, 66, 67, 69; an alternative to, 70
Tritonia, 243; flowering and resting times, 104
Tropaeolum, 243; from seed, 99
Tuberose, 222, 224
Tubular heating, 37
Tulipa, 244
Turutu, 166, 244

INDEX

Umbrella plant, 244
Unicorn plant, 201, 245

Vallota, 101, 102, 245
Veltheimia, 245; flowering and resting times, 104
Ventilation: automatic, 21, 48–51; fan and pad, 52; paraffin heaters and, 34; points for beginners, 20–1; purposes of, 20–1, 47–8, 51; and humidity, 47–53; use of extractor fans, 21, 49; with lean-to or span roofs, 20–1; with plastic-sheeting insulation, 24; with side-wall ventilator, 21; method of measuring, 50; value of adjustability, 21
Vermiculite, 64, 83, 97
Virus diseases, 118
Viscaria, 200, 245

Wandering Jew, 242, 245
'Warm White' fluorescent tubes, 74
Watering, 105–8; capillary bench, 66–72; excessive, 54, 84, 101, 106, 107; of newly potted plants, 72; three methods described, 66 seqq.
Waterproofing of greenhouse, 22
Wattle, 127, 245
Wax flower, 185, 245
Waxy-flowered species, 100, 185
Western red cedar wood, 22
White fly, 116; biological control of, 113
White oil insecticides, 112, 115
Wilt, 117
Winter cherry, 236, 245
Woodlice, 116–17
Woods, for greenhouse construction, 22
Woolly-leaved plants, cuttings of, 84

Zantedeschia, 101, 246
Zebrina, 246
Zephyranthes, 246; flowering and resting times, 104
Zephyr flower, 246
Zinnia, 247
Zonal pelargoniums, 122, 216, 217; blackleg affecting, 117
Zygocactus, 247; *Z. truncatus* as free-flowering, 110